# CONTENTS

# U.S. Posts First Sales Increase in 4 Years, Second Worst Year Since 1982

The sluggish U.S. market and turmoil that beset Detroit auto makers in 2009 set the stage for a notably different North American International Auto Show in 2010. The year's inaugural exhibition was marked by the absence of such hometown brands as Pontiac and Saturn, victims of General Motors Corp.'s bankruptcy.

Only 40 world debuts were present, down from 53 the previous year, and Chrysler Group LLC bowed out of the show's press conference schedule completely.

In 2010, U.S. auto makers delivered 11,554,576 light vehicles, an 11.1% increase over the prior year's tally but still the second-worst year since 1982. The increase, the first in four years, comes as the initial step to recovery after dramatic 18% and 21% drop-offs in 2008 and 2009 and points to the L-shaped nature of the recovery thus far.

General Motors Co. was again the top-selling auto maker in the U.S., despite having shed four of its brands in 2009. But its market share declined for the eighth straight year, to a record-low of 19.1% on sales of 2,211,262 – its lowest volume since 1952.

Ford Motor Co. enjoyed its second-consecutive year of improving sales and market share, taking 16.5% of industry demand (its highest penetration since 2005) on a volume of 1,905,372 cars and light trucks. That total, its highest in three years, nonetheless marked only the third year since 1961 that Ford sold fewer than 2 million LVs.

Still, the increased share lifted Ford into second place for 2010, a spot Toyota Motor Sales U.S.A. Inc. had held for the previous three years.

GM and Ford, heavy players in the commercial-fleet sector, were helped by the fact that fleet sales led retail sales on the path to recovery, claiming a larger-than-usual share of the overall market.

Toyota was the only top-seven auto maker to record a year-to-year sales drop, its third in a row. Prior to 2009, the company had never recorded two straight years of declines.

In the shadow of massive recalls that nearly shut down sales for the month of February, and hindered by its relatively small participation in the fleet market, Toyota's penetration fell from a record high of 17% in 2009 to 15.3% – still its fourth-largest share ever – on a volume of 1,763,595 - several thousand units below year-ago.

American Honda Motor Co. Inc. increased deliveries 6.9% to 1,230,480, to remain the country's fourth-largest vehicle seller, but saw its share drop for the year from 11.1% to 10.6%.

Five auto makers registered all-time high shares, including Nissan North America (7.9%) and Hyundai Group (7.7%), locking them in a year-long battle for sixth place in the market.

Subaru of America Inc. claimed a record 2.3% penetration, on the strength of its best sales year ever, at 263,820 units. Porsche Cars of North America Inc. (0.2%) and Daimler AG (2.0%) both set company share records as the luxury market led other consumer segments toward recovery.

Last year marked the first since 1999 that all three Detroit auto makers posted year-over-year sales increases, with the U.S.-based companies accounting for 45% of LV deliveries, up from 44.1% in 2009.

Asian auto makers dropped more than a point of market share, taking 47.3% of sales, compared with 48.5% year-ago. The Europeans claimed the remaining 7.7% of the market, up from 7.4% in 2009.

In Europe, government-sponsored scrappage programs initiated in 2009 jolted consumers out of their funk and spurred enough market interest to hold the region's 2010 vehicle sales slide to 8.8%, according to *Ward's* data.

European Commission research indicated the programs, which rewarded buyers with rebates for trading up, were responsible for nearly 2.2 million additional sales and saved some 120,000 jobs.

The road to recovery appeared rocky, at least for the European Union markets that used the euro. Those 16 nations were on track for 1.7% growth in 2010, on average, and 1.5% in 2011, according to an International Monetary Fund forecast.

In contrast, the global economy expanded by 4.8% in 2010 and is forecast to increase 4.2% in 2011, the IMF said. Against this backdrop, debt crises loomed in once-vibrant markets such as Ireland, which, in October, suffered three credit-rating downgrades in less than 10 days.

Spain took a similar hit. But its trials paled beside those of Greece, where coffers were so empty that the government staged an asset fire-sale that attracted investment promises from China, Libya and Qatar.

Globally, the auto industry still was sorting through the rubble of the worldwide economic crisis that started in the U.S. in late 2008 and permeated overseas markets throughout much of 2010, driving major car makers toward a renewed focus on emerging markets as consumer confidence lost momentum at home.

But shifting resources away from flailing domestic economies and toward regions with unpredictable political regimes, many armed with protectionist measures, brought a new 4-letter word to executive lips: "Risk."

While key emerging markets such as China, India and Brazil only were lightly scathed by the financial meltdown, mature regions such as the U.S. and Europe still were recovering. Japan – already suffering from falling domestic demand – remained flat, and for the first time auto makers there began to build passenger vehicles in other countries to be exported back to their home turf. ❏

# U.S. Production of Cars and Trucks

## U.S. VEHICLE PRODUCTION

| Year | Cars | Trucks | Total | Year | Cars | Trucks | Total |
|------|------|--------|-------|------|------|--------|-------|
| 2010 | 2,731,105 | 5,011,988 | 7,743,093 | 1957 | 6,115,458 | 1,090,200 | 7,205,658 |
| 2009 | 2,195,588 | 3,513,843 | 5,709,431 | 1956 | 5,801,864 | 1,104,325 | 6,906,189 |
| 2008 | 3,731,241 | 4,940,900 | 8,672,141 | 1955 | 7,942,132 | 1,246,442 | 9,188,574 |
| 2007 | 3,867,268 | 6,885,042 | 10,752,310 | 1954 | 5,509,550 | 1,022,609 | 6,532,159 |
| 2006 | 4,311,696 | 6,948,581 | 11,260,277 | 1953 | 6,134,534 | 1,203,835 | 7,338,369 |
| 2005 | 4,265,872 | 7,680,781 | 11,946,653 | 1952 | 4,337,481 | 1,218,045 | 5,555,526 |
| 2004 | 4,165,925 | 7,794,429 | 11,960,354 | 1951 | 5,338,820 | 1,412,149 | 6,750,969 |
| 2003 | 4,453,369 | 7,633,659 | 12,087,028 | 1950 | 6,672,132 | 1,344,227 | 8,016,359 |
| 2002 | 4,957,377 | 7,322,205 | 12,279,582 | 1949 | 5,126,060 | 1,132,138 | 6,258,198 |
| 2001 | 4,808,019 | 6,616,670 | 11,424,689 | 1948 | 3,910,213 | 1,369,472 | 5,279,685 |
| 2000 | 5,470,917 | 7,302,797 | 12,773,714 | 1947 | 3,555,924 | 1,236,703 | 4,792,627 |
| 1999 | 5,577,749 | 7,447,229 | 13,024,978 | 1946 | 2,155,924 | 942,317 | 3,098,241 |
| 1998 | 5,492,473 | 6,510,190 | 12,002,663 | 1945 | 83,786 | 701,090 | 784,876 |
| 1997 | 5,878,221 | 6,252,354 | 12,130,575 | 1944 | NA | 791,357 | 791,357 |
| 1996 | 6,035,235 | 5,794,922 | 11,830,157 | 1943 | NA | 751,698 | 751,698 |
| 1995 | 6,325,967 | 5,669,281 | 11,995,248 | 1942 | 206,274 | 876,812 | 1,083,086 |
| 1994 | 6,601,220 | 5,638,068 | 12,239,288 | 1941 | 3,760,501 | 1,093,868 | 4,854,369 |
| 1993 | 5,982,120 | 4,873,342 | 10,855,462 | 1940 | 3,728,491 | 784,404 | 4,512,895 |
| 1992 | 5,666,891 | 4,024,552 | 9,691,443 | 1939 | 2,866,796 | 710,496 | 3,577,292 |
| 1991 | 5,439,864 | 3,349,976 | 8,789,840 | 1938 | 2,000,985 | 488,100 | 2,489,085 |
| 1990 | 6,077,903 | 3,689,536 | 9,767,439 | 1937 | 3,915,889 | 893,085 | 4,808,974 |
| 1989 | 6,821,291 | 4,035,501 | 10,856,792 | 1936 | 3,669,528 | 784,587 | 4,454,115 |
| 1988 | 7,137,433 | 4,084,575 | 11,222,008 | 1935 | 3,252,244 | 694,690 | 3,946,934 |
| 1987 | 7,099,854 | 3,812,074 | 10,911,928 | 1934 | 2,177,919 | 575,192 | 2,753,111 |
| 1986 | 7,829,271 | 3,490,853 | 11,320,124 | 1933 | 1,573,512 | 346,545 | 1,920,057 |
| 1985 | 8,186,043 | 3,452,094 | 11,638,137 | 1932 | 1,135,491 | 235,187 | 1,370,678 |
| 1984 | 7,773,342 | 3,165,716 | 10,939,058 | 1931 | 1,973,090 | 416,648 | 2,389,738 |
| 1983 | 6,782,061 | 2,443,637 | 9,225,698 | 1930 | 2,784,745 | 571,241 | 3,355,986 |
| 1982 | 5,073,214 | 1,912,099 | 6,985,313 | 1929 | 4,587,400 | 771,020 | 5,358,420 |
| 1981 | 6,251,003 | 1,689,778 | 7,940,781 | 1928 | 3,815,417 | 543,342 | 4,358,759 |
| 1980 | 6,372,304 | 1,638,259 | 8,010,563 | 1927 | 2,936,533 | 464,793 | 3,401,326 |
| 1979 | 8,422,074 | 3,053,033 | 11,475,107 | 1926 | 3,783,987 | 516,947 | 4,300,934 |
| 1978 | 9,173,606 | 3,721,680 | 12,895,286 | 1925 | 3,735,171 | 530,659 | 4,265,830 |
| 1977 | 9,211,411 | 3,487,675 | 12,699,086 | 1924 | 3,185,881 | 416,659 | 3,602,540 |
| 1976 | 8,492,473 | 2,993,063 | 11,485,536 | 1923 | 3,624,717 | 409,295 | 4,034,012 |
| 1975 | 6,705,837 | 2,259,576 | 8,965,413 | 1922 | 2,274,185 | 269,991 | 2,544,176 |
| 1974 | 7,290,258 | 2,693,676 | 9,983,934 | 1921 | 1,468,067 | 148,052 | 1,616,119 |
| 1973 | 9,660,821 | 3,002,098 | 12,662,919 | 1920 | 1,905,560 | 321,789 | 2,227,349 |
| 1972 | 8,821,737 | 2,475,786 | 11,297,523 | 1919 | 1,651,625 | 224,731 | 1,876,356 |
| 1971 | 8,578,349 | 2,071,407 | 10,649,756 | 1918 | 943,436 | 227,250 | 1,170,686 |
| 1970 | 6,545,908 | 1,716,749 | 8,262,657 | 1917 | 1,745,792 | 128,157 | 1,873,949 |
| 1969 | 8,219,463 | 1,963,099 | 10,182,562 | 1916 | 1,525,578 | 92,130 | 1,617,708 |
| 1968 | 8,843,031 | 1,950,713 | 10,793,744 | 1915 | 895,930 | 74,000 | 969,930 |
| 1967 | 7,406,788 | 1,585,481 | 8,992,269 | 1914 | 548,139 | 24,900 | 573,039 |
| 1966 | 8,598,917 | 1,764,337 | 10,363,254 | 1913 | 461,500 | 23,500 | 485,000 |
| 1965 | 9,329,104 | 1,785,109 | 11,114,213 | 1912 | 356,000 | 22,000 | 378,000 |
| 1964 | 7,739,034 | 1,560,644 | 9,299,678 | 1911 | 199,319 | 10,681 | 210,000 |
| 1963 | 7,637,173 | 1,463,412 | 9,100,585 | 1910 | 181,000 | 6,000 | 187,000 |
| 1962 | 6,935,182 | 1,254,220 | 8,189,402 | 1909 | 123,990 | 3,297 | 127,287 |
| 1961 | 5,516,317 | 1,127,505 | 6,643,822 | 1908 | 63,500 | 1,500 | 65,000 |
| 1960 | 6,696,108 | 1,198,112 | 7,894,220 | 1907 | 43,000 | 1,000 | 44,000 |
| 1959 | 5,593,707 | 1,139,958 | 6,733,665 | 1906 | 33,200 | 800 | 34,000 |
| 1958 | 4,244,045 | 871,330 | 5,115,375 | 1905 | 24,250 | 750 | 25,000 |

N.A. - Not available.
SOURCE: Ward's Automotive Group.

# N. America Vehicle Production by Model

## NORTH AMERICA VEHICLE PRODUCTION BY MODEL

| | Canada | | Mexico | | United States | | North America | |
|---|---|---|---|---|---|---|---|---|
| | 2010 | 2009 | 2010 | 2009 | 2010 | 2009 | 2010 | 2009 |
| Ford Mustang | — | — | — | — | 77,586 | 69,921 | 77,586 | 69,921 |
| Mazda6 | — | — | — | — | 45,168 | 32,082 | 45,168 | 32,082 |
| **AUTOALLIANCE TOTAL** | **—** | **—** | **—** | **—** | **122,754** | **102,003** | **122,754** | **102,003** |
| Chrysler 200 Series | — | — | — | — | 2,197 | — | 2,197 | — |
| Chrysler 300 Series | 39,688 | 36,154 | — | — | — | — | 39,688 | 36,154 |
| Chrysler Sebring Convertible | — | — | — | — | 7,829 | 4,489 | 7,829 | 4,489 |
| Chrysler Sebring Sedan | — | — | — | — | 32,157 | 18,907 | 32,157 | 18,907 |
| Dodge Avenger | — | — | — | — | 59,170 | 35,315 | 59,170 | 35,315 |
| Dodge Caliber | — | — | — | — | 67,586 | 25,020 | 67,586 | 25,020 |
| Dodge Challenger | 40,042 | 32,600 | — | — | — | — | 40,042 | 32,600 |
| Dodge Charger | 83,527 | 52,961 | — | — | — | — | 83,527 | 52,961 |
| Dodge Viper | — | — | — | — | 459 | 338 | 459 | 338 |
| Fiat 500 | — | — | 724 | — | — | — | 724 | — |
| **CHRYSLER TOTAL** | **163,257** | **121,715** | **724** | **—** | **169,398** | **84,069** | **333,379** | **205,784** |
| Ford Crown Victoria | 52,148 | 43,507 | — | — | — | — | 52,148 | 43,507 |
| Ford Fiesta | — | — | 77,358 | — | — | — | 77,358 | — |
| Ford Focus | — | — | — | — | 199,502 | 166,453 | 199,502 | 166,453 |
| Ford Fusion | — | — | 267,533 | 187,052 | — | — | 267,533 | 187,052 |
| Ford Taurus | — | — | — | — | 83,052 | 50,976 | 83,052 | 50,976 |
| Lincoln MKS | — | — | — | — | 16,085 | 15,378 | 16,085 | 15,378 |
| Lincoln MKZ | — | — | 24,342 | 19,399 | — | — | 24,342 | 19,399 |
| Lincoln Town Car | 12,088 | 10,221 | — | — | — | — | 12,088 | 10,221 |
| Mercury Grand Marquis | 31,765 | 26,740 | — | — | — | — | 31,765 | 26,740 |
| Mercury Milan | — | — | 21,155 | 24,964 | — | — | 21,155 | 24,964 |
| Mercury Sable | — | — | — | — | — | 3,799 | — | 3,799 |
| **FORD TOTAL** | **96,001** | **80,468** | **390,388** | **231,415** | **298,639** | **236,606** | **785,028** | **548,489** |
| Buick LaCrosse | — | 11 | — | — | 73,480 | 25,632 | 73,480 | 25,643 |
| Buick Lucerne | — | — | — | — | 29,654 | 22,957 | 29,654 | 22,957 |
| Cadillac CTS | — | — | — | — | 60,688 | 36,496 | 60,688 | 36,496 |
| Cadillac DTS | — | — | — | — | 21,023 | 12,807 | 21,023 | 12,807 |
| Cadillac STS | — | — | — | — | 4,792 | 2,945 | 4,792 | 2,945 |
| Cadillac XLR | — | — | — | — | — | 234 | — | 234 |
| Chevrolet Aveo | — | — | 55,141 | 33,390 | — | — | 55,141 | 33,390 |
| Chevrolet Camaro | 94,433 | 82,188 | — | — | — | — | 94,433 | 82,188 |
| Chevrolet Chevy | — | — | 48,971 | 31,699 | — | — | 48,971 | 31,699 |
| Chevrolet Cobalt | — | — | — | — | 91,796 | 79,314 | 91,796 | 79,314 |
| Chevrolet Corvette | — | — | — | — | 15,791 | 7,355 | 15,791 | 7,355 |
| Chevrolet Cruze | — | — | — | — | 66,303 | — | 66,303 | — |
| Chevrolet Impala | 177,772 | 134,280 | — | — | — | — | 177,772 | 134,280 |
| Chevrolet Malibu | — | — | — | — | 235,956 | 160,855 | 235,956 | 160,855 |
| Chevrolet Volt | — | — | — | — | 1,219 | — | 1,219 | — |
| Opel GT | — | — | — | — | — | 21 | — | 21 |
| Pontiac G3 | — | — | — | 3,411 | — | — | — | 3,411 |
| Pontiac G5 | — | — | — | — | — | 8,603 | — | 8,603 |
| Pontiac G6 | — | — | — | — | 1 | 50,758 | 1 | 50,758 |
| Pontiac Solstice | — | — | — | — | — | 1,771 | — | 1,771 |
| Saturn Aura | — | — | — | — | — | 3,727 | — | 3,727 |
| Saturn Sky | — | — | — | — | — | 275 | — | 275 |
| **GM TOTAL** | **272,205** | **216,479** | **104,112** | **68,500** | **600,703** | **413,750** | **977,020** | **698,729** |
| Acura CSX | 1,979 | 1,890 | — | — | — | — | 1,979 | 1,890 |
| Acura TL | — | — | — | — | 35,294 | 28,841 | 35,294 | 28,841 |
| Honda Accord | — | — | — | — | 295,709 | 279,408 | 295,709 | 279,408 |
| Honda Civic | 207,555 | 224,527 | — | — | 95,116 | 83,301 | 302,671 | 307,828 |
| **HONDA TOTAL** | **209,534** | **226,417** | **—** | **—** | **426,119** | **391,550** | **635,653** | **617,967** |
| Hyundai Elantra | — | — | — | — | 19,780 | — | 19,780 | — |
| Hyundai Sonata | — | — | — | — | 218,607 | 103,876 | 218,607 | 103,876 |
| **HYUNDAI TOTAL** | **—** | **—** | **—** | **—** | **238,387** | **103,876** | **238,387** | **103,876** |
| Mitsubishi Eclipse | — | — | — | — | 6,424 | 2,653 | 6,424 | 2,653 |
| Mitsubishi Galant | — | — | — | — | 16,545 | 12,145 | 16,545 | 12,145 |

# N. America Vehicle Production by Model

**NORTH AMERICA VEHICLE PRODUCTION BY MODEL – continued**

| | Canada | | Mexico | | United States | | North America | |
|---|---|---|---|---|---|---|---|---|
| | 2010 | 2009 | 2010 | 2009 | 2010 | 2009 | 2010 | 2009 |
| **MITSUBISHI TOTAL** | — | — | — | — | **22,969** | **14,798** | **22,969** | **14,798** |
| Nissan Altima | — | — | — | — | 275,115 | 205,637 | 275,115 | 205,637 |
| Nissan Maxima | — | — | — | — | 71,776 | 53,456 | 71,776 | 53,456 |
| Nissan Platina | — | — | — | 1,996 | — | — | — | 1,996 |
| Nissan Sentra | — | — | 146,753 | 126,576 | — | — | 146,753 | 126,576 |
| Nissan Tsuru | — | — | 74,618 | 66,334 | — | — | 74,618 | 66,334 |
| Nissan Versa | — | — | 234,868 | 125,916 | — | — | 234,868 | 125,916 |
| Renault Clio | — | — | — | 2,396 | — | — | — | 2,396 |
| **NISSAN TOTAL** | — | — | **456,239** | **323,218** | **346,891** | **259,093** | **803,130** | **582,311** |
| Pontiac Vibe | — | — | — | — | — | 28,449 | — | 28,449 |
| Toyota Corolla | — | — | — | — | 63,319 | 172,988 | 63,319 | 172,988 |
| **NUMMI TOTAL** | — | — | — | — | **63,319** | **201,437** | **63,319** | **201,437** |
| Subaru Legacy | — | — | — | — | 43,791 | 28,139 | 43,791 | 28,139 |
| Toyota Camry | — | — | — | — | 87,731 | 87,926 | 87,731 | 87,926 |
| **SUBARU TOTAL** | — | — | — | — | **131,522** | **116,065** | **131,522** | **116,065** |
| Toyota Avalon | — | — | — | — | 40,155 | 27,513 | 40,155 | 27,513 |
| Toyota Camry | — | — | — | — | 270,249 | 244,828 | 270,249 | 244,828 |
| Toyota Corolla | 192,271 | 138,650 | — | — | — | — | 192,271 | 138,650 |
| Toyota Matrix | 33,809 | 38,538 | — | — | — | — | 33,809 | 38,538 |
| **TOYOTA TOTAL** | **226,080** | **177,188** | — | — | **310,404** | **272,341** | **536,484** | **449,529** |
| Volkswagen Beetle | — | — | 31,447 | 24,328 | — | — | 31,447 | 24,328 |
| Volkswagen Beetle Cabrio | — | — | 8,640 | 7,631 | — | — | 8,640 | 7,631 |
| Volkswagen Bora | — | — | 12,249 | 20,440 | — | — | 12,249 | 20,440 |
| Volkswagen Jetta | — | — | 382,349 | 267,344 | — | — | 382,349 | 267,344 |
| **VOLKSWAGEN TOTAL** | — | — | **434,685** | **319,743** | — | — | **434,685** | **319,743** |
| **TOTAL CARS** | **967,077** | **822,267** | **1,386,148** | **942,876** | **2,731,105** | **2,195,588** | **5,084,330** | **3,960,731** |
| Hummer H2 | — | — | — | — | — | 393 | — | 393 |
| **AM GENERAL TOTAL** | — | — | — | — | — | **393** | — | **393** |
| BMW X3 | — | — | — | — | 16,078 | — | 16,078 | — |
| BMW X5 | — | — | — | — | 98,245 | 79,015 | 98,245 | 79,015 |
| BMW X6 | — | — | — | — | 43,380 | 42,651 | 43,380 | 42,651 |
| **BMW TOTAL** | — | — | — | — | **157,703** | **121,666** | **157,703** | **121,666** |
| Chevrolet Equinox | — | 76,940 | — | — | — | — | — | 76,940 |
| GMC Terrain | — | 21,548 | — | — | — | — | — | 21,548 |
| Pontiac Torrent | — | 5,289 | — | — | — | — | — | 5,289 |
| Suzuki XL7 | — | 5 | — | — | — | — | — | 5 |
| **CAMI TOTAL** | — | **103,782** | — | — | — | — | — | **103,782** |
| Chrysler PT Cruiser | — | — | 11,083 | 14,067 | — | — | 11,083 | 14,067 |
| Chrysler Town & Country | 130,845 | 78,006 | — | — | — | — | 130,845 | 78,006 |
| Dodge Caravan | 165,594 | 110,904 | — | — | — | — | 165,594 | 110,904 |
| Dodge Durango | — | — | — | — | 3,429 | — | 3,429 | — |
| Dodge Journey | — | — | 128,203 | 73,909 | — | — | 128,203 | 73,909 |
| Dodge Nitro | — | — | — | — | 27,562 | 16,066 | 27,562 | 16,066 |
| Jeep Commander | — | — | — | — | 5,582 | 10,966 | 5,582 | 10,966 |
| Jeep Compass | — | — | — | — | 34,412 | 20,494 | 34,412 | 20,494 |
| Jeep Grand Cherokee | — | — | — | — | 125,142 | 49,646 | 125,142 | 49,646 |
| Jeep Liberty | — | — | — | — | 64,411 | 42,867 | 64,411 | 42,867 |
| Jeep Patriot | — | — | — | — | 66,427 | 39,095 | 66,427 | 39,095 |
| Jeep Wrangler | — | — | — | — | 59,181 | 34,776 | 59,181 | 34,776 |
| Jeep Wrangler Unlimited | — | — | — | — | 85,504 | 50,176 | 85,504 | 50,176 |
| Mitsubishi Raider | — | — | — | — | 178,406 | 117,608 | 178,406 | 117,608 |
| Ram Dakota | — | — | — | — | — | 1 | — | 1 |
| Ram Pickup | — | — | 110,673 | 66,331 | 19,043 | 15,419 | 129,716 | 81,750 |
| Volkswagen Routan | 15,686 | 3,879 | — | — | — | — | 15,686 | 3,879 |
| **CHRYSLER TOTAL** | **312,125** | **192,789** | **249,959** | **154,307** | **669,099** | **397,114** | **1,231,183** | **744,210** |
| Ford Econoline | — | — | — | — | 121,471 | 88,054 | 121,471 | 88,054 |
| Ford Edge | 15u,157 | 95,105 | — | — | — | — | 150,157 | 95,105 |
| Ford Escape | — | — | — | — | 275,646 | 208,057 | 275,646 | 208,057 |

# N. America Vehicle Production by Model

## NORTH AMERICA VEHICLE PRODUCTION BY MODEL – continued

| | Canada | | Mexico | | United States | | North America | |
|---|---|---|---|---|---|---|---|---|
| | 2010 | 2009 | 2010 | 2009 | 2010 | 2009 | 2010 | 2009 |
| Ford Expedition | — | — | — | — | 51,295 | 34,485 | 51,295 | 34,485 |
| Ford Explorer | — | — | — | — | 97,312 | 66,430 | 97,312 | 66,430 |
| Ford F-Series | — | — | — | — | 616,541 | 531,757 | 616,541 | 531,757 |
| Ford Flex | 41,081 | 33,692 | — | — | — | — | 41,081 | 33,692 |
| Ford Ranger | — | — | — | — | 70,666 | 73,625 | 70,666 | 73,625 |
| Ford Taurus X | — | — | — | — | — | 1,649 | — | 1,649 |
| Lincoln Mark LT | — | — | — | — | 847 | 608 | 847 | 608 |
| Lincoln MKT | 5,961 | 7,273 | — | — | — | — | 5,961 | 7,273 |
| Lincoln MKX | 27,408 | 21,414 | — | — | — | — | 27,408 | 21,414 |
| Lincoln Navigator | — | — | — | — | 9,636 | 7,902 | 9,636 | 7,902 |
| Mercury Mariner | — | — | — | — | 25,050 | 27,673 | 25,050 | 27,673 |
| Mercury Mountaineer | — | — | — | — | 4,564 | 5,210 | 4,564 | 5,210 |
| Mazda Pickup | — | — | — | — | 2,395 | 1,905 | 2,395 | 1,905 |
| Mazda Tribute | — | — | — | — | 9,273 | 7,396 | 9,273 | 7,396 |
| **FORD TOTAL** | **224,607** | **157,484** | **—** | **—** | **1,284,696** | **1,054,751** | **1,509,303** | **1,212,235** |
| Buick Enclave | — | — | — | — | 74,414 | 44,616 | 74,414 | 44,616 |
| Cadillac Escalade | — | — | — | — | 22,753 | 12,981 | 22,753 | 12,981 |
| Cadillac Escalade ESV | — | — | — | — | 12,693 | 5,321 | 12,693 | 5,321 |
| Cadillac Escalade EXT | — | — | 2,649 | 1,704 | — | — | 2,649 | 1,704 |
| Cadillac SRX | — | — | 76,589 | 22,994 | — | 5 | 76,589 | 22,999 |
| Chevrolet Avalanche | — | — | 26,956 | 18,820 | — | — | 26,956 | 18,820 |
| Chevrolet Captiva Sport | — | — | 30,618 | 20,571 | — | — | 30,618 | 20,571 |
| Chevrolet Colorado | — | — | — | — | 34,509 | 25,305 | 34,509 | 25,305 |
| Chevrolet Equinox | 180,522 | — | — | — | — | — | 180,522 | — |
| Chevrolet Express | — | — | — | — | 69,328 | 50,510 | 69,328 | 50,510 |
| Chevrolet HHR | — | — | 72,892 | 53,699 | — | — | 72,892 | 53,699 |
| Chevrolet Silverado | — | 18,546 | 162,141 | 109,176 | 294,802 | 215,771 | 456,943 | 343,493 |
| Chevrolet Suburban | — | — | — | — | 58,889 | 41,192 | 58,889 | 41,192 |
| Chevrolet Tahoe | — | — | — | — | 101,499 | 65,290 | 101,499 | 65,290 |
| Chevrolet Tiltmaster | — | — | — | — | — | 119 | — | 119 |
| Chevrolet TrailBlazer | — | — | — | — | — | 5 | — | 5 |
| Chevrolet Traverse | — | — | — | — | 118,220 | 95,450 | 118,220 | 95,450 |
| GMC Acadia | — | — | — | — | 82,555 | 46,353 | 82,555 | 46,353 |
| GMC Canyon | — | — | — | — | 12,436 | 8,374 | 12,436 | 8,374 |
| GMC Envoy | — | — | — | — | — | 3 | — | 3 |
| GMC Forward | — | — | — | — | — | 168 | — | 168 |
| GMC Savana | — | — | — | — | 21,688 | 13,753 | 21,688 | 13,753 |
| GMC Sierra | — | 8,555 | 80,594 | 49,500 | 124,846 | 82,768 | 205,440 | 140,823 |
| GMC Terrain | 76,841 | — | — | — | — | — | 76,841 | — |
| GMC Yukon | — | — | — | — | 50,402 | 30,913 | 50,402 | 30,913 |
| GMC Yukon XL | — | — | — | — | 35,793 | 17,797 | 35,793 | 17,797 |
| Hummer H3 | — | — | — | — | 1,183 | 3,175 | 1,183 | 3,175 |
| Hummer H3T | — | — | — | — | 321 | 1,652 | 321 | 1,652 |
| Isuzu NPR | — | — | — | — | — | 401 | — | 401 |
| Saab 9-7X | — | — | — | — | — | 2 | — | 2 |
| Saturn Outlook | — | — | — | — | 2,507 | 4,983 | 2,507 | 4,983 |
| Saturn Vue | — | — | 2,886 | 5,591 | — | — | 2,886 | 5,591 |
| **GM TOTAL** | **257,363** | **27,101** | **455,325** | **282,055** | **1,118,838** | **766,907** | **1,831,526** | **1,076,063** |
| Acura MDX | 63,859 | 32,784 | — | — | — | — | 63,859 | 32,784 |
| Acura RDX | — | — | — | — | 20,550 | 9,899 | 20,550 | 9,899 |
| Acura ZDX | 4,879 | 595 | — | — | — | — | 4,879 | 595 |
| Honda CR-V | — | — | 55,001 | 47,787 | 196,743 | 133,361 | 251,744 | 181,148 |
| Honda Crosstour | — | — | — | — | 33,200 | 9,158 | 33,200 | 9,158 |
| Honda Element | — | — | — | — | 16,800 | 13,920 | 16,800 | 13,920 |
| Honda Odyssey | — | — | — | — | 119,580 | 83,873 | 119,580 | 83,873 |
| Honda Pilot | — | — | — | — | 121,330 | 65,434 | 121,330 | 65,434 |
| Honda Ridgeline | — | — | — | — | 20,180 | 16,180 | 20,180 | 16,180 |
| **HONDA TOTAL** | **68,738** | **33,379** | **55,001** | **47,787** | **528,383** | **331,825** | **652,122** | **412,991** |

# N. America Vehicle Production by Model

## NORTH AMERICA VEHICLE PRODUCTION BY MODEL – continued

| | Canada | | Mexico | | United States | | North America | |
|---|---|---|---|---|---|---|---|---|
| | 2010 | 2009 | 2010 | 2009 | 2010 | 2009 | 2010 | 2009 |
| Hyundai Santa Fe | — | — | — | — | 62,113 | 91,685 | 62,113 | 91,685 |
| **HYUNDAI TOTAL** | **—** | **—** | **—** | **—** | **62,113** | **91,685** | **62,113** | **91,685** |
| Hyundai Santa Fe | — | — | — | — | 30,093 | — | 30,093 | — |
| Kia Sorento | — | — | — | — | 122,268 | 15,500 | 122,268 | 15,500 |
| **KIA TOTAL** | **—** | **—** | **—** | **—** | **152,361** | **15,500** | **152,361** | **15,500** |
| Mercedes GL | — | — | — | — | 31,995 | 19,348 | 31,995 | 19,348 |
| Mercedes M-Class | — | — | — | — | 76,472 | 61,028 | 76,472 | 61,028 |
| Mercedes R-Class | — | — | — | — | 16,870 | 10,206 | 16,870 | 10,206 |
| **MERCEDES TOTAL** | **—** | **—** | **—** | **—** | **125,337** | **90,582** | **125,337** | **90,582** |
| Mitsubishi Endeavor | — | — | — | — | 6,406 | 3,703 | 6,406 | 3,703 |
| **MITSUBISHI TOTAL** | **—** | **—** | **—** | **—** | **6,406** | **3,703** | **6,406** | **3,703** |
| Infiniti QX56 | — | — | — | — | 3,466 | 7,401 | 3,466 | 7,401 |
| Nissan Armada | — | — | — | — | 26,260 | 11,606 | 26,260 | 11,606 |
| Nissan Chassis | — | — | 20,907 | 16,263 | — | — | 20,907 | 16,263 |
| Nissan Frontier | — | — | 589 | — | 48,658 | 29,212 | 49,247 | 29,212 |
| Nissan Pathfinder | — | — | — | — | 29,786 | 22,860 | 29,786 | 22,860 |
| Nissan Pickup | — | — | 28,755 | 15,933 | — | — | 28,755 | 15,933 |
| Nissan Quest | — | — | — | — | — | 5,490 | — | 5,490 |
| Nissan Titan | — | — | — | — | 28,022 | 16,473 | 28,022 | 16,473 |
| Nissan Xterra | — | — | — | — | 26,180 | 19,563 | 26,180 | 19,563 |
| Suzuki Equator | — | — | — | — | 1,630 | 2,600 | 1,630 | 2,600 |
| **NISSAN TOTAL** | **—** | **—** | **50,251** | **32,196** | **164,002** | **115,205** | **214,253** | **147,401** |
| Toyota Tacoma | — | — | — | — | 27,495 | 67,435 | 27,495 | 67,435 |
| **NUMMI TOTAL** | **—** | **—** | **—** | **—** | **27,495** | **67,435** | **27,495** | **67,435** |
| Subaru Outback | — | — | — | — | 108,686 | 50,893 | 108,686 | 50,893 |
| Subaru Tribeca | — | — | — | — | 5,543 | 3,921 | 5,543 | 3,921 |
| **SUBARU TOTAL** | **—** | **—** | **—** | **—** | **114,229** | **54,814** | **114,229** | **54,814** |
| Lexus RX350 | 81,618 | 64,282 | — | — | — | — | 81,618 | 64,282 |
| Toyota Highlander | — | — | — | — | 86,527 | 17,503 | 86,527 | 17,503 |
| Toyota RAV4 | 151,031 | 78,077 | — | — | — | — | 151,031 | 78,077 |
| Toyota Sequoia | — | — | — | — | 24,685 | 18,376 | 24,685 | 18,376 |
| Toyota Sienna | — | — | — | — | 132,780 | 72,205 | 132,780 | 72,205 |
| Toyota Tacoma | — | — | 53,829 | 42,696 | 42,139 | — | 95,968 | 42,696 |
| Toyota Tundra | — | — | — | — | 107,959 | 86,000 | 107,959 | 86,000 |
| Toyota Venza | — | — | — | — | 61,290 | 75,896 | 61,290 | 75,896 |
| **TOYOTA TOTAL** | **232,649** | **142,359** | **53,829** | **42,696** | **455,380** | **269,980** | **741,858** | **455,035** |
| **TOTAL LIGHT TRUCKS** | **1,095,482** | **656,894** | **864,365** | **559,041** | **4,866,042** | **3,381,560** | **6,825,889** | **4,597,495** |
| **TOTAL LIGHT VEHICLES** | **2,062,559** | **1,479,161** | **2,250,513** | **1,501,917** | **7,597,147** | **5,577,148** | **11,910,219** | **8,558,226** |
| Blue Diamond | — | — | 340 | 3,603 | — | — | 340 | 3,603 |
| Chrysler | — | — | 7,100 | 3,700 | — | — | 7,100 | 3,700 |
| Dina Camiones | — | — | 143 | 132 | — | — | 143 | 132 |
| Ford | — | — | — | — | 30,052 | 29,502 | 30,052 | 29,502 |
| Freightliner | — | 1,611 | 46,643 | 27,687 | 24,756 | 21,116 | 71,399 | 50,414 |
| General Motors | — | — | — | — | — | 5,004 | — | 5,004 |
| Hino | — | — | 354 | 89 | 3,484 | 2,710 | 3,838 | 2,799 |
| International | 8 | 3,892 | 26,128 | 16,661 | 32,479 | 30,483 | 58,615 | 51,036 |
| Kenworth | 5,622 | 5,818 | 10,325 | 6,037 | 14,916 | 12,679 | 30,863 | 24,534 |
| Mack | — | — | — | — | 13,546 | 10,376 | 13,546 | 10,376 |
| MAN | — | — | 651 | 958 | — | — | 651 | 958 |
| Peterbilt | — | — | — | — | 13,853 | 12,814 | 13,853 | 12,814 |
| Scania | — | — | — | 3 | — | — | — | 3 |
| Volvo Truck | — | — | 85 | 265 | 12,836 | 7,575 | 12,921 | 7,840 |
| Other | — | — | — | — | 24 | 24 | 24 | 24 |
| **TOTAL MED.HVY. TRUCKS** | **5,630** | **11,321** | **91,769** | **59,135** | **145,946** | **132,283** | **243,345** | **202,739** |
| **TOTAL TRUCKS** | **1,101,112** | **668,215** | **956,134** | **618,176** | **5,011,988** | **3,513,843** | **7,069,234** | **4,800,234** |
| **TOTAL VEHICLES** | **2,068,189** | **1,490,482** | **2,342,282** | **1,561,052** | **7,743,093** | **5,709,431** | **12,153,564** | **8,760,965** |

SOURCE: *Ward's AutoInfoBank.*

# U.S. Factory Sales of Trucks and Buses by Gross Vehicle Weight Rating

## U.S. FACTORY SALES OF TRUCKS AND BUSES BY GROSS VEHICLE WEIGHT RATING

| | Gross Vehicle Weight Rating (Pounds) | | | | | | | | |
|---|---|---|---|---|---|---|---|---|---|
| | 6,000 & Less | 6,001- 10,000 | 10,001- 14,000 | 14,001- 16,000 | 16,001- 19,500 | 19,501- 26,000 | 26,001- 33,000 | 33,001 & Over | Total |
| **U.S. TOTAL** | | | | | | | | | |
| 2010 | 2,051,050 | 1,820,898 | 94,777 | 3,979 | 16,342 | 26,466 | 28,063 | 90,618 | 4,132,193 |
| 2009 | 1,624,363 | 1,248,435 | 80,176 | 15,301 | 15,215 | 16,443 | 31,100 | 76,393 | 3,107,426 |
| 2008 | 2,317,625 | 1,655,766 | 99,692 | 21,420 | 27,558 | 27,977 | 44,943 | 127,880 | 4,322,861 |
| 2007 | 3,232,324 | 2,504,072 | 156,610 | 35,293 | 34,478 | 46,158 | 54,761 | 137,016 | 6,200,712 |
| 2006 | 3,459,190 | 2,381,970 | 115,140 | 31,471 | 33,757 | 68,069 | 78,754 | 274,480 | 6,442,831 |
| 2005 | 4,059,286 | 2,585,660 | 146,809 | 36,812 | 37,359 | 55,666 | 71,305 | 253,840 | 7,246,737 |
| 2004 | 4,176,947 | 2,767,305 | 136,229 | 36,203 | 26,058 | 67,252 | 61,918 | 194,827 | 7,466,739 |
| 2003 | 4,238,125 | 2,503,395 | 116,416 | 26,888 | 20,086 | 46,211 | 56,225 | 136,083 | 7,143,429 |
| 2002 | 4,279,792 | 2,274,661 | 121,867 | 29,277 | 15,913 | 40,507 | 62,070 | 139,633 | 6,963,720 |
| 2001 | 3,915,731 | 1,968,010 | 66,787 | 29,876 | 22,616 | 35,815 | 69,749 | 115,002 | 6,223,586 |
| 2000 | 4,533,600 | 1,973,801 | 100,293 | 48,572 | 25,137 | 36,874 | 106,750 | 197,451 | 7,022,478 |
| 1999 | 4,876,534 | 1,891,397 | 116,868 | 44,250 | 19,699 | 25,528 | 122,411 | 248,332 | 7,345,019 |
| 1998 | 4,458,970 | 1,431,110 | 147,839 | 33,513 | 17,441 | 19,850 | 116,412 | 210,050 | 6,435,185 |
| 1997 | 4,377,340 | 1,366,899 | 47,022 | 32,286 | 4,056 | 16,687 | 128,245 | 180,282 | 6,152,817 |
| 1996 | 4,073,778 | 1,344,826 | 38,525 | 32,912 | 4,127 | 12,379 | 106,657 | 162,526 | 5,775,730 |
| 1995 | 3,742,739 | 1,583,878 | 901 | 37,073 | 1,549 | 16,369 | 125,703 | 205,257 | 5,713,469 |
| 1994 | 3,811,837 | 1,478,854 | 848 | 29,585 | 550 | 13,559 | 115,334 | 189,708 | 5,640,275 |
| 1993 | 3,488,278 | 1,124,106 | — | 8,149 | — | 21,943 | 93,939 | 158,809 | 4,895,224 |
| 1992 | 2,978,214 | 850,876 | — | 7,193 | 2 | 21,993 | 81,601 | 122,123 | 4,062,002 |
| 1991 | 2,533,904 | 658,425 | — | 3,820 | 56 | 19,498 | 77,850 | 93,950 | 3,387,503 |
| 1990 | 2,574,071 | 906,423 | — | 789 | 1,726 | 38,123 | 87,107 | 116,966 | 3,725,205 |
| **U.S. DOMESTIC** | | | | | | | | | |
| 2010 | 1,823,848 | 1,568,311 | 87,855 | 3,561 | 14,674 | 25,763 | 25,651 | 68,461 | 3,618,124 |
| 2009 | 1,485,453 | 1,069,687 | 74,899 | 13,994 | 13,428 | 15,772 | 29,317 | 61,769 | 2,764,319 |
| 2008 | 1,975,203 | 1,392,987 | 92,105 | 19,680 | 25,311 | 26,929 | 39,315 | 97,015 | 3,668,545 |
| 2007 | 2,745,028 | 2,185,881 | 146,794 | 32,162 | 31,123 | 45,195 | 50,747 | 102,614 | 5,339,544 |
| 2006 | 3,005,776 | 2,125,307 | 111,461 | 29,255 | 30,804 | 66,753 | 73,039 | 231,418 | 5,673,813 |
| 2005 | 3,569,546 | 2,333,147 | 142,116 | 33,926 | 33,446 | 54,557 | 65,524 | 213,873 | 6,446,135 |
| 2004 | 3,795,422 | 2,530,711 | 131,889 | 33,870 | 23,702 | 65,869 | 56,579 | 164,711 | 6,802,753 |
| 2003 | 3,818,750 | 2,300,058 | 112,745 | 24,960 | 18,304 | 45,515 | 50,927 | 114,990 | 6,486,249 |
| 2002 | 3,827,782 | 2,073,553 | 117,927 | 26,986 | 14,279 | 39,607 | 56,691 | 120,409 | 6,277,234 |
| 2001 | 3,511,326 | 1,794,251 | 61,168 | 27,038 | 20,216 | 34,905 | 64,454 | 99,422 | 5,612,780 |
| 2000 | 4,070,026 | 1,757,683 | 97,697 | 35,407 | 22,602 | 35,752 | 100,175 | 171,565 | 6,290,907 |
| 1999 | 4,453,332 | 1,723,012 | 112,349 | 37,328 | 17,542 | 24,362 | 113,147 | 218,041 | 6,699,113 |
| 1998 | 4,053,521 | 1,303,786 | 141,781 | 29,629 | 15,779 | 18,989 | 105,874 | 177,852 | 5,847,211 |
| 1997 | 3,894,222 | 1,236,119 | 44,893 | 28,428 | 3,931 | 15,609 | 116,922 | 149,183 | 5,489,307 |
| 1996 | 3,699,385 | 1,225,792 | 37,559 | 30,309 | 4,056 | 11,717 | 97,720 | 141,941 | 5,248,479 |
| 1995 | 3,405,062 | 1,458,713 | 780 | 35,427 | 1,471 | 15,046 | 114,194 | 180,652 | 5,211,345 |
| 1994 | 3,475,044 | 1,353,576 | 848 | 28,437 | 533 | 12,123 | 102,745 | 165,375 | 5,138,681 |
| 1993 | 3,187,731 | 1,031,829 | -- | 7,630 | -- | 19,277 | 84,779 | 140,247 | 4,471,493 |
| 1992 | 2,711,172 | 785,198 | -- | 6,612 | 2 | 19,160 | 71,899 | 108,003 | 3,702,046 |
| 1991 | 2,281,761 | 594,435 | -- | 3,547 | 28 | 16,536 | 69,703 | 83,875 | 3,049,885 |
| 1990 | 2,383,892 | 848,690 | -- | 693 | 1,644 | 34,141 | 78,553 | 107,025 | 3,454,638 |

\* Reporting firms do not represent the entire industry.
SOURCE: *Ward's* Automotive Group.

### U.S. FACTORY SALES OF TRUCKS AND BUSES BY GROSS VEHICLE WEIGHT RATING, 1990-2010

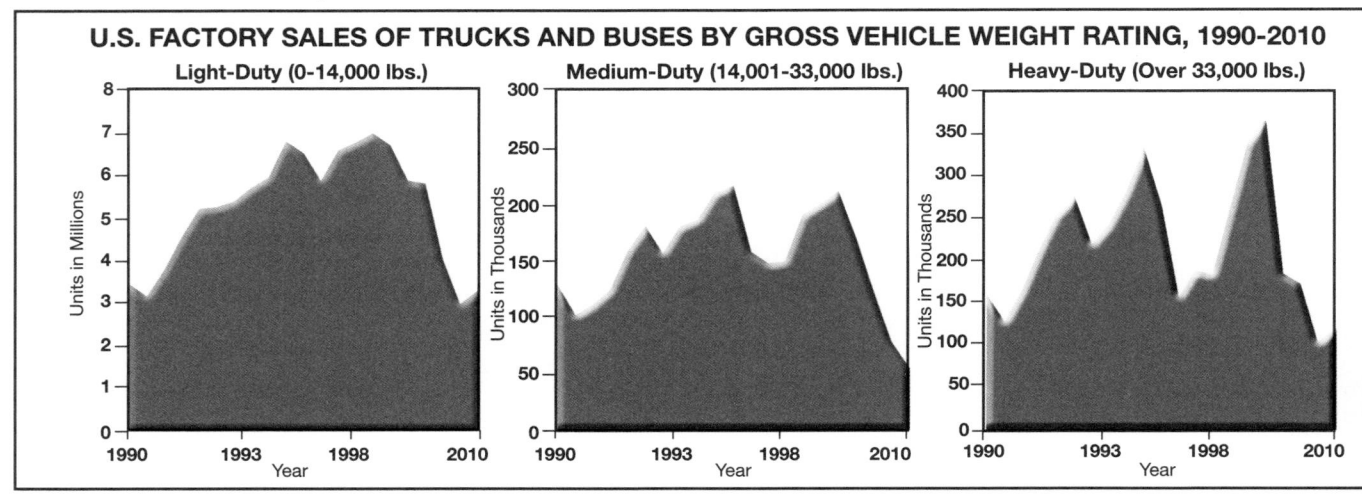

# U.S. Factory Sales of Diesel Trucks and Vehicle Factory Sales from U.S. and Canadian Plants

## U.S. FACTORY SALES OF DIESEL TRUCKS BY GROSS VEHICLE WEIGHT RATING

| | Gross Vehicle Weight Rating (Pounds) | | | | | | | | |
|---|---|---|---|---|---|---|---|---|---|
| | 6,000 & Less | 6,001-10,000 | 10,001-14,000 | 14,001-16,000 | 16,001-19,500 | 19,501-26,000 | 26,001-33,000 | 33,001 & Over | Total |
| **U.S. TOTAL** | | | | | | | | | |
| 2010 | 635 | 282,134 | 45,476 | 3,739 | 15,140 | 24,346 | 10,893 | 90,547 | 472,910 |
| 2009 | 492 | 201,621 | 37,277 | 13,350 | 13,894 | 9,148 | 11,090 | 76,335 | 363,207 |
| 2008 | 1,126 | 213,647 | 44,000 | 17,320 | 25,441 | 16,238 | 22,588 | 127,549 | 467,909 |
| 2007 | 1,292 | 260,435 | 66,575 | 27,631 | 31,665 | 24,170 | 27,592 | 136,839 | 576,199 |
| 2006 | 1,598 | 240,289 | 78,943 | 23,817 | 30,935 | 51,224 | 46,103 | 274,459 | 747,368 |
| 2005 | 2,258 | 246,744 | 100,773 | 27,158 | 34,457 | 40,869 | 39,820 | 253,828 | 745,907 |
| 2000 | 2,580 | 279,224 | 50,571 | 30,223 | 23,422 | 19,807 | 72,509 | 197,451 | 675,787 |
| 1995 | 5,995 | 225,968 | 150 | 25,241 | 1,346 | 11,403 | 93,237 | 205,254 | 568,594 |
| 1990 | 449 | 102,051 | — | 81 | 51 | 12,567 | 61,010 | 116,931 | 293,140 |
| 1985 | 15,447 | 132,871 | 5,870 | — | — | 16,537 | 57,238 | 132,429 | 360,392 |
| 1980 | 72,501 | 4,973 | — | — | — | 15,268 | 34,544 | 116,860 | 244,146 |
| **U.S. DOMESTIC** | | | | | | | | | |
| 2010 | 54 | 222,846 | 43,966 | 3,333 | 13,498 | 22,633 | 9,508 | 68,447 | 384,285 |
| 2009 | 38 | 159,701 | 36,039 | 12,084 | 12,434 | 8,827 | 10,015 | 61,761 | 300,899 |
| 2008 | 81 | 164,700 | 42,539 | 15,674 | 23,267 | 15,626 | 18,689 | 96,899 | 377,475 |
| 2007 | 105 | 207,668 | 64,365 | 24,632 | 28,425 | 23,645 | 24,836 | 102,570 | 476,246 |
| 2006 | 135 | 194,968 | 76,322 | 21,707 | 28,109 | 50,372 | 41,881 | 231,397 | 644,891 |
| 2005 | 192 | 204,413 | 97,427 | 24,431 | 30,692 | 39,939 | 36,183 | 213,861 | 647,138 |
| 2000 | 271 | 221,830 | 48,911 | 26,997 | 20,921 | 18,812 | 68,678 | 171,565 | 577,985 |
| 1995 | 4,579 | 191,758 | 92 | 23,913 | 1,272 | 10,597 | 84,213 | 180,652 | 497,076 |
| 1990 | 337 | 94,030 | — | 55 | 51 | 11,458 | 53,957 | 107,002 | 266,890 |
| 1985 | 9,663 | 123,882 | 5,870 | — | — | 14,253 | 50,492 | 120,311 | 324,471 |
| 1980 | 68,868 | 4,397 | — | — | — | 12,337 | 30,958 | 98,002 | 214,562 |

* Reporting firms do not represent the entire industry.
SOURCE: *Ward's* Automotive Group.

## U.S. AND CANADA TRUCK AND BUS FACTORY SALES

| | U.S. Plants | | | | Canadian Plants | | | |
|---|---|---|---|---|---|---|---|---|
| | U.S Total | Exports to Canada | Other Exports | U.S. Domestic | Canada Total | Exports to U.S. | Other Exports | Canada Domestic |
| 2010 | 4,132,193 | 255,408 | 258,661 | 3,618,124 | 785,087 | 648,199 | 16,704 | 120,184 |
| 2009 | 3,107,426 | 190,641 | 152,466 | 2,764,319 | 493,856 | 407,087 | 11,534 | 75,235 |
| 2008 | 4,322,861 | 296,702 | 357,614 | 3,668,545 | 684,183 | 555,449 | 24,896 | 103,838 |
| 2007 | 6,200,712 | 374,739 | 486,429 | 5,339,544 | 861,711 | 746,417 | 13,004 | 102,290 |
| 2006 | 6,442,831 | 388,689 | 380,329 | 5,673,813 | 713,960 | 626,986 | 9,841 | 77,133 |
| 2005 | 7,246,737 | 424,819 | 375,783 | 6,446,135 | 830,683 | 747,926 | 7,558 | 75,199 |
| 2004 | 7,466,739 | 419,384 | 244,602 | 6,802,753 | 923,873 | 837,521 | 8,542 | 77,810 |
| 2003 | 7,143,429 | 411,539 | 245,641 | 6,486,249 | 917,240 | 806,830 | 8,648 | 101,762 |
| 2002 | 6,963,720 | 446,775 | 239,711 | 6,277,234 | 1,003,861 | 845,602 | 8,187 | 150,072 |
| 2001 | 6,223,586 | 384,775 | 226,031 | 5,612,780 | 982,983 | 851,884 | 5,868 | 125,231 |
| 2000 | 7,022,478 | 410,698 | 320,873 | 6,290,907 | 1,161,654 | 954,641 | 8,899 | 198,114 |
| 1999 | 7,345,059 | 416,010 | 229,936 | 6,699,113 | 1,241,442 | 1,017,982 | 11,814 | 211,646 |
| 1998 | 6,435,185 | 364,865 | 223,109 | 5,847,211 | 1,041,626 | 814,961 | 10,223 | 216,442 |
| 1997 | 6,152,817 | 402,138 | 261,372 | 5,489,307 | 1,153,540 | 924,837 | 11,329 | 217,374 |
| 1996 | 5,775,730 | 327,701 | 199,550 | 5,248,479 | 1,058,106 | 891,117 | 11,772 | 155,217 |
| 1995 | 5,713,469 | 318,470 | 183,654 | 5,211,345 | 1,004,717 | 871,134 | 5,180 | 128,403 |
| 1994 | 5,640,275 | 340,606 | 160,988 | 5,138,681 | 1,031,795 | 896,608 | 5,408 | 129,779 |
| 1993 | 4,895,224 | 286,348 | 137,383 | 4,471,493 | 842,468 | 732,189 | 5,297 | 104,982 |
| 1992 | 4,062,002 | 242,944 | 117,012 | 3,702,046 | 907,346 | 779,824 | 24,725 | 102,797 |
| 1991 | 3,387,503 | 235,432 | 102,186 | 3,049,885 | 790,485 | 648,973 | 33,621 | 107,891 |
| 1990 | 3,725,205 | 207,559 | 63,008 | 3,454,638 | 812,467 | 660,176 | 26,441 | 125,850 |

* Reporting firms do not represent the entire industry.
SOURCE: Ward's Automotive Group.

# Vehicle Production by State and Make

## U.S. VEHICLE PRODUCTION  BY STATE AND PLANT, 2010

| Location | Type | Make/Model | Number |
|---|---|---|---|
| **ALABAMA** | | | |
| Lincoln | Car | Honda Accord | 10,992 |
| Lincoln | Light Truck | Honda Odyssey | 119,580 |
| Lincoln | Light Truck | Honda Pilot | 121,330 |
| Lincoln | Light Truck | Honda Ridgeline | 20,180 |
| **Honda Total** | | | **272,082** |
| Montgomery | Car | Hyundai Elantra | 19,780 |
| Montgomery | Car | Hyundai Sonata | 218,607 |
| Montgomery | Light Truck | Hyundai Santa Fe | 62,113 |
| **Hyundai Total** | | | **300,500** |
| Vance | Light Truck | Mercedes GL | 31,995 |
| Vance | Light Truck | Mercedes M-Class | 76,472 |
| Vance | Light Truck | Mercedes R-Class | 16,870 |
| **Mercedes Total** | | | **125,337** |
| **Total Alabama** | | | **697,919** |
| **CALIFORNIA** | | | |
| Fremont | Car | Toyota Corolla | 63,319 |
| Fremont | Light Truck | Toyota Tacoma | 27,495 |
| **NUMMI Total** | | | **90,814** |
| **Total California** | | | **90,814** |
| **GEORGIA** | | | |
| West Point | Light Truck | Hyundai Santa Fe | 30,093 |
| West Point | Light Truck | Kia Sorento | 122,268 |
| **Kia Total** | | | **152,361** |
| **Total Georgia** | | | **152,361** |
| **ILLINOIS** | | | |
| Belvidere | Car | Dodge Caliber | 67,586 |
| Belvidere | Light Truck | Jeep Compass | 34,412 |
| Belvidere | Light Truck | Jeep Patriot | 66,427 |
| **Chrysler Total** | | | **168,425** |
| Chicago | Car | Ford Taurus | 83,052 |
| Chicago | Car | Lincoln MKS | 16,085 |
| Chicago | Light Truck | Ford Explorer | 11,905 |
| **Ford Total** | | | **111,042** |
| Normal | Car | Mitsubishi Eclipse | 6,424 |
| Normal | Car | Mitsubishi Galant | 16,545 |
| Normal | Light Truck | Mitsubishi Endeavor | 6,406 |
| **Mitsubishi Total** | | | **29,375** |
| **Total Illinois** | | | **308,842** |
| **INDIANA** | | | |
| Fort Wayne | Light Truck | Chevrolet Silverado | 214,842 |
| Fort Wayne | Light Truck | GMC Sierra | 89,837 |
| **GM Total** | | | **304,679** |
| Greensburg | Car | Honda Civic | 95,116 |
| **Honda Total** | | | **95,116** |
| Lafayette | Car | Subaru Legacy | 43,791 |
| Lafayette | Car | Toyota Camry | 87,731 |
| Lafayette | Light Truck | Subaru Outback | 108,686 |
| Lafayette | Light Truck | Subaru Tribeca | 5,543 |
| **Subaru Total** | | | **245,751** |
| Princeton | Light Truck | Toyota Highlander | 86,527 |
| Princeton | Light Truck | Toyota Sequoia | 24,685 |
| Princeton | Light Truck | Toyota Sienna | 132,780 |
| **Toyota Total** | | | **243,992** |
| **Total Indiana** | | | **889,538** |
| **KANSAS** | | | |
| Fairfax | Car | Buick LaCrosse | 73,480 |
| Fairfax | Car | Chevrolet Malibu | 235,956 |
| **GM Total** | | | **309,436** |
| **Total Kansas** | | | **309,436** |
| **KENTUCKY** | | | |
| Kentucky Truck | Light Truck | Ford Expedition | 51,295 |
| Kentucky Truck | Light Truck | Ford F-Series | 177,475 |
| Kentucky Truck | Light Truck | Lincoln Navigator | 9,636 |
| Kentucky Truck | Med./Hvy. Truck | Ford F-Series | 22,909 |
| Louisville | Light Truck | Ford Explorer | 85,407 |
| Louisville | Light Truck | Mercury Mountaineer | 4,564 |
| **Ford Total** | | | **351,286** |
| Bowling Green | Car | Chevrolet Corvette | 15,791 |
| **GM Total** | | | **15,791** |
| Georgetown | Car | Toyota Avalon | 40,155 |
| Georgetown | Car | Toyota Camry | 270,249 |
| Georgetown | Light Truck | Toyota Venza | 61,290 |
| **Toyota Total** | | | **371,694** |
| **Total Kentucky** | | | **738,771** |
| **LOUISIANA** | | | |
| Shreveport | Light Truck | Chevrolet Colorado | 34,509 |
| Shreveport | Light Truck | GMC Canyon | 12,436 |
| Shreveport | Light Truck | Hummer H3 | 1,183 |
| Shreveport | Light Truck | Hummer H3T | 321 |
| **GM Total** | | | **48,449** |
| **Total Louisiana** | | | **48,449** |
| **MICHIGAN** | | | |
| Flat Rock | Car | Ford Mustang | 77,586 |
| Flat Rock | Car | Mazda6 | 45,168 |
| **AutoAlliance Total** | | | **122,754** |
| Detroit (Conner) | Car | Dodge Viper | 459 |
| Detroit (Jefferson N.) | Light Truck | Dodge Durango | 3,429 |
| Detroit (Jefferson N.) | Light Truck | Jeep Commander | 5,582 |
| Detroit (Jefferson N.) | Light Truck | Jeep Grand Cherokee | 125,142 |
| Sterling Heights | Car | Chrysler 200 Series | 2,197 |
| Sterling Heights | Car | Chrysler Sebring Convertible | 7,829 |
| Sterling Heights | Car | Chrysler Sebring Sedan | 32,157 |
| Sterling Heights | Car | Dodge Avenger | 59,170 |
| Warren | Light Truck | Ram Dakota | 19,043 |
| Warren | Light Truck | Ram Pickup | 178,406 |
| **Chrysler Total** | | | **433,414** |
| Dearborn Truck | Light Truck | Ford F-Series | 312,480 |
| Dearborn Truck | Light Truck | Lincoln Mark LT | 847 |
| Detroit | Med./Hvy. Truck | Ford Chassis | 7,143 |
| Wayne | Car | Ford Focus | 199,185 |
| Wayne (MI Assembly) | Car | Ford Focus | 317 |
| **Ford Total** | | | **519,972** |
| Flint 1 | Light Truck | Chevrolet Silverado | 79,960 |

# Vehicle Production by State and Make

## U.S. VEHICLE PRODUCTION BY STATE AND PLANT, 2010 — continued

| Plant | Type | Make/Model | Units |
|---|---|---|---|
| Flint 1 | Light Truck | GMC Sierra | 35,009 |
| Hamtramck | Car | Buick Lucerne | 29,654 |
| Hamtramck | Car | Cadillac DTS | 21,023 |
| Hamtramck | Car | Chevrolet Volt | 1,219 |
| Lansing Delta | Light Truck | Buick Enclave | 74,414 |
| Lansing Delta | Light Truck | Chevrolet Traverse | 118,220 |
| Lansing Delta | Light Truck | GMC Acadia | 82,555 |
| Lansing Delta | Light Truck | Saturn Outlook | 2,507 |
| Lansing Grand River | Car | Cadillac CTS | 60,688 |
| Lansing Grand River | Car | Cadillac STS | 4,792 |
| Orion | Car | Pontiac G6 | 1 |
| **GM Total** | | | **510,042** |
| **Total Michigan** | | | **1,586,182** |
| **MINNESOTA** | | | |
| Twin Cities | Light Truck | Ford Ranger | 70,666 |
| Twin Cities | Light Truck | Mazda Pickup | 2,395 |
| **Ford Total** | | | **73,061** |
| **Total Minnesota** | | | **73,061** |
| **MISSISSIPPI** | | | |
| Canton | Car | Nissan Altima | 171,240 |
| Canton | Light Truck | Infiniti QX56 | 3,466 |
| Canton | Light Truck | Nissan Armada | 26,260 |
| Canton | Light Truck | Nissan Titan | 28,022 |
| **Nissan Total** | | | **228,988** |
| **Total Mississippi** | | | **228,988** |
| **MISSOURI** | | | |
| Kansas City 1 | Light Truck | Ford Escape | 275,646 |
| Kansas City 1 | Light Truck | Mazda Tribute | 9,273 |
| Kansas City 1 | Light Truck | Mercury Mariner | 25,050 |
| Kansas City 2 | Light Truck | Ford F-Series | 126,586 |
| **Ford Total** | | | **436,555** |
| Wentzville | Light Truck | Chevrolet Express | 69,328 |
| Wentzville | Light Truck | GMC Savana | 21,688 |
| **GM Total** | | | **91,016** |
| **Total Missouri** | | | **527,571** |
| **OHIO** | | | |
| Toledo North | Light Truck | Dodge Nitro | 27,562 |
| Toledo North | Light Truck | Jeep Liberty | 64,411 |
| Toledo South | Light Truck | Jeep Wrangler | 59,181 |
| Toledo South | Light Truck | Jeep Wrangler Unlimited | 85,504 |
| **Chrysler Total** | | | **236,658** |
| Avon Lake | Light Truck | Ford Econoline | 121,471 |
| **Ford Total** | | | **121,471** |
| Lordstown | Car | Chevrolet Cobalt | 91,796 |
| Lordstown | Car | Pontiac G5 | 66,303 |
| **GM Total** | | | **158,099** |
| East Liberty | Light Truck | Honda CR-V | 196,743 |
| East Liberty | Light Truck | Honda Crosstour | 33,200 |
| East Liberty | Light Truck | Honda Element | 16,800 |
| Marysville | Car | Acura TL | 35,294 |
| Marysville | Car | Honda Accord | 284,717 |
| Marysville | Light Truck | Acura RDX | 20,550 |
| **Honda Total** | | | **587,304** |
| **Total Ohio** | | | **1,103,532** |
| **SOUTH CAROLINA** | | | |
| Spartanburg | Light Truck | BMW X3 | 16,078 |
| Spartanburg | Light Truck | BMW X5 | 98,245 |
| Spartanburg | Light Truck | BMW X6 | 43,380 |
| **BMW Total** | | | **157,703** |
| **Total South Carolina** | | | **157,703** |
| **TENNESSEE** | | | |
| Smyrna | Car | Nissan Altima | 103,875 |
| Smyrna | Car | Nissan Maxima | 71,776 |
| Smyrna | Light Truck | Nissan Frontier | 48,658 |
| Smyrna | Light Truck | Nissan Pathfinder | 29,786 |
| Smyrna | Light Truck | Nissan Xterra | 26,180 |
| Smyrna | Light Truck | Suzuki Equator | 1,630 |
| **Nissan Total** | | | **281,905** |
| **Total Tennessee** | | | **281,905** |
| **TEXAS** | | | |
| Arlington | Light Truck | Cadillac Escalade | 22,753 |
| Arlington | Light Truck | Cadillac Escalade ESV | 12,693 |
| Arlington | Light Truck | Chevrolet Suburban | 58,889 |
| Arlington | Light Truck | Chevrolet Tahoe | 101,499 |
| Arlington | Light Truck | GMC Yukon | 50,402 |
| Arlington | Light Truck | GMC Yukon XL | 35,793 |
| **GM Total** | | | **282,029** |
| San Antonio | Light Truck | Toyota Tacoma | 42,139 |
| San Antonio | Light Truck | Toyota Tundra | 107,959 |
| **Toyota Total** | | | **150,098** |
| **Total Texas** | | | **432,127** |
| **OTHER** | | | |
| Freightliner | Med./Hvy. Truck | | 24,756 |
| Hino | Med./Hvy. Truck | | 3,484 |
| International | Med./Hvy. Truck | | 32,479 |
| Kenworth | Med./Hvy. Truck | | 14,916 |
| Mack | Med./Hvy. Truck | | 13,546 |
| Peterbilt | Med./Hvy. Truck | | 13,853 |
| Volvo Truck | Med./Hvy. Truck | | 12,836 |
| Other | Med./Hvy. Truck | | 24 |
| **TOTAL U.S. CARS** | | | **2,731,105** |
| **TOTAL U.S. LIGHT TRUCKS** | | | **4,866,042** |
| **TOTAL U.S. MED./HVY. TRUCKS** | | | **145,946** |
| **TOTAL U.S. VEHICLES** | | | **7,743,093** |

## TOP STATES IN CALENDAR 2010 U.S. PRODUCTION

| Rank | Cars | Rank | Trucks |
|---|---|---|---|
| 1. Michigan | 541,445 | 1. Michigan | 1,044,737 |
| 2. Ohio | 478,110 | 2. Indiana | 662,900 |
| 3. Kentucky | 326,195 | 3. Ohio | 657,901 |
| 4. Kansas | 309,436 | 4. Missouri | 527,571 |
| 5. Alabama | 249,379 | 5. Alabama | 448,540 |

SOURCE: *Ward's AutoInfoBank.*

# Factory Installations of Selected Equipment

## FACTORY INSTALLATIONS OF SELECTED EQUIPMENT BY MODEL YEAR

| | 2010 | | 2009 | | 2008 | | 2007 | |
|---|---|---|---|---|---|---|---|---|
| | Units (000) | % of Total | Units (000) | % of Total | Units (000) | % of Total | Units (000) | % of Total |
| **CARS** | | | | | | | | |
| Automatic Transmission | 4,171 | 91.1 | 3,556 | 91.4 | 5,281 | 91.5 | 5,253 | 90.4 |
| 5-Speed Transmission | 174 | 3.8 | 241 | 6.2 | 373 | 6.5 | 408 | 7.0 |
| 6-Speed Transmission | 236 | 5.1 | 93 | 2.4 | 115 | 2.0 | 154 | 2.6 |
| All-Wheel Drive | 141 | 3.1 | 150 | 3.9 | 158 | 2.7 | 159 | 2.7 |
| 4-Cylinder Engine | 2,953 | 64.5 | 2,539 | 65.3 | 3,186 | 55.2 | 3,059 | 52.6 |
| 6-Cylinder Engine | 1,147 | 25.0 | 938 | 24.1 | 1,804 | 31.3 | 2,015 | 34.6 |
| 8-Cylinder Engine | 260 | 5.7 | 191 | 4.9 | 341 | 5.9 | 419 | 7.2 |
| Stability Control | 3,563 | 77.8 | 1,690 | 43.5 | 953 | 16.5 | 693 | 11.9 |
| Antilock Brakes | 4,484 | 97.9 | 3,494 | 89.8 | 4,524 | 78.4 | 4,186 | 72.0 |
| Power Door Locks | 4,474 | 97.7 | 3,756 | 96.6 | 5,571 | 96.6 | 5,544 | 95.3 |
| Power Seats, 4 or 6 way | 2,057 | 44.9 | 2,038 | 52.4 | 2,761 | 47.9 | 2,676 | 46.0 |
| Memory Seats | 188 | 4.1 | 220 | 5.5 | 384 | 6.7 | 365 | 6.3 |
| Power Windows | 4,474 | 97.7 | 3,750 | 96.4 | 5,561 | 96.4 | 5,564 | 95.7 |
| Sun Roof | 1,246 | 27.2 | 1,006 | 25.9 | 1,531 | 26.5 | 1,499 | 25.8 |
| Side Airbags | 4,436 | 96.8 | 3,455 | 88.8 | 4,190 | 72.6 | 3,633 | 62.5 |
| Side Curtain Airbags | 4,332 | 94.6 | 3,561 | 91.5 | 4,603 | 79.8 | 3,846 | 66.1 |
| Navigation System | 292 | 6.4 | 191 | 4.9 | 262 | 4.5 | 216 | 3.7 |
| Keyless Remote | 4,384 | 95.7 | 3,663 | 94.2 | 5,341 | 92.6 | 5,278 | 90.8 |
| Air Conditioning,Automatic Temp. Control | 1,011 | 22.1 | 843 | 21.7 | 1,196 | 20.7 | 1,256 | 21.6 |
| Air Conditioning, Manual Temp. Control | 3,550 | 77.5 | 3,020 | 77.6 | 4,532 | 78.6 | 4,517 | 77.7 |
| Limited-Slip Differential | 234 | 5.1 | 157 | 4.0 | 256 | 4.4 | 270 | 4.6 |
| Styled Wheels | 2,765 | 60.3 | 2,499 | 64.3 | 3,603 | 62.5 | 3,675 | 63.2 |
| Automatic Headlamp | 2,829 | 61.7 | 2,050 | 52.7 | 3,365 | 58.3 | 2,968 | 51.0 |
| Cruise Control | 4,392 | 95.9 | 3,653 | 93.9 | 5,369 | 93.1 | 5,278 | 90.8 |
| **LIGHT TRUCKS (0-10,000 lbs. G.V.W.R.)** | | | | | | | | |
| AutomaticTransmission | 5,192 | 98.1 | 3,983 | 98.2 | 6,860 | 97.8 | 7,373 | 96.5 |
| Four Wheel Antilock Brakes | 5,284 | 99.8 | 4,024 | 99.3 | 6,690 | 95.3 | 7,158 | 93.7 |
| Rear Antilock Brakes | 9,191 | 0.2 | 5 | 0.1 | 203 | 2.9 | 247 | 3.2 |
| Keyless Entry | 4,740 | 89.6 | 3,549 | 87.5 | 6,135 | 87.4 | 6,533 | 85.5 |
| Side Airbag | 3,207 | 60.6 | 2,068 | 51.0 | 3,471 | 49.5 | 2,396 | 31.4 |
| Four-Wheel Drive | 2,561 | 48.4 | 1,913 | 47.2 | 3,411 | 48.6 | 3,565 | 46.7 |
| Diesel Engine | 177 | 3.3 | 236 | 5.8 | 459 | 6.5 | 392 | 5.1 |
| 4-Cylinder Gasoline Engine | 940 | 17.8 | 600 | 14.8 | 706 | 10.1 | 754 | 9.9 |
| 5-Cylinder Gasoline Engine | 41 | 0.8 | 36 | 0.9 | 88 | 1.3 | 112 | 1.5 |
| 6-Cylinder Gasoline Engine | 2,513 | 47.5 | 1,742 | 43.0 | 3,248 | 46.3 | 3,461 | 45.3 |
| 8-Cylinder Gasoline Engine | 1,788 | 33.8 | 1,429 | 35.3 | 2,487 | 35.5 | 3,275 | 42.9 |
| 10-Cylinder Gasoline Engine | 12 | 0.2 | 11 | 0.3 | 29 | 0.4 | 35 | 0.5 |
| Air Conditioning | 5,224 | 98.7 | 4,032 | 99.5 | 7,006 | 99.8 | 7,619 | 99.8 |
| Cruise Control | 4,982 | 94.1 | 3,751 | 92.5 | 6,422 | 91.5 | 6,856 | 89.8 |
| Limited-Slip Differential | 1,165 | 22.0 | 1,149 | 28.4 | 2,049 | 29.2 | 2,413 | 31.6 |

NOTE: Based on production in the United States, Canada and Mexico for the United States market.
SOURCE: Ward's Automotive Group.

# Recreation Vehicle Shipments

## U.S. RECREATION VEHICLE SHIPMENTS BY TYPE

| Year | Total All Types | Travel Trailers Conven-tional | Fifth Wheel[1] | Folding Camping Trailers | Truck Campers | Motor Homes Type A Conven-tional | Type B Van Campers[2] | Type C Chopped Vans[3] | Multi-use Van Con-versions |
|------|------|------|------|------|------|------|------|------|------|
| 2010 | 242,300 | 144,500 | 54,700 | 15,000 | 2,900 | 13,100 | 1,600 | 10,500 | NA |
| 2009 | 165,700 | 101,500 | 36,800 | 12,300 | 1,900 | 5,900 | 1,200 | 6,100 | NA |
| 2008 | 237,000 | 128,100 | 57,000 | 18,900 | 4,700 | 14,900 | 1,900 | 11,500 | NA |
| 2007 | 353,500 | 180,200 | 81,500 | 28,800 | 7,500 | 32,900 | 3,100 | 19,500 | NA |
| 2006 | 416,800 | 203,600 | 88,800 | 34,000 | 8,200 | 32,700 | 3,000 | 20,200 | 26,300 |
| 2005 | 419,500 | 196,600 | 84,800 | 32,800 | 8,800 | 37,900 | 2,600 | 20,900 | 35,100 |
| 2004 | 412,100 | 163,600 | 91,000 | 34,100 | 9,600 | 46,300 | 2,500 | 23,000 | 42,000 |
| 2003 | 377,800 | 139,800 | 74,600 | 35,700 | 8,800 | 41,500 | 2,100 | 18,300 | 57,000 |
| 2002 | 378,700 | 129,700 | 66,100 | 44,800 | 10,000 | 39,600 | 2,800 | 18,000 | 67,700 |
| 2001 | 321,000 | 102,200 | 54,700 | 40,800 | 9,900 | 33,400 | 2,600 | 13,200 | 64,200 |
| 2000 | 418,300 | 114,500 | 62,300 | 51,300 | 11,100 | 41,000 | 3,400 | 16,500 | 118,200 |
| 1999 | 473,800 | 117,500 | 60,500 | 60,100 | 11,500 | 49,400 | 3,600 | 18,600 | 152,600 |
| 1998 | 441,300 | 98,600 | 56,500 | 63,300 | 10,800 | 42,900 | 3,600 | 17,000 | 148,600 |
| 1997 | 438,800 | 78,800 | 52,800 | 57,600 | 10,300 | 37,600 | 3,800 | 13,600 | 184,300 |
| 1996 | 466,800 | 75,400 | 48,500 | 57,300 | 11,000 | 36,500 | 4,100 | 14,700 | 219,300 |
| 1995 | 475,200 | 75,300 | 45,900 | 61,100 | 11,900 | 33,000 | 4,100 | 15,700 | 228,200 |
| 1994 | 518,800 | 79,100 | 48,900 | 61,700 | 11,400 | 37,300 | 3,500 | 17,300 | 259,600 |
| 1993 | 420,200 | 69,700 | 43,900 | 51,900 | 10,900 | 31,900 | 3,000 | 16,500 | 192,400 |
| 1992 | 382,700 | 63,600 | 38,900 | 43,300 | 10,600 | 27,300 | 2,900 | 16,800 | 179,300 |
| 1991 | 293,700 | 49,300 | 28,300 | 33,900 | 9,600 | 23,500 | 3,500 | 15,200 | 130,400 |
| 1990 | 347,300 | 52,500 | 27,900 | 30,700 | 9,700 | 29,000 | 5,900 | 17,400 | 174,200 |
| 1989 | 388,300 | 53,500 | 29,400 | 33,900 | 9,900 | 35,400 | 5,000 | 20,800 | 200,400 |
| 1988 | 420,000 | 58,300 | 31,300 | 42,300 | 11,000 | 41,500 | 5,200 | 26,200 | 204,200 |
| 1987 | 393,600 | 59,100 | 27,100 | 41,600 | 10,100 | 40,800 | 6,600 | 26,400 | 181,900 |
| 1986 | 371,700 | 55,100 | 23,100 | 36,500 | 7,400 | 33,300 | 6,200 | 28,200 | 181,900 |

(1) To be towed by pickup truck with fifth-wheel hitch mounted on the truck bed.
(2) Panel-type trucks with interior converted to living area.
(3) Chopped Vans: Mini - unit over 8' high attaches to van chassis of 6,500 lbs. GVWR or more; Low Profile - unit less than 8' high attaches to van chassis of 6,500 lbs. GVWR or more: Compact - unit attaches to van chassis less than 6,500 lbs. GVWR.
SOURCE: Recreation Vehicle Industry Assn.

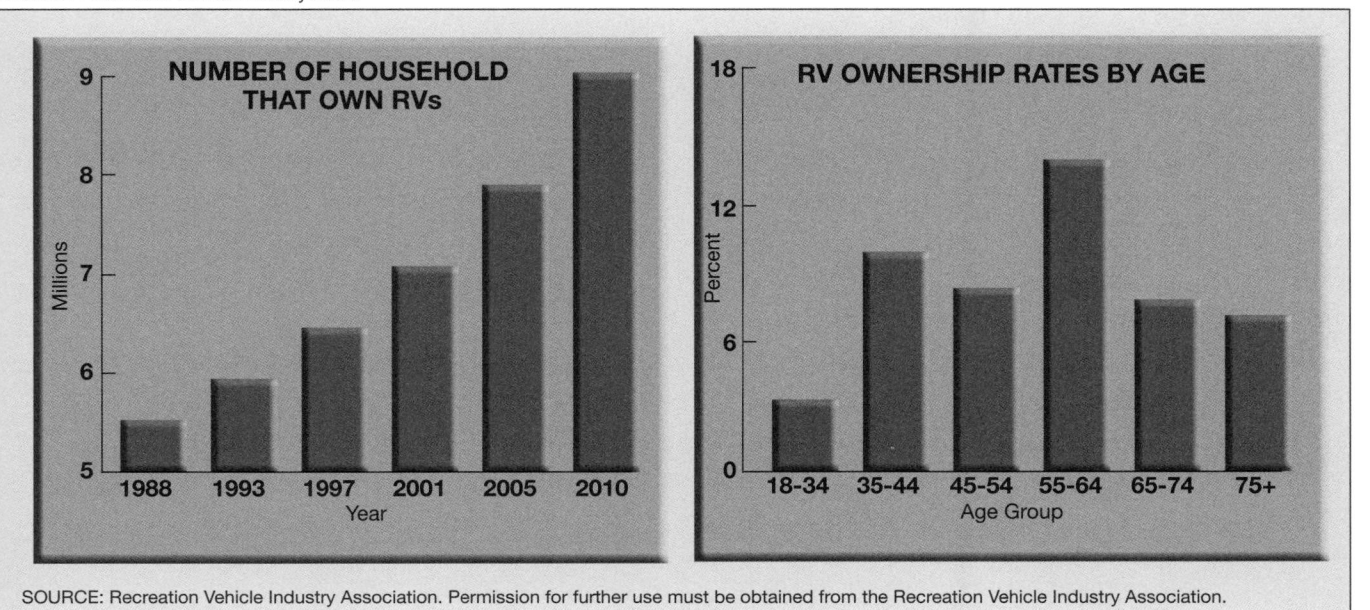

SOURCE: Recreation Vehicle Industry Association. Permission for further use must be obtained from the Recreation Vehicle Industry Association.

# World Vehicle Production by Country

## WORLD VEHICLE PRODUCTION IN MAJOR COUNTRIES, 2010

| Region/Country | Cars | Commercial Vehicles | Total |
|---|---|---|---|
| **North America** | | | |
| Canada | 967,077 | 1,101,112 | 2,068,189 |
| Mexico | 1,386,148 | 956,134 | 2,342,282 |
| United States | 2,731,105 | 5,011,988 | 7,743,093 |
| **Total** | **5,084,330** | **7,069,234** | **12,153,564** |
| **Western Europe** | | | |
| Austria | 86,183 | 18,814 | 104,997 |
| Belgium | 528,224 | 26,426 | 554,650 |
| France | 1,914,029 | 304,729 | 2,218,758 |
| Germany | 5,552,409 | 353,576 | 5,905,985 |
| Italy | 573,169 | 263,096 | 836,265 |
| Netherlands | 48,025 | 46,107 | 94,132 |
| Portugal | 114,563 | 44,160 | 158,723 |
| Spain | 1,951,380 | 436,519 | 2,387,899 |
| Sweden | 177,084 | 31,343 | 208,427 |
| United Kingdom | 1,274,291 | 119,200 | 1,393,491 |
| **Total** | **12,219,357** | **1,643,970** | **13,863,327** |
| **Eastern/Central Europe** | | | |
| Czech Republic | 1,069,518 | 6,867 | 1,076,385 |
| Poland | 799,255 | 95,552 | 894,807 |
| Russia | 1,208,362 | 195,489 | 1,403,851 |
| Slovakia | 562,612 | 0 | 562,612 |
| Turkey | 603,394 | 491,163 | 1,094,557 |
| Other | 759,013 | 63,790 | 822,803 |
| **Total** | **5,002,154** | **852,861** | **5,855,015** |
| **Asia/Pacific** | | | |
| Australia | 205,334 | 34,109 | 239,443 |
| China | 9,494,018 | 8,770,649 | 18,264,667 |
| India | 2,316,931 | 1,236,872 | 3,553,803 |
| Japan | 8,307,382 | 1,318,558 | 9,625,940 |
| South Korea | 2,792,210 | 1,479,531 | 4,271,741 |
| Other | 1,815,547 | 1,556,406 | 3,371,953 |
| **Total** | **24,931,422** | **14,396,125** | **39,327,547** |
| **South America** | | | |
| Argentina | 515,884 | 208,139 | 724,023 |
| Brazil | 2,828,273 | 820,085 | 3,648,358 |
| Venezuela | 60,810 | 43,547 | 104,357 |
| **Total** | **3,404,967** | **1,071,771** | **4,476,738** |
| **South Africa** | **295,394** | **176,655** | **472,049** |
| **Total Vehicles** | **50,937,624** | **25,210,616** | **76,148,240** |

NOTE: North America excludes buses. Table excludes smaller non-reporting countries.
SOURCE: Compiled by *Ward's* from various industry sources.

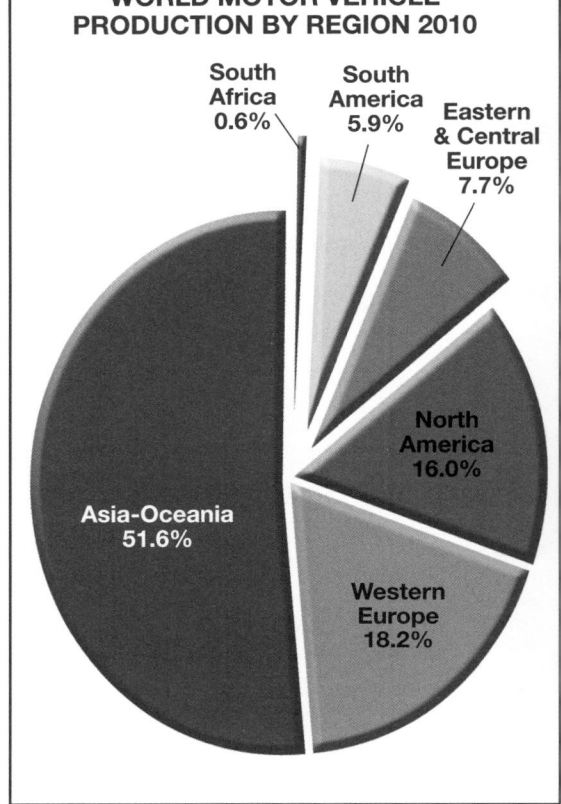

**WORLD MOTOR VEHICLE PRODUCTION BY REGION 2010**

South Africa 0.6%
South America 5.9%
Eastern & Central Europe 7.7%
North America 16.0%
Western Europe 18.2%
Asia-Oceania 51.6%

## WORLD VEHICLE PRODUCTION

| Year | United States | Canada | U.S. & Canada Total | Western Europe | China | Japan | Other | World Total | Percent of World Total United States | Percent of World Total U.S. & Canada |
|---|---|---|---|---|---|---|---|---|---|---|
| 2010 | 7,743 | 2,068 | 9,811 | 13,863 | 18,265 | 9,626 | 24,583 | 76,148 | 10.2 | 12.9 |
| 2009 | 5,709 | 1,490 | 7,199 | 12,315 | 13,649 | 7,935 | 19,156 | 60,254 | 9.5 | 11.9 |
| 2008 | 8,673 | 2,082 | 10,755 | 15,310 | 9,233 | 11,564 | 22,722 | 69,584 | 12.5 | 15.5 |
| 2007 | 10,752 | 2,579 | 13,331 | 16,892 | 8,885 | 11,596 | 21,936 | 72,640 | 14.8 | 18.4 |
| 2006 | 11,260 | 2,571 | 13,831 | 16,540 | 7,566 | 11,484 | 19,703 | 69,124 | 16.3 | 20.0 |
| 2005 | 11,947 | 2,688 | 14,635 | 16,806 | 5,668 | 10,780 | 18,196 | 66,085 | 18.1 | 22.1 |
| 2000 | 12,771 | 2,962 | 15,732 | 16,749 | 2,069 | 10,145 | 14,251 | 58,946 | 21.7 | 26.7 |
| 1995 | 11,985 | 2,408 | 14,393 | 17,045 | 1,435 | 10,196 | 6,914 | 49,983 | 24.0 | 28.8 |
| 1990 | 9,783 | 1,928 | 11,711 | 18,866 | 509 | 13,487 | 3,981 | 48,554 | 20.1 | 24.1 |
| 1985 | 11,653 | 1,933 | 13,586 | 16,113 | 443 | 12,271 | 2,496 | 44,909 | 25.9 | 30.3 |
| 1980 | 8,010 | 1,324 | 9,334 | 15,496 | 141 | 11,043 | 2,551 | 38,565 | 20.8 | 24.2 |
| 1975 | 8,987 | 1,385 | 10,372 | 13,581 | NA | 6,942 | 2,211 | 33,106 | 27.1 | 31.3 |
| 1970 | 8,284 | 1,160 | 9,444 | 13,049 | NA | 5,289 | 1,637 | 29,419 | 28.2 | 32.1 |
| 1965 | 11,138 | 847 | 11,985 | 9,576 | NA | 1,876 | 834 | 24,271 | 45.9 | 49.4 |
| 1960 | 7,905 | 398 | 8,303 | 6,837 | NA | 482 | 866 | 16,488 | 47.9 | 50.4 |
| 1955 | 9,204 | 452 | 9,656 | 3,741 | NA | 68 | 163 | 13,628 | 67.5 | 70.9 |
| 1950 | 8,006 | 388 | 8,394 | 1,991 | NA | 32 | 160 | 10,577 | 75.7 | 79.4 |

NA - Not available.
NOTE: Units in thousands.
SOURCE: Ward's Automotive Group.

# World Vehicle Production by Manufacturer

## WORLD VEHICLE PRODUCTION FOR SELECT MANUFACTURERS BY REGION

| Manufacturer/Region | 2009 Cars | 2009 Commercial Vehicles | 2009 Total | 2008 Cars | 2008 Commercial Vehicles | 2008 Total |
|---|---|---|---|---|---|---|
| **BMW** | | | | | | |
| Africa | 47,749 | — | 47,749 | 50,465 | — | 50,465 |
| Asia/Pacific | 7,602 | — | 7,602 | 7,221 | — | 7,221 |
| North America | — | 121,666 | 121,666 | 9,771 | 160,968 | 170,739 |
| Western Europe | 1,087,017 | — | 1,087,017 | 1,218,366 | — | 1,218,366 |
| **Total BMW** | **1,142,368** | **121,666** | **1,264,034** | **1,285,823** | **160,968** | **1,446,791** |
| **Chrysler** | | | | | | |
| Africa | 655 | — | 655 | 575 | — | 575 |
| Europe | 5,376 | — | 5,376 | 28,207 | — | 28,207 |
| North America | 205,784 | 747,910 | 953,694 | 501,251 | 1,363,610 | 1,864,861 |
| South America | 2,734 | 10,311 | 13,045 | 2,814 | 9,860 | 12,674 |
| **Total Chrysler** | **214,549** | **758,221** | **972,770** | **532,847** | **1,373,470** | **1,906,317** |
| **Daimler** | | | | | | |
| Africa | 42,585 | 3,113 | 45,698 | 52,365 | 6,995 | 59,360 |
| Asia/Pacific | 11,249 | 129,092 | 140,341 | 12,572 | 217,320 | 229,892 |
| Europe | 888,579 | 198,041 | 1,086,620 | 1,124,539 | 399,312 | 1,523,851 |
| North America | — | 140,996 | 140,996 | — | 246,131 | 246,131 |
| South America | 15,211 | 66,962 | 82,173 | 27,095 | 100,000 | 127,095 |
| **Total Daimler** | **957,624** | **538,204** | **1,495,828** | **1,216,571** | **969,758** | **2,186,329** |
| **Fiat** | | | | | | |
| Africa | — | 1,550 | 1,550 | — | 1,950 | 1,950 |
| Asia/Pacific | 23,677 | — | 23,677 | 5,048 | — | 5,048 |
| Europe | 1,348,830 | 345,569 | 1,694,399 | 1,184,046 | 591,250 | 1,775,296 |
| South America | 681,681 | 148,546 | 830,227 | 631,789 | 144,881 | 776,670 |
| **Total Fiat** | **2,054,188** | **495,665** | **2,549,853** | **1,820,883** | **738,081** | **2,558,964** |
| **Ford** | | | | | | |
| Africa | 15,200 | 24,822 | 40,022 | 13,566 | 41,957 | 55,523 |
| Asia/Pacific | 85,783 | 120,972 | 206,755 | 74,038 | 167,957 | 241,995 |
| Europe | 1,269,297 | 201,146 | 1,470,443 | 1,484,225 | 344,789 | 1,829,014 |
| North America | 650,492 | 1,241,737 | 1,892,229 | 868,246 | 1,424,192 | 2,292,438 |
| South America | 290,806 | 157,100 | 447,906 | 253,280 | 185,687 | 438,967 |
| **Total Ford** | **2,311,578** | **1,745,777** | **4,057,355** | **2,693,355** | **2,164,582** | **4,857,937** |
| **General Motors** | | | | | | |
| Africa | 42,526 | 40,234 | 82,760 | 47,428 | 33,392 | 80,820 |
| Asia/Pacific | 583,985 | 119,290 | 703,275 | 865,879 | 233,158 | 1,099,037 |
| Europe | 1,176,702 | 86,836 | 1,263,538 | 1,644,403 | 153,446 | 1,797,849 |
| North America | 698,729 | 1,185,242 | 1,883,971 | 1,472,781 | 1,918,189 | 3,390,970 |
| South America | 601,924 | 124,587 | 726,511 | 630,457 | 140,704 | 771,161 |
| **Total General Motors** | **3,103,866** | **1,556,189** | **4,660,055** | **4,660,948** | **2,478,889** | **7,139,837** |
| **Honda** | | | | | | |
| Asia/Pacific | 1,130,221 | 33,186 | 1,163,407 | 1,594,611 | 40,247 | 1,634,858 |
| Europe | 93,847 | — | 93,847 | 280,496 | — | 280,496 |
| North America | 617,967 | 412,991 | 1,030,958 | 855,029 | 566,398 | 1,421,427 |
| South America | 132,122 | — | 132,122 | 131,139 | — | 131,139 |
| **Total Honda** | **1,974,157** | **446,177** | **2,420,334** | **2,861,275** | **606,645** | **3,467,920** |
| **Hyundai-Kia** | | | | | | |
| Africa | 15,354 | 86 | 15,440 | 20,530 | 101 | 20,631 |
| Asia/Pacific | 2,311,240 | 1,017,167 | 3,328,407 | 2,104,453 | 1,141,899 | 3,246,352 |
| Europe | 316,667 | — | 316,667 | 295,147 | — | 295,147 |
| North America | 103,876 | 107,185 | 211,061 | 152,588 | 84,454 | 237,042 |
| South America | 3,061 | 6,814 | 9,875 | 6,069 | — | 6,069 |

# World Vehicle Production by Manufacturer

## WORLD VEHICLE PRODUCTION FOR SELECT MANUFACTURERS BY REGION — continued

| Manufacturer/Region | 2009 Cars | 2009 Commercial Vehicles | 2009 Total | 2008 Cars | 2008 Commercial Vehicles | 2008 Total |
|---|---|---|---|---|---|---|
| **Total Hyundai-Kia** | **2,750,198** | **1,131,252** | **3,881,450** | **2,578,787** | **1,226,454** | **3,805,241** |
| **Mitsubishi** | | | | | | |
| Africa | — | 2,500 | 2,500 | — | 73,333 | 73,333 |
| Asia/Pacific | 382,537 | 158,339 | 540,876 | 784,479 | 248,923 | 1,033,402 |
| Europe | 50,620 | — | 50,620 | 59,223 | — | 59,223 |
| North America | 14,798 | 3,703 | 18,501 | 54,480 | 4,538 | 59,018 |
| South America | 2,005 | 32,560 | 34,565 | 3,679 | 37,643 | 41,322 |
| **Total Mitsubishi** | **449,960** | **197,102** | **647,062** | **901,861** | **364,437** | **1,266,298** |
| **Nissan** | | | | | | |
| Africa | 9,063 | 26,897 | 35,960 | 12,983 | 40,695 | 53,678 |
| Asia/Pacific | 852,702 | 186,294 | 1,038,996 | 1,179,466 | 276,004 | 1,455,470 |
| Europe | 361,054 | 33,207 | 394,261 | 452,853 | 90,873 | 543,726 |
| North America | 582,311 | 147,401 | 729,712 | 775,341 | 217,388 | 992,729 |
| South America | 11,966 | 6,942 | 18,908 | — | 5,316 | 5,316 |
| **Total Nissan** | **1,817,096** | **400,741** | **2,217,837** | **2,420,643** | **630,276** | **3,050,919** |
| **PSA** | | | | | | |
| Africa | 688 | — | 688 | 556 | — | 556 |
| Asia/Pacific | 1,673 | — | 1,673 | 359 | — | 359 |
| Europe | 1,581,851 | 343,493 | 1,925,344 | 1,770,765 | 502,098 | 2,272,863 |
| South America | 191,486 | 13,648 | 205,134 | 260,060 | 18,473 | 278,533 |
| **Total PSA** | **1,775,698** | **357,141** | **2,132,839** | **2,031,740** | **520,571** | **2,552,311** |
| **Renault** | | | | | | |
| Asia/Pacific | 161,098 | 28,733 | 189,831 | 132,855 | 55,092 | 187,947 |
| Europe | 1,335,309 | 135,204 | 1,470,513 | 1,294,917 | 209,264 | 1,504,181 |
| South America | 168,978 | 18,021 | 186,999 | 172,327 | 23,169 | 195,496 |
| **Total Renault** | **1,665,385** | **181,958** | **1,847,343** | **1,600,099** | **287,525** | **1,887,624** |
| **Suzuki** | | | | | | |
| Africa | 569 | 2,584 | 3,153 | 475 | 3,148 | 3,623 |
| Asia/Pacific | 1,701,184 | 277,769 | 1,978,953 | 1,859,158 | 307,818 | 2,166,976 |
| Europe | — | — | — | — | — | — |
| North America | — | — | — | — | — | — |
| **Total Suzuki** | **1,701,753** | **280,353** | **1,982,106** | **1,859,633** | **310,966** | **2,170,599** |
| **Toyota** | | | | | | |
| Africa | 40,018 | 62,804 | 102,822 | 84,576 | 94,591 | 179,167 |
| Asia/Pacific | 3,741,050 | 889,257 | 4,630,307 | 4,991,532 | 1,207,085 | 6,198,617 |
| Europe | 744,548 | 1,967 | 746,515 | 902,961 | 5,947 | 908,908 |
| North America | 650,966 | 525,269 | 1,176,235 | 885,792 | 553,147 | 1,438,939 |
| South America | 71,977 | 68,528 | 140,505 | 80,035 | 73,924 | 153,959 |
| **Total Toyota** | **5,248,559** | **1,547,825** | **6,796,384** | **6,944,896** | **1,934,694** | **8,879,590** |
| **Volkswagen** | | | | | | |
| Africa | 59,529 | 309 | 59,838 | 96,109 | 571 | 96,680 |
| Asia/Pacific | 8,920 | — | 8,920 | 18,345 | — | 18,345 |
| Europe | 3,510,486 | 129,388 | 3,639,874 | 3,982,006 | 228,424 | 4,210,430 |
| North America | 319,743 | — | 319,743 | 449,096 | — | 449,096 |
| South America | 842,434 | 67,070 | 909,504 | 840,651 | 71,394 | 912,045 |
| **Total Volkswagen** | **4,741,112** | **196,767** | **4,937,879** | **5,386,207** | **300,389** | **5,686,596** |
| **Other Manufacturers** | **10,388,345** | **8,002,193** | **18,390,538** | **9,992,644** | **6,728,105** | **16,720,749** |
| **Total World** | **42,296,436** | **17,957,231** | **60,253,667** | **48,788,212** | **20,795,810** | **69,584,022** |

Compiled by *Ward's* from various industry sources.

# U.S. Sales of Cars and Trucks

## U.S. VEHICLE SALES

| Year | Cars | | | Trucks | | | Total Vehicles | | |
|---|---|---|---|---|---|---|---|---|---|
| | Domestic | Import | Total | Domestic | Import | Total | Domestic | Import | Total |
| 2010 | 3,791,877 | 1,843,556 | 5,635,433 | 5,228,589 | 908,198 | 6,136,787 | 9,020,466 | 2,751,754 | 11,772,220 |
| 2009 | 3,557,608 | 1,843,282 | 5,400,890 | 4,309,483 | 890,995 | 5,200,478 | 7,867,091 | 2,734,277 | 10,601,368 |
| 2008 | 4,490,836 | 2,278,271 | 6,769,107 | 5,616,890 | 1,107,168 | 6,724,058 | 10,107,726 | 3,385,439 | 13,493,165 |
| 2007 | 5,197,271 | 2,365,063 | 7,562,334 | 7,489,745 | 1,408,236 | 8,897,981 | 12,687,016 | 3,773,299 | 16,460,315 |
| 2006 | 5,416,828 | 2,344,764 | 7,761,592 | 7,918,015 | 1,369,374 | 9,287,389 | 13,334,843 | 3,714,138 | 17,048,981 |
| 2005 | 5,473,450 | 2,186,533 | 7,659,983 | 8,547,078 | 1,237,268 | 9,784,346 | 14,020,528 | 3,423,801 | 17,444,329 |
| 2004 | 5,333,496 | 2,149,059 | 7,482,555 | 8,546,755 | 1,269,263 | 9,816,018 | 13,880,251 | 3,418,322 | 17,298,573 |
| 2003 | 5,472,500 | 2,083,051 | 7,555,551 | 8,165,851 | 1,246,040 | 9,411,891 | 13,638,351 | 3,329,091 | 16,967,442 |
| 2002 | 5,816,671 | 2,225,584 | 8,042,255 | 8,012,897 | 1,083,500 | 9,096,397 | 13,829,568 | 3,309,084 | 17,138,652 |
| 2001 | 6,254,371 | 2,097,629 | 8,352,000 | 8,118,253 | 1,002,125 | 9,120,378 | 14,372,624 | 3,099,754 | 17,472,378 |
| 2000 | 6,761,603 | 2,016,120 | 8,777,723 | 8,161,045 | 872,905 | 9,033,950 | 14,922,648 | 2,889,025 | 17,811,673 |
| 1999 | 6,918,781 | 1,718,927 | 8,637,708 | 7,982,485 | 794,535 | 8,777,020 | 14,901,266 | 2,513,462 | 17,414,728 |
| 1998 | 6,705,208 | 1,379,781 | 8,084,989 | 7,207,820 | 674,478 | 7,882,298 | 13,913,028 | 2,054,259 | 15,967,287 |
| 1997 | 6,862,175 | 1,355,305 | 8,217,480 | 6,687,076 | 593,304 | 7,280,380 | 13,549,251 | 1,948,609 | 15,497,860 |
| 1996 | 7,206,349 | 1,272,196 | 8,478,545 | 6,526,030 | 451,537 | 6,977,567 | 13,732,379 | 1,723,733 | 15,456,112 |
| 1995 | 7,113,902 | 1,506,257 | 8,620,159 | 6,078,959 | 417,207 | 6,496,166 | 13,192,861 | 1,923,464 | 15,116,325 |
| 1994 | 7,255,303 | 1,735,214 | 8,990,517 | 5,995,895 | 424,962 | 6,420,857 | 13,251,198 | 2,160,176 | 15,411,374 |
| 1993 | 6,741,667 | 1,776,192 | 8,517,859 | 5,287,384 | 393,611 | 5,680,995 | 12,029,051 | 2,169,803 | 14,198,854 |
| 1992 | 6,285,916 | 1,927,197 | 8,213,113 | 4,481,769 | 422,562 | 4,904,331 | 10,767,685 | 2,349,759 | 13,117,444 |
| 1991 | 6,161,573 | 2,023,406 | 8,184,979 | 3,814,225 | 550,319 | 4,364,544 | 9,975,798 | 2,573,725 | 12,549,523 |
| 1990 | 6,918,869 | 2,384,346 | 9,303,215 | 4,216,644 | 629,519 | 4,846,163 | 11,135,513 | 3,013,865 | 14,149,378 |
| 1989 | 7,098,098 | 2,680,419 | 9,778,517 | 4,405,286 | 661,458 | 5,066,744 | 11,503,384 | 3,341,877 | 14,845,261 |
| 1988 | 7,543,116 | 3,003,692 | 10,546,808 | 4,511,065 | 733,671 | 5,244,736 | 12,054,181 | 3,737,363 | 15,791,544 |
| 1987 | 7,085,279 | 3,106,598 | 10,191,877 | 4,058,996 | 942,073 | 5,001,069 | 11,144,275 | 4,048,671 | 15,192,946 |
| 1986 | 8,215,017 | 3,189,222 | 11,404,239 | 3,930,067 | 988,715 | 4,918,782 | 12,145,084 | 4,177,937 | 16,323,021 |
| 1985 | 8,204,670 | 2,774,517 | 10,979,187 | 3,905,329 | 840,775 | 4,746,104 | 12,109,999 | 3,615,292 | 15,725,291 |
| 1984 | 7,951,523 | 2,372,172 | 10,323,695 | 3,480,209 | 679,237 | 4,159,446 | 11,431,732 | 3,051,409 | 14,483,141 |
| 1983 | 6,795,299 | 2,352,739 | 9,148,038 | 2,663,022 | 500,456 | 3,163,478 | 9,458,321 | 2,853,195 | 12,311,516 |
| 1982 | 5,756,658 | 2,199,802 | 7,956,460 | 2,145,793 | 436,109 | 2,581,902 | 7,902,451 | 2,635,911 | 10,538,362 |
| 1981 | 6,180,784 | 2,308,418 | 8,489,202 | 1,820,693 | 468,085 | 2,288,778 | 8,001,477 | 2,776,503 | 10,777,980 |
| 1980 | 6,579,778 | 2,369,457 | 8,949,235 | 2,014,709 | 479,669 | 2,494,378 | 8,594,487 | 2,849,126 | 11,443,613 |
| 1979 | 8,341,000 | 2,332,000 | 10,673,000 | 3,010,000 | 470,000 | 3,480,000 | 11,351,000 | 2,802,000 | 14,153,000 |
| 1978 | 9,312,000 | 2,002,000 | 11,314,000 | 3,773,000 | 336,000 | 4,109,000 | 13,085,000 | 2,338,000 | 15,423,000 |
| 1977 | 9,109,000 | 2,074,000 | 11,183,000 | 3,352,000 | 323,000 | 3,675,000 | 12,461,000 | 2,397,000 | 14,859,000 |
| 1976 | 8,611,000 | 1,499,000 | 10,110,000 | 2,944,000 | 237,000 | 3,181,000 | 11,555,000 | 1,736,000 | 13,291,000 |
| 1975 | 7,053,000 | 1,571,000 | 8,624,000 | 2,249,000 | 229,000 | 2,478,000 | 9,302,000 | 1,800,000 | 11,103,000 |
| 1974 | 7,454,000 | 1,399,000 | 8,853,000 | 2,512,000 | 176,000 | 2,688,000 | 9,966,000 | 1,575,000 | 11,541,000 |
| 1973 | 9,676,000 | 1,748,000 | 11,424,000 | 2,916,000 | 233,000 | 3,148,000 | 12,592,000 | 1,981,000 | 14,572,000 |
| 1972 | 9,327,000 | 1,614,000 | 10,940,000 | 2,486,000 | 143,000 | 2,629,000 | 11,813,000 | 1,757,000 | 13,569,000 |
| 1971 | 8,681,000 | 1,561,000 | 10,242,000 | 2,011,000 | 85,000 | 2,096,000 | 10,692,000 | 1,646,000 | 12,338,000 |
| 1970 | 7,119,000 | 1,280,000 | 8,400,000 | 1,746,000 | 65,000 | 1,811,000 | 8,865,000 | 1,345,000 | 10,211,000 |
| 1969 | 8,464,000 | 1,118,000 | 9,582,000 | 1,936,000 | 34,000 | 1,970,000 | 10,400,000 | 1,152,000 | 11,552,000 |
| 1968 | 8,625,000 | 1,031,000 | 9,656,000 | 1,807,000 | 24,000 | 1,831,000 | 10,432,000 | 1,055,000 | 11,487,000 |
| 1967 | 7,568,000 | 769,000 | 8,337,000 | 1,524,000 | 21,000 | 1,545,000 | 9,092,000 | 790,000 | 9,882,000 |
| 1966 | 8,377,000 | 651,000 | 9,028,000 | 1,619,000 | 17,000 | 1,636,000 | 9,996,000 | 668,000 | 10,664,000 |
| 1965 | 8,763,000 | 569,000 | 9,332,000 | 1,539,000 | 14,000 | 1,553,000 | 10,302,000 | 583,000 | 10,885,000 |
| 1964 | 7,617,000 | 484,000 | 8,101,000 | 1,351,000 | 42,000 | 1,393,000 | 8,968,000 | 526,000 | 9,494,000 |
| 1963 | 7,334,000 | 386,000 | 7,720,000 | 1,230,000 | 40,000 | 1,270,000 | 8,564,000 | 426,000 | 8,990,000 |
| 1961 | 5,556,000 | 379,000 | 5,935,000 | 908,000 | 29,000 | 937,000 | 6,464,000 | 408,000 | 6,872,000 |
| 1959 | 5,486,000 | 614,000 | 6,100,000 | 928,000 | 37,000 | 965,000 | 6,414,000 | 651,000 | 7,065,000 |
| 1957 | 5,826,000 | 207,000 | 6,033,000 | 878,000 | 16,000 | 894,000 | 6,704,000 | 223,000 | 6,927,000 |
| 1955 | 7,408,000 | 58,000 | 7,466,000 | 1,012,000 | 3,000 | 1,015,000 | 8,420,000 | 61,000 | 8,481,000 |
| 1953 | 5,775,000 | 33,000 | 5,808,000 | 965,000 | NA | 965,000 | 6,740,000 | 33,000 | 6,773,000 |
| 1951 | 5,143,000 | 21,000 | 5,164,000 | 1,111,000 | NA | 1,111,000 | 6,254,000 | 21,000 | 6,275,000 |
| 1942-1950 | NA | NA | NA | NA | NA | NA | NA | NA | NA |
| 1941 | 3,763,000 | NA | 3,763,000 | 902,000 | NA | 902,000 | 4,665,000 | NA | 4,665,000 |

NOTE: NA is not available.

# U.S. Vehicle Sales by Model

## U.S. VEHICLE SALES BY MODEL

| Model | 2010 | 2009 | 2008 | 2007 | 2006 |
|---|---|---|---|---|---|
| A3* | 6,558 | 3,874 | 4,759 | 6,354 | 8,040 |
| A4* | 30,816 | 31,461 | 36,930 | 35,606 | 40,230 |
| A4 Cabrio* | 107 | 4,501 | 4,709 | 6,975 | 6,599 |
| A5* | 12,206 | 6,845 | 4,120 | — | — |
| A6* | 8,465 | 6,606 | 11,406 | 11,239 | 15,819 |
| A8* | 1,515 | 1,334 | 2,433 | 3,059 | 4,686 |
| R8* | 799 | 699 | 900 | 241 | — |
| S4* | 3,749 | 1,108 | 1,705 | 2,830 | 3,033 |
| S5* | 4,173 | 2,955 | 2,162 | 625 | — |
| S6* | 210 | 180 | 550 | 762 | 397 |
| S8* | 6 | 129 | 392 | 767 | 352 |
| TT* | 1,531 | 1,935 | 4,486 | 4,355 | 954 |
| **AUDI TOTAL** | **70,135** | **61,627** | **74,552** | **72,813** | **80,110** |
| 1-Series* | 13,132 | 11,182 | 12,018 | — | — |
| 3-Series* | 100,910 | 90,960 | 112,464 | 142,490 | 120,180 |
| 5-Series* | 39,488 | 40,109 | 45,915 | 54,142 | 56,756 |
| 6-Series* | 2,418 | 3,549 | 6,533 | 9,033 | 9,322 |
| 7-Series* | 12,253 | 9,254 | 12,276 | 14,773 | 17,796 |
| Z4 | — | 125 | 5,879 | 10,097 | 12,284 |
| Z4* | 3,804 | 3,398 | — | — | — |
| Z8* | — | — | — | — | 5 |
| **BMW Total** | **172,005** | **158,577** | **195,085** | **230,535** | **216,343** |
| Mini Cooper* | 45,644 | 45,225 | 54,077 | 42,045 | 39,171 |
| **BMW TOTAL** | **217,649** | **203,802** | **249,162** | **272,580** | **255,514** |
| 300 Series | 37,116 | 38,606 | 62,352 | 120,636 | 143,647 |
| Crossfire* | — | 499 | 2,021 | 8,774 | 8,216 |
| PT Cruiser Convertible | — | 2 | 1,094 | 10,978 | 12,502 |
| Sebring Convertible | 7,027 | 5,139 | 27,437 | 21,599 | 18,457 |
| Sebring Coupe | — | — | — | — | 856 |
| Sebring Sedan | 31,558 | 22,321 | 44,226 | 71,531 | 50,044 |
| **Chrysler Total** | **75,701** | **66,567** | **137,130** | **233,518** | **233,722** |
| Avenger | 50,923 | 38,922 | 61,963 | 83,804 | — |
| Caliber | 45,082 | 36,098 | 84,158 | 101,079 | 92,224 |
| Challenger | 36,791 | 25,852 | 17,423 | — | — |
| Charger | 75,397 | 60,651 | 97,367 | 119,289 | 114,201 |
| Magnum | — | 113 | 6,912 | 30,256 | 40,095 |
| Neon | — | — | — | — | 17,239 |
| Stratus Coupe | — | — | — | — | 400 |
| Stratus Sedan | — | — | — | 1,478 | 50,993 |
| Viper | 392 | 482 | 1,172 | 435 | 1,455 |
| **Dodge Total** | **208,585** | **162,118** | **268,995** | **336,341** | **316,607** |
| **CHRYSLER TOTAL** | **284,286** | **228,685** | **406,125** | **569,859** | **550,329** |
| B-Class* | 1 | — | — | — | — |
| C-Class* | 58,785 | 52,427 | 72,471 | 63,701 | 50,187 |
| CL* | 1,035 | 1,220 | 2,733 | 3,672 | 1,312 |
| CLK* | 585 | 7,150 | 10,844 | 15,009 | 16,415 |
| CLS* | 2,135 | 2,527 | 5,775 | 7,906 | 10,763 |
| E-Class* | 60,922 | 43,072 | 38,576 | 48,950 | 50,195 |
| S-Class* | 13,608 | 11,199 | 17,787 | 26,081 | 30,886 |
| SL* | 2,385 | 4,025 | 5,464 | 6,126 | 8,462 |
| SLK* | 1,980 | 2,566 | 4,941 | 7,270 | 10,410 |
| SLS* | 499 | — | — | — | — |
| **Mercedes Total** | **141,935** | **124,186** | **158,591** | **178,715** | **178,630** |
| Smart Fortwo* | 5,927 | 14,595 | 24,622 | — | — |
| **DAIMLER TOTAL** | **147,862** | **138,781** | **183,213** | **178,715** | **178,630** |
| Crown Victoria | 33,722 | 33,255 | 48,557 | 60,901 | 62,976 |
| Fiesta | 23,273 | — | — | — | — |
| Five Hundred | — | — | — | 35,146 | 84,218 |
| Focus | 172,421 | 160,433 | 195,823 | 173,213 | 177,006 |
| Ford GT | — | — | — | 231 | 1,919 |
| Fusion | 219,219 | 180,671 | 147,569 | 149,552 | 142,502 |
| Mustang | 73,716 | 66,623 | 91,251 | 134,626 | 166,530 |
| Taurus | 68,859 | 45,617 | 52,667 | 33,032 | 174,803 |
| Thunderbird | — | — | — | — | 469 |
| **Ford Total** | **591,210** | **486,599** | **535,867** | **586,701** | **810,423** |
| LS | — | — | — | — | 8,797 |
| MKS | 14,417 | 17,174 | 12,982 | — | — |
| MKZ | 22,535 | 22,081 | 30,117 | 34,363 | 11,176 |
| Town Car | 11,264 | 11,375 | 15,653 | 26,739 | 39,295 |
| Zephyr | — | — | — | — | 21,938 |
| **Lincoln Total** | **48,216** | **50,630** | **58,752** | **61,102** | **81,206** |
| Grand Marquis | 28,543 | 24,783 | 29,766 | 50,664 | 54,688 |
| Milan | 28,912 | 27,403 | 31,393 | 37,244 | 35,853 |

# U.S. Vehicle Sales by Model

## U.S. VEHICLE SALES  BY MODEL — continued

| Model | 2010 | 2009 | 2008 | 2007 | 2006 |
|---|---|---|---|---|---|
| Montego | — | — | — | 10,755 | 22,332 |
| Sable | 37 | 6,256 | 16,187 | 10,366 | — |
| **Mercury Total** | **57,492** | **58,442** | **77,346** | **109,029** | **112,873** |
| **FORD TOTAL** | **696,918** | **595,671** | **671,965** | **756,832** | **1,004,502** |
| Century | — | — | — | 5 | 83 |
| LaCrosse | 61,178 | 27,818 | 36,873 | 47,747 | 71,072 |
| LeSabre | — | — | — | 121 | 2,313 |
| Lucerne | 26,459 | 31,292 | 54,930 | 82,923 | 96,515 |
| Park Ave | — | — | — | 26 | 51 |
| Regal | — | — | — | — | 30 |
| Regal* | 12,326 | — | — | — | — |
| **Buick Total** | **99,963** | **59,110** | **91,803** | **130,822** | **170,064** |
| CTS | 45,656 | 38,817 | 58,774 | 57,029 | 54,846 |
| Deville | — | — | — | 71 | 807 |
| DTS | 18,640 | 17,330 | 30,479 | 51,469 | 58,224 |
| Seville | — | — | — | — | 9 |
| STS | 4,473 | 6,037 | 14,790 | 20,873 | 25,676 |
| XLR | 188 | 787 | 1,250 | 1,750 | 3,203 |
| **Cadillac Total** | **68,957** | **62,971** | **105,293** | **131,192** | **142,765** |
| Aveo* | 48,623 | 38,516 | 55,360 | 67,028 | 58,244 |
| Camaro | 81,299 | 61,648 | — | — | — |
| Cavalier | — | — | — | 57 | 355 |
| Classic | — | — | — | 17 | 18 |
| Cobalt | 97,376 | 104,724 | 188,045 | 200,620 | 211,449 |
| Corvette | 12,624 | 13,934 | 26,971 | 33,685 | 36,518 |
| Cruze | 24,495 | — | — | — | — |
| Impala | 172,078 | 165,565 | 265,840 | 311,128 | 289,868 |
| Malibu | 198,770 | 161,568 | 178,253 | 128,312 | 163,853 |
| Monte Carlo | — | 6 | 711 | 15,784 | 34,113 |
| Volt | 326 | — | — | — | — |
| **Chevrolet Total** | **635,591** | **545,961** | **715,180** | **756,631** | **794,418** |
| Alero | — | — | — | — | 67 |
| **Oldsmobile Total** | **—** | **—** | **—** | **—** | **67** |
| Bonneville | — | — | — | 130 | 1,160 |
| G3* | 14 | 6,223 | — | — | — |
| G5 | 86 | 12,362 | 25,439 | 27,928 | 7,902 |
| G6 | 479 | 87,171 | 140,240 | 150,001 | 157,644 |
| G8* | 274 | 23,157 | 15,002 | — | — |
| Grand Am | — | — | — | 99 | 828 |
| Grand Prix | 7 | 265 | 8,636 | 87,622 | 108,634 |
| GTO* | — | — | 52 | 4,200 | 11,268 |
| Solstice | 157 | 5,642 | 10,739 | 16,779 | 19,710 |
| Sunfire | — | — | — | 39 | 853 |
| Vibe | 97 | 33,842 | 46,551 | 37,170 | 45,221 |
| **Pontiac Total** | **1,114** | **168,662** | **246,659** | **323,968** | **353,220** |
| Astra* | 25 | 6,298 | 11,968 | — | — |
| Aura | 644 | 21,395 | 59,380 | 59,964 | 19,746 |
| Ion | — | 12 | 315 | 47,873 | 102,042 |
| Saturn L | — | — | — | 2 | 20 |
| Sky | 179 | 3,399 | 9,162 | 11,263 | 8,671 |
| **Saturn Total** | **848** | **31,104** | **80,825** | **119,102** | **130,479** |
| **GM TOTAL** | **806,473** | **867,808** | **1,239,760** | **1,461,715** | **1,591,013** |
| NSX* | — | — | — | 2 | 58 |
| RL* | 2,037 | 2,043 | 4,517 | 6,262 | 11,501 |
| RSX* | — | — | 1 | 296 | 16,996 |
| TL | 34,049 | 33,620 | 46,766 | 58,545 | 71,348 |
| TSX* | 32,076 | 28,650 | 31,998 | 33,037 | 38,035 |
| **Acura Total** | **68,162** | **64,313** | **83,282** | **98,142** | **137,938** |
| Accord | 282,360 | 273,466 | 309,461 | 355,767 | 323,079 |
| Accord* | 170 | 14,026 | 63,328 | 36,464 | 31,362 |
| Civic | 252,882 | 244,271 | 305,509 | 292,192 | 272,899 |
| Civic* | 7,336 | 15,451 | 33,780 | 38,903 | 43,739 |
| CR-Z* | 5,249 | — | — | — | — |
| FCX* | — | — | — | 10 | — |
| FCX Clarity* | 17 | 5 | 11 | — | — |
| Fit* | 54,354 | 67,315 | 79,794 | 56,432 | 27,934 |
| Insight* | 20,962 | 20,572 | — | 3 | 728 |
| S2000* | 85 | 795 | 2,538 | 4,302 | 6,271 |
| **Honda Total** | **623,415** | **635,901** | **794,421** | **784,073** | **706,012** |
| **HONDA TOTAL** | **691,577** | **700,214** | **877,703** | **882,215** | **843,950** |
| Accent* | 51,975 | 68,086 | 50,431 | 36,055 | 34,735 |
| Azera* | 3,051 | 3,808 | 14,461 | 21,948 | 24,057 |
| Elantra | 4,724 | — | — | — | — |

# U.S. Vehicle Sales by Model

## U.S. VEHICLE SALES BY MODEL — continued

| Model | 2010 | 2009 | 2008 | 2007 | 2006 |
|---|---|---|---|---|---|
| Elantra* | 127,522 | 103,269 | 94,720 | 85,724 | 98,853 |
| Equus* | 196 | — | — | — | — |
| Genesis* | 29,122 | 21,889 | 6,167 | — | — |
| Sonata | 196,623 | 120,028 | 117,357 | 145,568 | 149,463 |
| Sonata* | — | — | — | — | 50 |
| Tiburon* | — | 8,587 | 9,111 | 14,073 | 17,382 |
| XG350* | — | — | — | — | 2,776 |
| **HYUNDAI TOTAL** | **413,213** | **325,667** | **292,247** | **303,368** | **327,316** |
| Jaguar S-Type* | — | 24 | 904 | 3,524 | 5,875 |
| Jaguar Vanden Plas* | 8 | 272 | 853 | 1,512 | 1,614 |
| Jaguar X-Type* | — | 9 | 431 | 3,198 | 5,214 |
| Jaguar XF* | 6,925 | 8,487 | 8,578 | — | — |
| Jaguar XJ6/8* | 4,267 | 872 | 1,471 | 2,638 | 3,078 |
| Jaguar XJR* | 3 | 17 | 128 | 324 | 335 |
| Jaguar XK8* | 2,137 | 2,274 | 2,459 | 4,487 | 4,567 |
| **JAGUAR LAND ROVER TOTAL** | **13,340** | **11,955** | **14,824** | **15,683** | **20,683** |
| Amanti* | 281 | 3,704 | 3,614 | 5,522 | 9,594 |
| Forte* | 68,500 | 26,328 | — | — | — |
| Optima* | 27,382 | 37,527 | 44,904 | 40,901 | 38,408 |
| Rio* | 24,619 | 34,666 | 36,532 | 33,370 | 28,388 |
| Soul* | 67,110 | 31,621 | — | — | — |
| Spectra* | 272 | 47,114 | 68,465 | 73,474 | 72,557 |
| **KIA TOTAL** | **188,164** | **180,960** | **153,515** | **153,267** | **148,947** |
| Mazda2* | 3,021 | — | — | — | — |
| Mazda3* | 106,353 | 96,466 | 109,957 | 120,291 | 94,437 |
| Mazda6 | 35,662 | 34,866 | 52,590 | 57,575 | 66,203 |
| MX-5 Miata* | 6,370 | 7,917 | 10,977 | 15,075 | 16,897 |
| RX-8* | 1,134 | 2,217 | 3,368 | 5,767 | 9,344 |
| **MAZDA TOTAL** | **152,540** | **141,466** | **176,892** | **198,708** | **186,881** |
| Eclipse | 4,282 | 6,672 | 20,107 | 27,292 | 33,003 |
| Galant | 11,492 | 11,740 | 26,941 | 26,491 | 27,673 |
| Lancer* | 21,416 | 20,117 | 27,861 | 31,376 | 23,167 |
| **MITSUBISHI TOTAL** | **37,190** | **38,529** | **74,909** | **85,159** | **83,843** |
| G35/37* | 58,143 | 47,174 | 64,181 | 71,811 | 60,745 |
| M35/45* | 14,618 | 8,501 | 15,618 | 21,885 | 25,658 |
| Q45* | — | — | — | 22 | 393 |
| **Infiniti Total** | **72,761** | **55,675** | **79,799** | **93,718** | **86,796** |
| 350Z* | — | 3,875 | 10,337 | 18,957 | 24,635 |
| 370Z* | 10,215 | 9,242 | — | — | — |
| Altima | 229,263 | 203,568 | 269,668 | 284,762 | 232,457 |
| Cube* | 22,968 | 21,471 | — | — | — |
| GT-R* | 877 | 1,534 | 1,730 | — | — |
| Leaf* | 19 | — | — | — | — |
| Maxima | 60,569 | 53,351 | 47,072 | 52,574 | 69,763 |
| Sentra | 94,065 | 82,706 | 99,797 | 106,522 | 117,922 |
| Versa | 99,705 | 82,906 | 85,182 | 79,443 | 22,044 |
| **Nissan Total** | **517,681** | **458,653** | **513,786** | **542,258** | **466,821** |
| **NISSAN TOTAL** | **590,442** | **514,328** | **593,585** | **635,976** | **553,617** |
| 911* | 5,737 | 6,839 | 8,324 | 12,493 | 12,045 |
| Boxster* | 2,177 | 1,909 | 2,982 | 3,622 | 4,503 |
| Carrera GT* | — | — | — | 4 | 85 |
| Cayman* | 1,322 | 1,966 | 3,513 | 6,027 | 7,025 |
| Panamera* | 7,741 | 1,247 | — | — | — |
| **PORSCHE TOTAL** | **16,977** | **11,961** | **14,819** | **22,146** | **23,658** |
| 9-2X* | — | — | 3 | 118 | 1,435 |
| 9-3* | 4,533 | 5,428 | 15,167 | 22,979 | 24,134 |
| 9-5* | 811 | 1,034 | 2,538 | 4,357 | 4,991 |
| **SAAB TOTAL** | **5,344** | **6,462** | **17,708** | **27,454** | **30,560** |
| Impreza* | 44,395 | 46,611 | 49,098 | 46,333 | 41,148 |
| Legacy | 38,725 | 30,974 | 22,614 | 22,349 | 25,180 |
| **SUBARU TOTAL** | **83,120** | **77,585** | **71,712** | **68,682** | **66,328** |
| Aerio* | — | 9 | 80 | 1,531 | 8,769 |
| Forenza* | 12 | 3,769 | 20,796 | 42,113 | 48,579 |
| Kizashi* | 6,138 | 71 | — | — | — |
| SX4* | 11,606 | 20,704 | 29,483 | 15,209 | 3,453 |
| Verona* | — | 1 | 3 | 315 | 2,302 |
| **SUZUKI TOTAL** | **17,756** | **24,554** | **50,362** | **59,168** | **63,103** |
| ES* | 48,652 | 48,485 | 64,135 | 82,867 | 75,987 |
| GS* | 7,059 | 7,430 | 15,759 | 23,381 | 27,390 |
| HS* | 10,663 | 6,699 | — | — | — |
| IS* | 34,129 | 38,077 | 49,432 | 54,933 | 54,267 |
| LS* | 12,275 | 11,334 | 20,255 | 35,226 | 19,546 |
| SC* | 328 | 720 | 1,986 | 3,927 | 5,847 |

# U.S. Vehicle Sales by Model

## U.S. VEHICLE SALES BY MODEL — continued

| Model | 2010 | 2009 | 2008 | 2007 | 2006 |
|---|---|---|---|---|---|
| Lexus Total | 113,106 | 112,745 | 151,567 | 200,334 | 183,037 |
| tC* | 15,204 | 17,998 | 40,980 | 63,852 | 79,125 |
| xA* | — | 3 | 39 | 9,547 | 32,603 |
| xB* | 20,364 | 25,461 | 45,220 | 45,834 | 61,306 |
| xD* | 10,110 | 14,499 | 27,665 | 10,948 | — |
| Scion Total | 45,678 | 57,961 | 113,904 | 130,181 | 173,034 |
| Avalon | 28,390 | 26,935 | 42,790 | 72,945 | 88,938 |
| Camry | 324,756 | 346,957 | 428,841 | 418,757 | 362,961 |
| Camry* | 3,048 | 9,867 | 7,776 | 54,351 | 85,484 |
| Celica* | — | 1 | 1 | 4 | 14 |
| Corolla/Matrix | 228,165 | 265,440 | 252,877 | 348,016 | 335,054 |
| Corolla* | 37,917 | 31,434 | 98,130 | 23,374 | 52,334 |
| Echo* | — | 1 | — | 3 | 16 |
| MR2 Spyder* | — | — | 1 | — | 5 |
| Prius* | 140,928 | 139,682 | 158,884 | 181,221 | 106,971 |
| Yaris* | 40,076 | 63,743 | 102,328 | 84,799 | 70,308 |
| Toyota Total | 803,280 | 884,060 | 1,091,628 | 1,183,470 | 1,102,085 |
| TOYOTA TOTAL | 962,064 | 1,054,766 | 1,357,099 | 1,513,985 | 1,458,156 |
| Beetle | 11,874 | 9,581 | 15,520 | 17,155 | 18,166 |
| Beetle Cabrio | 4,663 | 4,504 | 10,957 | 13,866 | 16,944 |
| CC* | 27,987 | 23,872 | 2,105 | — | — |
| Eos* | 6,690 | 7,204 | 12,837 | 12,744 | 3,394 |
| Golf* | 13,426 | 1,211 | — | 25 | 3,132 |
| GTI* | 13,755 | 7,932 | 12,232 | 14,618 | 13,957 |
| Jetta | 123,213 | 108,427 | 97,461 | 98,951 | 103,331 |
| Passat* | 12,497 | 11,138 | 30,034 | 37,183 | 54,208 |
| Phaeton* | — | — | — | 17 | 235 |
| R32* | — | 139 | 3,106 | 1,756 | — |
| Rabbit* | 1,105 | 6,470 | 20,070 | 25,445 | 11,610 |
| VOLKSWAGEN TOTAL | 215,210 | 180,478 | 204,322 | 221,760 | 224,977 |
| 30-Series* | 3,906 | 4,267 | 4,299 | 2,090 | — |
| 40-Series* | 5,623 | 7,957 | 9,687 | 18,141 | 24,566 |
| 50-Series* | 1,720 | 2,155 | 1,856 | 2,850 | 4,138 |
| 60-Series* | 1,437 | 5,895 | 8,966 | 18,511 | 25,753 |
| 70-Series* | 5,263 | 6,986 | 8,787 | 8,310 | 9,549 |
| 80-Series* | 7,224 | 8,331 | 11,038 | 12,347 | 5,469 |
| VOLVO TOTAL | 25,173 | 35,591 | 44,633 | 62,249 | 69,475 |
| TOTAL CARS | 5,635,433 | 5,400,890 | 6,769,107 | 7,562,334 | 7,761,592 |
| Allroad* | — | — | — | — | 3 |
| Q5* | 23,518 | 13,790 | — | — | — |
| Q7* | 7,976 | 7,299 | 13,209 | 20,695 | 10,003 |
| AUDI TOTAL | 31,494 | 21,089 | 13,209 | 20,695 | 10,006 |
| X3 | 940 | — | — | — | — |
| X3* | 5,135 | 6,067 | 17,622 | 28,058 | 31,291 |
| X5 | 35,776 | 27,071 | 31,858 | 35,202 | 26,798 |
| X6 | 6,257 | 4,787 | 4,548 | — | — |
| BMW TOTAL | 48,108 | 37,925 | 54,028 | 63,260 | 58,089 |
| Aspen | 30 | 5,996 | 22,254 | 28,788 | 7,656 |
| Pacifica | — | 1,955 | 7,345 | 53,947 | 78,243 |
| PT Cruiser | 9,440 | 17,939 | 49,816 | 88,607 | 126,148 |
| Town & Country | 112,275 | 84,558 | 118,563 | 138,151 | 159,105 |
| Chrysler Total | 121,745 | 110,448 | 197,978 | 309,493 | 371,152 |
| Caravan | 103,323 | 90,666 | 123,749 | 176,150 | 211,140 |
| Durango | 572 | 3,521 | 21,420 | 45,503 | 70,606 |
| Journey | 48,577 | 53,826 | 47,097 | — | — |
| Nitro | 22,618 | 17,443 | 36,368 | 74,825 | 16,990 |
| Dodge Total | 175,090 | 165,456 | 228,634 | 296,478 | 298,736 |
| Commander | 8,115 | 12,655 | 27,694 | 63,027 | 88,497 |
| Compass | 15,894 | 11,739 | 25,349 | 39,491 | 18,579 |
| Grand Cherokee | 84,635 | 50,328 | 73,678 | 120,937 | 139,148 |
| Liberty | 49,564 | 43,503 | 66,911 | 92,105 | 133,557 |
| Patriot | 38,620 | 31,432 | 55,654 | 40,434 | — |
| Wrangler | 94,310 | 82,044 | 84,615 | 119,243 | 80,271 |
| Jeep Total | 291,138 | 231,701 | 333,901 | 475,237 | 460,052 |
| Dakota | 13,047 | 10,690 | 26,044 | 50,702 | 76,098 |
| Ram Pickup Light-Duty | 194,175 | 173,066 | 240,454 | 357,707 | 364,177 |
| Sprinter Van* | 248 | 6,819 | 13,505 | 14,869 | 20,379 |
| Sprinter Wagon* | 5 | 335 | 1,095 | 1,717 | 1,582 |
| Ram Total | 207,475 | 190,910 | 281,098 | 424,995 | 462,236 |
| CHRYSLER TOTAL | 795,448 | 698,515 | 1,041,611 | 1,506,203 | 1,592,176 |
| G-Class* | 919 | 662 | 931 | 1,152 | 587 |
| GL | 19,943 | 15,012 | 23,328 | 26,396 | 18,776 |
| GLK* | 20,946 | 21,944 | — | — | — |

# U.S. Vehicle Sales by Model

## U.S. VEHICLE SALES BY MODEL — continued

| Model | 2010 | 2009 | 2008 | 2007 | 2006 |
|---|---|---|---|---|---|
| M-Class | 29,698 | 25,799 | 34,320 | 33,879 | 31,632 |
| R-Class | 2,937 | 2,825 | 7,733 | 13,031 | 18,168 |
| Sprinter Van* | 8,559 | — | — | — | — |
| **Mercedes Total** | **83,002** | **66,242** | **66,312** | **74,458** | **69,163** |
| Mitsubishi Fuso Light-Duty* | 311 | 275 | 202 | 52 | 93 |
| Sterling Light-Duty* | 1 | 103 | 12 | — | — |
| **DAIMLER TOTAL** | **83,314** | **66,620** | **66,526** | **74,510** | **69,256** |
| Club Wagon | 23,799 | 20,948 | 26,677 | 31,973 | 32,414 |
| Econoline | 84,459 | 64,787 | 97,919 | 136,749 | 148,043 |
| Edge | 118,637 | 88,548 | 110,798 | 130,125 | 2,201 |
| Escape | 191,026 | 173,044 | 156,544 | 165,596 | 157,395 |
| Excursion | — | — | — | — | 965 |
| Expedition | 37,336 | 31,655 | 55,123 | 90,287 | 87,203 |
| Explorer | 60,687 | 52,190 | 78,439 | 137,817 | 179,229 |
| F-Series Light-Duty | 502,125 | 392,112 | 476,469 | 633,949 | 744,996 |
| Flex | 34,227 | 38,717 | 14,457 | — | — |
| Freestar | — | — | — | 2,390 | 50,125 |
| Freestyle | — | — | — | 23,765 | 58,602 |
| Ranger | 55,364 | 55,600 | 65,872 | 72,711 | 92,420 |
| Taurus X | 12 | 6,106 | 23,112 | 18,345 | — |
| Transit Connect* | 27,405 | 8,834 | — | — | — |
| **Ford Total** | **1,135,077** | **932,541** | **1,105,410** | **1,443,707** | **1,553,593** |
| Aviator | — | — | — | — | 1,711 |
| Mark LT | — | 147 | 4,631 | 8,382 | 12,753 |
| MKT | 7,435 | 2,580 | — | — | — |
| MKX | 21,932 | 21,433 | 29,076 | 37,953 | 859 |
| Navigator | 8,245 | 8,057 | 14,836 | 24,050 | 23,947 |
| **Lincoln Total** | **37,612** | **32,217** | **48,543** | **70,385** | **39,270** |
| Mariner | 29,912 | 28,688 | 32,306 | 34,844 | 33,941 |
| Monterey | — | — | — | 700 | 4,467 |
| Mountaineer | 5,791 | 5,169 | 10,596 | 23,849 | 29,567 |
| **Mercury Total** | **35,703** | **33,857** | **42,902** | **59,393** | **67,975** |
| **FORD TOTAL** | **1,208,392** | **998,615** | **1,196,855** | **1,573,485** | **1,660,838** |
| Enclave | 55,426 | 43,150 | 44,706 | 29,286 | — |
| Rainier | — | 4 | 117 | 4,819 | 12,691 |
| Rendezvous | — | 9 | 27 | 15,295 | 45,954 |
| Terraza | — | 33 | 544 | 5,569 | 11,948 |
| **Buick Total** | **55,426** | **43,196** | **45,394** | **54,969** | **70,593** |
| Escalade | 16,118 | 16,873 | 23,947 | 36,654 | 39,017 |
| Escalade ESV | 8,674 | 6,588 | 11,054 | 16,370 | 16,170 |
| Escalade EXT | 2,082 | 2,423 | 4,709 | 7,967 | 7,019 |
| SRX | 51,094 | 20,237 | 16,156 | 22,543 | 22,043 |
| **Cadillac Total** | **77,968** | **46,121** | **55,866** | **83,534** | **84,249** |
| Astro | — | — | — | 25 | 386 |
| Avalanche | 20,515 | 16,432 | 35,003 | 55,550 | 57,076 |
| Colorado | 24,642 | 32,413 | 54,346 | 75,716 | 93,876 |
| Equinox | 149,979 | 86,148 | 67,447 | 89,552 | 113,888 |
| Express | 59,753 | 54,302 | 86,986 | 114,730 | 123,195 |
| HHR | 75,401 | 70,842 | 96,053 | 105,175 | 101,298 |
| S Blazer | — | — | — | 7 | 114 |
| S10 Pickup | — | — | — | — | 4 |
| Silverado | 370,135 | 316,544 | 465,065 | 618,257 | 636,069 |
| SSR | — | — | 13 | 244 | 3,803 |
| Suburban | 45,152 | 41,055 | 54,058 | 83,673 | 77,211 |
| Tahoe | 75,675 | 73,254 | 91,578 | 146,256 | 161,491 |
| Tracker | — | — | — | — | 11 |
| TrailBlazer | 218 | 8,829 | 74,878 | 134,626 | 174,797 |
| Traverse | 106,744 | 91,074 | 9,456 | — | — |
| Uplander | 76 | 1,758 | 40,456 | 69,885 | 58,699 |
| Venture | — | — | — | 25 | 196 |
| W4 Tiltmaster | 54 | 142 | 293 | 432 | 407 |
| W4 Tiltmaster* | 28 | 62 | 144 | 379 | 469 |
| **Chevrolet Total** | **928,372** | **792,855** | **1,075,776** | **1,494,532** | **1,602,990** |
| Acadia | 68,295 | 53,820 | 66,440 | 72,765 | 480 |
| Canyon | 7,992 | 10,107 | 14,974 | 20,888 | 23,979 |
| Envoy | 84 | 4,857 | 23,876 | 48,586 | 74,452 |
| Safari | — | — | — | 13 | 56 |
| Savana | 13,942 | 12,164 | 22,437 | 25,706 | 29,973 |
| Sierra | 129,794 | 111,842 | 168,544 | 208,243 | 210,736 |
| Terrain | 60,519 | 14,033 | — | — | — |
| W4 Forward | 47 | 139 | 364 | 504 | 448 |
| W4 Forward* | 42 | 145 | 240 | 624 | 889 |
| Yukon | 28,781 | 29,411 | 39,064 | 63,428 | 71,476 |

# U.S. Vehicle Sales by Model

**U.S. VEHICLE SALES BY MODEL — continued**

| Model | 2010 | 2009 | 2008 | 2007 | 2006 |
|---|---|---|---|---|---|
| Yukon XL | 23,797 | 16,819 | 26,404 | 45,303 | 45,413 |
| **GMC Total** | **333,293** | **253,337** | **362,343** | **486,060** | **457,902** |
| H1 | — | — | 17 | 125 | 365 |
| H2 | 108 | 1,147 | 4,793 | 9,897 | 13,296 |
| H2 SUT | 43 | 366 | 1,302 | 2,534 | 3,811 |
| H3 | 2,713 | 5,487 | 20,681 | 43,430 | 54,052 |
| H3T | 948 | 2,046 | 692 | — | — |
| **Hummer Total** | **3,812** | **9,046** | **27,485** | **55,986** | **71,524** |
| Bravada | — | — | — | — | 19 |
| Silhouette | — | — | — | — | 10 |
| **Oldsmobile Total** | **—** | **—** | **—** | **—** | **29** |
| Aztek | — | — | — | 25 | 347 |
| Montana | — | — | — | 26 | 388 |
| Montana SV6 | — | — | 64 | 1,359 | 13,100 |
| Torrent | 68 | 9,638 | 20,625 | 32,644 | 43,174 |
| **Pontiac Total** | **68** | **9,638** | **20,689** | **34,054** | **57,009** |
| Outlook | 2,649 | 13,115 | 25,340 | 34,748 | 144 |
| Relay | — | 12 | 163 | 1,474 | 7,171 |
| Vue | 3,201 | 28,429 | 81,676 | 84,767 | 88,581 |
| **Saturn Total** | **5,850** | **41,556** | **107,179** | **120,989** | **95,896** |
| **GM TOTAL** | **1,404,789** | **1,195,749** | **1,694,732** | **2,330,124** | **2,440,192** |
| MDX | 47,210 | 31,178 | 45,377 | 58,606 | 54,121 |
| RDX | 14,975 | 10,153 | 15,845 | 23,356 | 9,164 |
| ZDX | 3,259 | 79 | — | — | — |
| **Acura Total** | **65,444** | **41,410** | **61,222** | **81,962** | **63,285** |
| CR-V | 166,334 | 153,431 | 90,480 | 26,130 | — |
| CR-V* | 37,380 | 37,783 | 106,799 | 193,030 | 170,028 |
| Crosstour | 28,851 | 2,564 | — | — | — |
| Element | 14,247 | 14,884 | 26,447 | 35,218 | 51,829 |
| Odyssey | 108,182 | 100,133 | 135,493 | 173,046 | 177,919 |
| Pilot | 102,323 | 83,901 | 96,746 | 117,146 | 152,154 |
| Ridgeline | 16,142 | 16,464 | 33,875 | 42,795 | 50,193 |
| **Honda Total** | **473,459** | **409,160** | **489,840** | **587,365** | **602,123** |
| **HONDA TOTAL** | **538,903** | **450,570** | **551,062** | **669,327** | **665,408** |
| Entourage* | — | 3,433 | 8,470 | 17,155 | 12,206 |
| Santa Fe | 76,680 | 80,343 | 70,994 | 92,421 | 45,898 |
| Santa Fe* | — | — | — | — | 18,033 |
| Tucson* | 39,594 | 15,411 | 19,027 | 41,476 | 52,067 |
| Veracruz* | 8,741 | 10,210 | 11,004 | 12,589 | — |
| **HYUNDAI TOTAL** | **125,015** | **109,397** | **109,495** | **163,641** | **128,204** |
| International Truck Light-Duty | 1,008 | 374 | 704 | — | — |
| **INTERNATIONAL TOTAL** | **1,008** | **374** | **704** | **—** | **—** |
| Ascender | — | 68 | 1,760 | 2,948 | 4,857 |
| Axiom | — | — | — | 8 | 124 |
| i-Series | — | 97 | 2,998 | 4,138 | 3,497 |
| Rodeo | — | — | — | 4 | 129 |
| Trooper* | — | — | — | — | 7 |
| **Isuzu Total** | **—** | **165** | **4,758** | **7,098** | **8,614** |
| Isuzu Truck Light-Duty | 608 | 666 | 1,034 | 1,153 | 1,270 |
| Isuzu Truck Light-Duty* | 1,082 | 807 | 1,534 | 3,197 | 3,659 |
| **ISUZU TOTAL** | **1,690** | **1,638** | **7,326** | **11,448** | **13,543** |
| Land Rover Discovery* | — | — | — | — | 1 |
| Land Rover Freelander* | — | — | — | 1 | 42 |
| Land Rover LR2* | 3,649 | 4,433 | 5,618 | 9,205 | — |
| Land Rover LR3* | — | 2,330 | 4,039 | 11,039 | 16,930 |
| Land Rover LR4* | 7,122 | 867 | — | — | — |
| Land Rover Range Rover* | 8,746 | 7,312 | 8,393 | 12,316 | 12,044 |
| Land Rover Range Rover Sport* | 12,347 | 11,364 | 11,668 | 16,989 | 18,757 |
| **JAGUAR LAND ROVER TOTAL** | **31,864** | **26,306** | **29,718** | **49,550** | **47,774** |
| Borrego* | 9,835 | 10,530 | 1,869 | — | — |
| Rondo* | 3,588 | 14,206 | 28,645 | 26,020 | 594 |
| Sedona* | 21,823 | 27,398 | 26,915 | 40,493 | 57,018 |
| Sorento | 108,202 | — | — | — | — |
| Sorento* | 783 | 24,460 | 29,699 | 36,300 | 50,672 |
| Sportage* | 23,873 | 42,509 | 32,754 | 49,393 | 37,071 |
| **KIA TOTAL** | **168,104** | **119,103** | **119,882** | **152,206** | **145,355** |
| B-Series | 10 | 573 | 1,319 | 2,657 | 4,086 |
| CX-7* | 28,788 | 20,583 | 26,811 | 41,659 | 22,325 |
| CX-9* | 28,908 | 21,132 | 26,100 | 25,566 | — |
| Mazda5* | 15,683 | 18,488 | 22,021 | 13,718 | 17,109 |
| MPV* | — | — | — | 122 | 11,600 |
| Tribute | 3,637 | 5,525 | 10,806 | 13,680 | 26,785 |
| **MAZDA TOTAL** | **77,026** | **66,301** | **87,057** | **97,402** | **81,905** |

# U.S. Vehicle Sales by Model

## U.S. VEHICLE SALES BY MODEL — continued

| Model | 2010 | 2009 | 2008 | 2007 | 2006 |
|---|---|---|---|---|---|
| Endeavor | 4,294 | 3,228 | 5,938 | 11,886 | 14,017 |
| Montero* | — | 2 | 4 | 401 | 1,610 |
| Outlander* | 12,500 | 10,283 | 13,471 | 23,285 | 11,493 |
| Outlander Sport* | 1,690 | — | — | — | — |
| Raider | 9 | 1,944 | 2,935 | 8,262 | 7,595 |
| **MITSUBISHI TOTAL** | **18,493** | **15,457** | **22,348** | **43,834** | **34,715** |
| EX* | 8,312 | 7,950 | 12,873 | 305 | — |
| FX* | 10,420 | 11,024 | 12,660 | 20,727 | 22,656 |
| QX56 | 5,064 | 6,440 | 7,657 | 12,288 | 11,694 |
| QX56* | 6,854 | — | — | — | — |
| **Infiniti Total** | **30,650** | **25,414** | **33,190** | **33,320** | **34,350** |
| Armada | 19,344 | 9,903 | 15,685 | 31,632 | 32,864 |
| Frontier | 40,427 | 28,415 | 44,997 | 64,397 | 77,510 |
| Juke* | 8,639 | — | — | — | — |
| Murano* | 53,999 | 52,546 | 71,401 | 76,358 | 81,362 |
| Pathfinder | 21,438 | 18,341 | 33,555 | 63,056 | 73,120 |
| Pathfinder* | — | — | — | — | 4 |
| Quest | 177 | 8,437 | 18,252 | 28,590 | 31,905 |
| Rogue* | 99,515 | 77,222 | 73,053 | 17,808 | — |
| Titan | 23,416 | 19,042 | 34,053 | 65,746 | 72,192 |
| Xterra | 20,523 | 16,455 | 33,579 | 51,355 | 62,325 |
| **Nissan Total** | **287,478** | **230,361** | **324,575** | **398,942** | **431,282** |
| **NISSAN TOTAL** | **318,128** | **255,775** | **357,765** | **432,262** | **465,632** |
| Cayenne* | 8,343 | 7,735 | 11,216 | 12,547 | 10,569 |
| **PORSCHE TOTAL** | **8,343** | **7,735** | **11,216** | **12,547** | **10,569** |
| 9-7X | 102 | 2,218 | 3,660 | 5,257 | 5,789 |
| **SAAB TOTAL** | **102** | **2,218** | **3,660** | **5,257** | **5,789** |
| Baja | — | — | 2 | 1,127 | 5,241 |
| Forester* | 85,080 | 77,781 | 60,748 | 44,530 | 51,258 |
| Outback | 93,148 | 55,356 | 44,262 | 56,079 | 59,262 |
| Tribeca | 2,472 | 5,930 | 10,975 | 16,790 | 18,614 |
| **SUBARU TOTAL** | **180,700** | **139,067** | **115,987** | **118,526** | **134,375** |
| Equator | 1,447 | 2,221 | 13 | — | — |
| Vitara | — | — | — | — | 8 |
| Vitara* | 4,478 | 7,557 | 11,936 | 19,540 | 26,931 |
| XL7 | 313 | 4,357 | 22,554 | 22,722 | 684 |
| XL7* | — | — | — | 454 | 10,264 |
| **SUZUKI TOTAL** | **6,238** | **14,135** | **34,503** | **42,716** | **37,887** |
| GX* | 16,450 | 6,235 | 16,424 | 23,035 | 25,454 |
| LX* | 3,983 | 3,616 | 7,915 | 2,468 | 5,595 |
| RX | 72,556 | 63,593 | 63,610 | 74,351 | 75,508 |
| RX* | 23,234 | 29,786 | 20,571 | 28,989 | 32,840 |
| **Lexus Total** | **116,223** | **103,230** | **108,520** | **128,843** | **139,397** |
| 4Runner* | 46,531 | 19,675 | 47,878 | 87,718 | 103,086 |
| FJ Cruiser* | 14,959 | 11,941 | 28,668 | 55,170 | 56,225 |
| Highlander | 70,767 | 10,948 | — | — | — |
| Highlander* | 21,354 | 72,170 | 104,661 | 127,878 | 129,794 |
| Land Cruiser* | 1,807 | 2,261 | 3,801 | 3,251 | 3,376 |
| RAV4 | 101,850 | 46,360 | 157 | — | — |
| RAV4* | 69,027 | 102,728 | 136,863 | 172,752 | 152,047 |
| Sequoia | 13,848 | 16,387 | 30,693 | 23,273 | 34,315 |
| Sienna | 98,337 | 84,064 | 115,944 | 138,162 | 163,269 |
| Tacoma | 106,198 | 111,824 | 144,655 | 173,238 | 178,351 |
| Tundra | 93,309 | 79,385 | 137,249 | 196,555 | 124,508 |
| Venza | 47,321 | 54,410 | 1,474 | — | — |
| **Toyota Total** | **685,308** | **612,153** | **752,043** | **977,997** | **944,971** |
| **TOYOTA TOTAL** | **801,531** | **715,383** | **860,563** | **1,106,840** | **1,084,368** |
| Routan | 15,961 | 14,681 | 3,387 | — | — |
| Tiguan* | 20,946 | 13,903 | 8,664 | — | — |
| Touareg* | 4,713 | 4,392 | 6,755 | 8,812 | 10,163 |
| **VOLKSWAGEN TOTAL** | **41,620** | **32,976** | **18,806** | **8,812** | **10,163** |
| XC60* | 12,030 | 9,262 | — | — | — |
| XC70* | 6,626 | 5,825 | 9,489 | 12,628 | 13,132 |
| XC90* | 10,119 | 10,757 | 18,980 | 31,336 | 33,200 |
| **VOLVO TOTAL** | **28,775** | **25,844** | **28,469** | **43,964** | **46,332** |
| UD Trucks Light-Duty* | — | — | 112 | 279 | 232 |
| **VOLVO TRUCK TOTAL** | — | — | **112** | **279** | **232** |
| **TOTAL LIGHT TRUCKS** | **5,919,085** | **5,000,792** | **6,425,634** | **8,526,888** | **8,742,808** |
| **TOTAL LIGHT VEHICLES** | **11,554,518** | **10,401,682** | **13,194,741** | **16,089,222** | **16,504,400** |
| **TOTAL MED./HVY. TRUCKS** | **217,702** | **199,686** | **298,424** | **371,093** | **544,581** |
| **TOTAL VEHICLES** | **11,772,220** | **10,601,368** | **13,493,165** | **16,460,315** | **17,048,981** |

*Units imported from outside North America.
SOURCE: *Ward's AutoInfoBank.*

# U.S. Sales of Vehicles by Source, Market Class and Purchasing Sector

## U.S. LIGHT VEHICLE SALES BY COUNTRY OF ORIGIN

| | 2010 | 2009 | 2008 | 2007 | 2006 | 2005 | 2004 | 2003 | 2002 | 2001 |
|---|---|---|---|---|---|---|---|---|---|---|
| Germany | 482,148 | 407,487 | 506,736 | 581,905 | 574,683 | 534,287 | 541,940 | 543,823 | 546,654 | 522,659 |
| Japan | 798,706 | 829,496 | 1,141,768 | 1,183,144 | 1,154,455 | 922,934 | 810,004 | 830,355 | 930,253 | 836,685 |
| South Korea | 448,679 | 435,108 | 404,564 | 420,523 | 435,925 | 524,496 | 550,314 | 447,660 | 485,061 | 494,798 |
| Others | 114,023 | 171,191 | 225,203 | 179,491 | 179,701 | 204,816 | 246,801 | 261,213 | 263,616 | 243,487 |
| **Imported Totals** | **1,843,556** | **1,843,282** | **2,278,271** | **2,365,063** | **2,344,764** | **2,186,533** | **2,149,059** | **2,083,051** | **2,225,584** | **2,097,629** |
| N. America (Domestics) | 3,791,877 | 3,557,608 | 4,490,836 | 5,197,271 | 5,416,828 | 5,473,450 | 5,333,496 | 5,472,500 | 5,816,671 | 6,254,371 |
| **TOTAL CARS** | **5,635,433** | **5,400,890** | **6,769,107** | **7,562,334** | **7,761,592** | **7,659,983** | **7,482,555** | **7,555,551** | **8,042,255** | **8,352,000** |
| Germany | 87,278 | 68,918 | 41,235 | 37,945 | 42,696 | 53,748 | 60,890 | 41,829 | 12,680 | 11,957 |
| Japan | 601,055 | 592,155 | 806,902 | 983,295 | 855,396 | 699,706 | 751,219 | 821,678 | 796,007 | 793,670 |
| South Korea | 108,237 | 148,157 | 158,383 | 223,426 | 227,661 | 258,510 | 232,668 | 198,309 | 165,254 | 123,454 |
| Others | 102,074 | 75,012 | 89,949 | 143,419 | 220,997 | 203,351 | 201,481 | 165,364 | 92,434 | 52,199 |
| **Imported Totals** | **898,644** | **884,242** | **1,096,469** | **1,388,085** | **1,346,750** | **1,215,315** | **1,246,258** | **1,227,180** | **1,066,375** | **981,280** |
| N.America (Domestics) | 5,020,441 | 4,116,550 | 5,329,165 | 7,138,803 | 7,396,058 | 8,072,456 | 8,138,107 | 7,856,322 | 7,707,738 | 7,789,089 |
| **TOTAL LIGHT TRUCKS** | **5,919,085** | **5,000,792** | **6,425,634** | **8,526,888** | **8,742,808** | **9,287,771** | **9,384,365** | **9,083,502** | **8,774,113** | **8,770,369** |
| Germany | 569,426 | 476,405 | 547,971 | 619,850 | 617,379 | 588,035 | 602,830 | 585,652 | 559,334 | 534,616 |
| Japan | 1,399,761 | 1,421,651 | 1,948,670 | 2,166,439 | 2,009,851 | 1,622,640 | 1,561,223 | 1,652,033 | 1,726,260 | 1,630,355 |
| South Korea | 556,916 | 583,265 | 562,947 | 643,949 | 663,586 | 783,006 | 782,982 | 645,969 | 650,315 | 618,252 |
| Others | 216,097 | 246,203 | 315,152 | 322,910 | 400,698 | 408,167 | 448,282 | 426,577 | 356,050 | 295,686 |
| **Imported Totals** | **2,742,200** | **2,727,524** | **3,374,740** | **3,753,148** | **3,691,514** | **3,401,848** | **3,395,317** | **3,310,231** | **3,291,959** | **3,078,909** |
| N. America (Domestics) | 8,812,318 | 7,674,158 | 9,820,001 | 12,336,074 | 12,812,886 | 13,545,906 | 13,471,603 | 13,328,822 | 13,524,409 | 14,043,460 |
| **TOTAL LIGHT VEHICLES** | **11,554,518** | **10,401,682** | **13,194,741** | **16,089,222** | **16,504,400** | **16,947,754** | **16,866,920** | **16,639,053** | **16,816,368** | **17,122,369** |

NOTE: North America is U.S., Canada, Mexico. Light vehicles are cars and light trucks (GVW Classes 1-3, under 14,001 lbs.).
SOURCE: *Ward's AutoInfoBank.*

## U.S. LIGHT VEHICLE SALES BY SEGMENT GROUP

| Year | Small Car | Middle Car | Large Car | Luxury Car | Cross Utility | Sport Utility | Van | Pickup | Comm. Chassis | Total |
|---|---|---|---|---|---|---|---|---|---|---|
| 2010 | 17.8 | 20.5 | 2.9 | 7.6 | 24.5 | 6.9 | 5.9 | 13.9 | — | 100.0 |
| 2009 | 19.6 | 21.7 | 3.1 | 7.5 | 22.3 | 6.9 | 5.6 | 13.3 | — | 100.0 |
| 2008 | 19.0 | 21.0 | 3.5 | 7.8 | 18.4 | 9.0 | 6.4 | 14.8 | — | 100.0 |
| 2007 | 15.8 | 19.3 | 4.3 | 7.6 | 17.3 | 12.1 | 7.0 | 16.6 | — | 100.0 |
| 2006 | 15.3 | 19.3 | 4.8 | 7.7 | 14.4 | 13.2 | 8.0 | 17.2 | — | 100.0 |
| 2005 | 14.2 | 18.8 | 4.7 | 7.6 | 12.9 | 14.5 | 8.7 | 18.8 | 0.1 | 100.0 |
| 2004 | 13.6 | 19.6 | 3.5 | 7.6 | 11.4 | 16.8 | 8.6 | 18.8 | — | 100.0 |
| 2003 | 14.1 | 20.5 | 2.9 | 7.9 | 10.2 | 17.4 | 8.4 | 18.6 | — | 100.0 |
| 2002 | 14.7 | 21.8 | 3.0 | 8.4 | 7.7 | 17.7 | 8.7 | 18.0 | — | 100.0 |
| 2001 | 15.1 | 22.3 | 3.2 | 8.3 | 6.3 | 17.3 | 9.0 | 18.7 | — | 100.0 |

SOURCE: *Ward's AutoInfoBank.*

## U.S. CAR SALES BY SECTOR

| | Units by Consuming Sector (000) | | | | % of Total Sales | | | Units by Consuming Sector (000) | | | | % of Total Sales | |
|---|---|---|---|---|---|---|---|---|---|---|---|---|---|
| Year | Consumer | Business | Government | Total | Consumer | Business | Year | Consumer | Business | Government | Total | Consumer | Business |
| 2010 | 2,944 | 2,621 | 70 | 5,635 | 52.2 | 46.5 | 1999 | 4,388 | 4,076 | 174 | 8,638 | 50.8 | 47.2 |
| 2009 | 3,228 | 2,042 | 131 | 5,401 | 59.8 | 37.8 | 1998 | 3,981 | 3,943 | 161 | 8,085 | 49.2 | 48.8 |
| 2008 | 3,759 | 2,821 | 189 | 6,769 | 55.5 | 41.7 | 1997 | 3,908 | 4,166 | 143 | 8,217 | 47.6 | 50.7 |
| 2007 | 4,113 | 3,255 | 194 | 7,562 | 54.4 | 43.0 | 1996 | 4,079 | 4,273 | 176 | 8,527 | 47.8 | 50.1 |
| 2006 | 4,330 | 3,239 | 193 | 7,762 | 55.8 | 41.7 | 1995 | 4,351 | 4,186 | 151 | 8,687 | 50.1 | 48.2 |
| 2005 | 4,335 | 3,169 | 156 | 7,660 | 56.6 | 41.4 | 1994 | 4,600 | 4,268 | 124 | 8,991 | 51.2 | 47.5 |
| 2004 | 4,275 | 3,078 | 130 | 7,483 | 57.1 | 41.1 | 1993 | 4,657 | 3,748 | 113 | 8,518 | 54.7 | 44.0 |
| 2003 | 4,341 | 3,074 | 141 | 7,556 | 57.5 | 40.7 | 1992 | 4,566 | 3,529 | 119 | 8,214 | 55.6 | 43.0 |
| 2002 | 4,523 | 3,374 | 145 | 8,042 | 56.2 | 42.0 | 1991 | 4,424 | 3,648 | 103 | 8,175 | 54.1 | 44.6 |
| 2001 | 4,629 | 3,570 | 153 | 8,352 | 55.4 | 42.7 | 1990 | 5,677 | 3,477 | 147 | 9,301 | 61.0 | 37.4 |
| 2000 | 4,678 | 3,950 | 150 | 8,778 | 53.3 | 45.0 | | | | | | | |

SOURCE: U.S. Department of Commerce, Bureau of Economic Analysis.

# U.S. Sales of Trucks by Manufacturer, Gross Vehicle Weight Rating, and Source

## U.S. TRUCK SALES BY GVW CLASS AND SOURCE, 2010

| | Gross Vehicle Weight Rating (Pounds) | | | | | | | | |
|---|---|---|---|---|---|---|---|---|---|
| | 6,000 & Less | 6,001- 10,000 | 10,001- 14,000 | 14,001- 16,000 | 16,001- 19,500 | 19,501- 26,000 | 26,001- 33,000 | 33,001 & Over | Total |
| **DOMESTIC\*** | | | | | | | | | |
| BMW | 42,973 | — | — | — | — | — | — | — | 42,973 |
| Chrysler | 600,418 | 114,608 | 80,169 | — | 5,477 | — | — | — | 800,672 |
| Ford | 517,588 | 609,759 | 53,640 | 3,412 | 18,295 | 5,781 | 2,664 | — | 1,211,139 |
| Freightliner/Sterling/Western Star | — | — | — | 997 | 396 | 6,253 | 14,366 | 36,345 | 58,357 |
| General Motors | 623,720 | 756,413 | 24,586 | 798 | 1,486 | 182 | 558 | — | 1,407,743 |
| Hino | — | — | — | 47 | 165 | 2,325 | 885 | — | 3,422 |
| Honda | 501,523 | — | — | — | — | — | — | — | 501,523 |
| Hyundai | 76,680 | — | — | — | — | — | — | — | 76,680 |
| International | — | 33 | 975 | 1,529 | 1,512 | 12,966 | 15,333 | 26,939 | 59,287 |
| Isuzu | — | — | 608 | 574 | — | 62 | 49 | — | 1,293 |
| Kenworth | — | — | — | — | 34 | 542 | 2,134 | 11,621 | 14,331 |
| Kia | 108,202 | — | — | — | — | — | — | — | 108,202 |
| Mack | — | — | — | — | — | — | — | 9,209 | 9,209 |
| Mazda | 3,647 | — | — | — | — | — | — | — | 3,647 |
| Mercedes-Benz | 52,578 | — | — | — | — | — | — | — | 52,578 |
| Mitsubishi | 4,303 | — | — | — | — | — | — | — | 4,303 |
| Nissan | 106,973 | 23,416 | — | — | — | — | — | — | 130,389 |
| Peterbilt | — | — | — | — | 25 | 160 | 1,989 | 12,980 | 15,154 |
| Saab | 102 | — | — | — | — | — | — | — | 102 |
| Subaru | 95,620 | — | — | — | — | — | — | — | 95,620 |
| Suzuki | 1,760 | — | — | — | — | — | — | — | 1,760 |
| Toyota | 604,186 | — | — | — | — | — | — | — | 604,186 |
| Volkswagen | 15,961 | — | — | — | — | — | — | — | 15,961 |
| Volvo Truck | — | — | — | — | — | — | — | 10,036 | 10,036 |
| Other Domestic | — | — | — | — | — | — | — | 22 | 22 |
| **Total Domestic** | **3,356,234** | **1,504,229** | **159,978** | **7,357** | **27,390** | **28,271** | **37,978** | **107,152** | **5,228,589** |
| **IMPORT** | | | | | | | | | |
| Audi | 31,494 | — | — | — | — | — | — | — | 31,494 |
| BMW | 5,135 | — | — | — | — | — | — | — | 5,135 |
| Chrysler | — | 253 | — | — | — | — | — | — | 253 |
| Ford | 27,405 | — | — | — | — | — | — | — | 27,405 |
| General Motors | — | — | 70 | 251 | 82 | — | — | — | 403 |
| Honda | 37,380 | — | — | — | — | — | — | — | 37,380 |
| Hyundai | 48,335 | — | — | — | — | — | — | — | 48,335 |
| Isuzu | — | — | 1,082 | 3,195 | 2,648 | — | — | — | 6,925 |
| Kia | 59,902 | — | — | — | — | — | — | — | 59,902 |
| Land Rover | 31,864 | — | — | — | — | — | — | — | 31,864 |
| Mazda | 73,379 | — | — | — | — | — | — | — | 73,379 |
| Mercedes-Benz | 21,865 | 8,559 | — | — | — | — | — | — | 30,424 |
| Mitsubishi | 14,190 | — | — | — | — | — | — | — | 14,190 |
| Mitsubishi Fuso | — | — | 311 | 1,163 | 624 | 427 | 61 | — | 2,586 |
| Nissan | 187,739 | — | — | — | — | — | — | — | 187,739 |
| Porsche | 8,343 | — | — | — | — | — | — | — | 8,343 |
| Sterling | — | — | 1 | 1 | 7 | — | — | — | 9 |
| Subaru | 85,080 | — | — | — | — | — | — | — | 85,080 |
| Suzuki | 4,478 | — | — | — | — | — | — | — | 4,478 |
| Toyota | 197,345 | — | — | — | — | — | — | — | 197,345 |
| UD Trucks | — | — | — | 114 | 225 | 445 | 311 | — | 1,095 |
| Volkswagen | 25,659 | — | — | — | — | — | — | — | 25,659 |
| Volvo | 28,775 | — | — | — | — | — | — | — | 28,775 |
| **Total Import** | **888,368** | **8,812** | **1,464** | **4,724** | **3,586** | **872** | **372** | **—** | **908,198** |
| **Total Trucks** | **4,244,602** | **1,513,041** | **161,442** | **12,081** | **30,976** | **29,143** | **38,350** | **107,152** | **6,136,787** |

\*Units produced in the United States, Canada and Mexico.
SOURCE: *Ward's AutoInfoBank.*

# U.S. Sales of Trucks by Gross Vehicle Weight Rating and Body Type

## U.S. LIGHT TRUCK SALES BY GVW AND BODY TYPE

| GVWR/Body type | 2010 | 2009 | 2008 | 2007 | 2006 |
|---|---|---|---|---|---|
| **0-6,000 Lbs.** | | | | | |
| Utility | 3,383,837 | 2,794,008 | 3,255,649 | 4,131,827 | 3,950,113 |
| Mini Van | 460,154 | 415,173 | 592,000 | 793,335 | 970,708 |
| Passenger Carrier | 3,158 | 2,695 | 3,670 | 1,939 | 2,228 |
| Van | 37,918 | 19,573 | 20,800 | 35,065 | 33,498 |
| Compact Pickup | 266,226 | 272,394 | 392,735 | 516,875 | 616,653 |
| Conventional Pickup | 93,309 | 79,424 | 137,744 | 259,372 | 581,610 |
| **Total 0-6,000 lbs.** | **4,244,602** | **3,583,267** | **4,402,598** | **5,738,413** | **6,154,810** |
| **6,001-10,000 Lbs.** | | | | | |
| Utility | 254,048 | 239,745 | 370,507 | 607,973 | 619,409 |
| Passenger Carrier | 33,427 | 29,637 | 40,060 | 50,397 | 53,955 |
| Van | 106,984 | 83,012 | 129,688 | 170,677 | 192,360 |
| Van Cutaway | 36,716 | 33,305 | 54,496 | 67,666 | 73,545 |
| Conventional Pickup | 1,081,866 | 920,122 | 1,293,446 | 1,725,866 | 1,498,885 |
| **Total 6,001-10,000 lbs.** | **1,513,041** | **1,305,821** | **1,888,197** | **2,622,579** | **2,438,154** |
| **10,001 - 14,000 lbs.** | | | | | |
| Conventional Pickup | 158,294 | 109,024 | 130,278 | 159,151 | 142,012 |
| Other Body Types | 3,148 | 2,680 | 4,561 | 6,745 | 7,832 |
| Total 10,001 - 14,000 lbs. | 161,442 | 111,704 | 134,839 | 165,896 | 149,844 |
| **Total Light Trucks** | **5,919,085** | **5,000,792** | **6,425,634** | **8,526,888** | **8,742,808** |

SOURCE: *Ward's AutoInfoBank.*

## U.S. TRUCK SALES BY COUNTRY OF ORIGIN

| | 2010 | 2009 | 2008 | 2007 | 2006 | 2005 | 2004 | 2003 | 2002 | 2001 |
|---|---|---|---|---|---|---|---|---|---|---|
| Germany | 87,278 | 68,918 | 41,235 | 37,945 | 42,696 | 53,748 | 60,890 | 41,829 | 12,680 | 11,957 |
| Japan | 601,055 | 592,155 | 806,902 | 983,295 | 855,396 | 699,706 | 751,219 | 821,678 | 796,007 | 793,670 |
| South Korea | 108,237 | 148,157 | 158,383 | 223,426 | 227,661 | 258,510 | 232,668 | 198,309 | 165,254 | 123,454 |
| Others | 102,074 | 75,012 | 89,949 | 143,419 | 220,997 | 203,351 | 201,481 | 165,364 | 92,434 | 52,199 |
| **Imported Totals** | **898,644** | **884,242** | **1,096,469** | **1,388,085** | **1,346,750** | **1,215,315** | **1,246,258** | **1,227,180** | **1,066,375** | **981,280** |
| North America (Domestic) | 5,020,441 | 4,116,550 | 5,329,165 | 7,138,803 | 7,396,058 | 8,072,456 | 8,138,107 | 7,856,322 | 7,707,738 | 7,789,089 |
| **TOTAL LIGHT TRUCKS** | **5,919,085** | **5,000,792** | **6,425,634** | **8,526,888** | **8,742,808** | **9,287,771** | **9,384,365** | **9,083,502** | **8,774,113** | **8,770,369** |
| Japan | 9,554 | 6,753 | 10,699 | 20,151 | 22,624 | 21,953 | 22,984 | 18,406 | 16,426 | 19,719 |
| South Korea | — | — | — | — | — | — | — | — | — | 524 |
| Others | — | — | — | — | — | — | 21 | 454 | 699 | 602 |
| **Imported Totals** | **9,554** | **6,753** | **10,699** | **20,151** | **22,624** | **21,953** | **23,005** | **18,860** | **17,125** | **20,845** |
| North America (Domestic) | 208,148 | 192,933 | 287,725 | 350,942 | 521,957 | 474,622 | 408,648 | 309,529 | 305,159 | 329,164 |
| **TOTAL MED./HVY. TRUCKS** | **217,702** | **199,686** | **298,424** | **371,093** | **544,581** | **496,575** | **431,653** | **328,389** | **322,284** | **350,009** |
| Germany | 87,278 | 68,918 | 41,235 | 37,945 | 42,696 | 53,748 | 60,890 | 41,829 | 12,680 | 11,957 |
| Japan | 610,609 | 598,908 | 817,601 | 1,003,446 | 878,020 | 721,659 | 774,203 | 840,084 | 812,433 | 813,389 |
| South Korea | 108,237 | 148,157 | 158,383 | 223,426 | 227,661 | 258,510 | 232,668 | 198,309 | 165,254 | 123,978 |
| Others | 102,074 | 75,012 | 89,949 | 143,419 | 220,997 | 203,351 | 201,502 | 165,818 | 93,133 | 52,801 |
| **Imported Totals** | **908,198** | **890,995** | **1,107,168** | **1,408,236** | **1,369,374** | **1,237,268** | **1,269,263** | **1,246,040** | **1,083,500** | **1,002,125** |
| North America (Domestic) | 5,228,589 | 4,309,483 | 5,616,890 | 7,489,745 | 7,918,015 | 8,547,078 | 8,546,755 | 8,165,851 | 8,012,897 | 8,118,253 |
| **TOTAL TRUCKS** | **6,136,787** | **5,200,478** | **6,724,058** | **8,897,981** | **9,287,389** | **9,784,346** | **9,816,018** | **9,411,891** | **9,096,397** | **9,120,378** |

NOTE: North America is U.S., Canada, Mexico.
SOURCE: *Ward's AutoInfoBank.*

# Annual and Monthly Records for U.S. Production and Sales

## RECORD U.S. PRODUCTION YEARS

| Cars | | Trucks | |
| --- | --- | --- | --- |
| Year | Units | Year | Units |
| 1973 | 9,660,821 | 2004 | 7,794,429 |
| 1965 | 9,329,104 | 2005 | 7,680,781 |
| 1977 | 9,211,411 | 2003 | 7,633,659 |
| 1978 | 9,173,606 | 1999 | 7,447,229 |
| 1968 | 8,843,031 | 2002 | 7,322,205 |
| 1972 | 8,821,737 | 2000 | 7,302,797 |
| 1966 | 8,598,917 | 2006 | 6,948,581 |

## RECORD U.S. SALES YEARS

| Cars | | Trucks | |
| --- | --- | --- | --- |
| Year | Units | Year | Units |
| 1973 | 11,423,851 | 2004 | 9,816,018 |
| 1986 | 11,404,239 | 2005 | 9,784,346 |
| 1978 | 11,314,079 | 2003 | 9,411,891 |
| 1977 | 11,183,412 | 2006 | 9,287,389 |
| 1985 | 10,979,187 | 2001 | 9,120,378 |
| 1972 | 10,940,482 | 2002 | 9,096,397 |
| 1979 | 10,672,768 | 2000 | 9,033,950 |

## RECORD U.S. PRODUCTION BY MONTH

| Month | Year | Units |
| --- | --- | --- |
| | Cars | |
| January | 1973 | 917,273 |
| February | 1973 | 856,117 |
| March | 1965 | 963,101 |
| April | 1978 | 870,689 |
| May | 1973 | 941,019 |
| June | 1977 | 949,440 |
| July | 1965 | 740,576 |
| August | 1950 | 684,970 |
| September | 1972 | 758,578 |
| October | 1973 | 951,434 |
| November | 1965 | 913,146 |
| December | 1964 | 866,632 |
| | Trucks | |
| January | 2003 | 636,722 |
| February | 2004 | 678,010 |
| March | 2004 | 786,195 |
| April | 2004 | 693,282 |
| May | 2000 | 713,996 |
| June | 2005 | 706,460 |
| July | 2003 | 428,676 |
| August | 2005 | 732,841 |
| September | 2005 | 721,291 |
| October | 2003 | 757,513 |
| November | 2004 | 626,000 |
| December | 2003 | 594,003 |

## RECORD U.S. SALES BY MONTH

| Month | Year | Units |
| --- | --- | --- |
| | Cars | |
| January | 1973 | 874,084 |
| February | 1973 | 918,681 |
| March | 1973 | 1,140,386 |
| April | 1978 | 1,043,341 |
| May | 1978 | 1,159,996 |
| June | 1978 | 1,138,504 |
| July | 1973 | 958,270 |
| August | 1985 | 994,926 |
| September | 1986 | 1,212,714 |
| October | 1972 | 1,068,400 |
| November | 1972 | 1,029,689 |
| December | 1986 | 987,744 |
| | Trucks | |
| January | 2004 | 658,568 |
| February | 2000 | 775,789 |
| March | 2005 | 897,083 |
| April | 2005 | 827,851 |
| May | 2004 | 920,354 |
| June | 2005 | 1,015,406 |
| July | 2005 | 1,134,313 |
| August | 2003 | 924,067 |
| September | 2004 | 864,381 |
| October | 2001 | 946,182 |
| November | 2001 | 750,766 |
| December | 2004 | 931,903 |

## U.S. PRODUCTION MILESTONES

| Cars | | Trucks | | Total Vehicles | |
| --- | --- | --- | --- | --- | --- |
| Year | Units | Year | Units | Year | Units |
| 2003 | 450 millionth | 2005 | 200 millionth | 2010 | 700 millionth |
| 1994 | 400 millionth | 1998 | 150 millionth | 2001 | 600 millionth |
| 1986 | 350 millionth | 1988 | 100 millionth | 1992 | 500 millionth |
| 1979 | 300 millionth | 1971 | 50 millionth | 1982 | 400 millionth |
| 1973 | 250 millionth | 1965 | 40 millionth | 1972 | 300 millionth |
| 1967 | 200 millionth | 1957 | 30 millionth | 1962 | 200 millionth |
| 1952 | 100 millionth | 1949 | 20 millionth | 1955 | 150 millionth |
| 1935 | 50 millionth | 1938 | 10 millionth | 1948 | 100 millionth |
| 1925 | 25 millionth | 1929 | 5 millionth | 1931 | 50 millionth |
| 1920 | 10 millionth | 1920 | 1 millionth | 1920 | 10 millionth |
| 1912 | 1 millionth | 1915 | 100,000th | 1912 | 1 millionth |

SOURCE: *Ward's* Automotive Group

# Top Selling Vehicles and Automotive Color Popularity

## TOP 10 CARS SOLD IN THE U.S.

| | 2010 | | | 2009 | |
|---|---|---|---|---|---|
| Rank | Model | Sales | Rank | Model | Sales |
| 1 | Toyota Camry | 327,804 | 1 | Toyota Camry | 356,824 |
| 2 | Honda Accord | 282,530 | 2 | Toyota Corolla/Matrix | 296,874 |
| 3 | Toyota Corolla/Matrix | 266,082 | 3 | Honda Accord | 287,492 |
| 4 | Honda Civic | 260,218 | 4 | Honda Civic | 259,722 |
| 5 | Nissan Altima | 229,263 | 5 | Nissan Altima | 203,568 |
| 6 | Ford Fusion | 219,219 | 6 | Ford Fusion | 180,671 |
| 7 | Chevrolet Malibu | 198,770 | 7 | Chevrolet Impala | 165,565 |
| 8 | Hyundai Sonata | 196,623 | 8 | Chevrolet Malibu | 161,568 |
| 9 | Ford Focus | 172,421 | 9 | Ford Focus | 160,433 |
| 10 | Chevrolet Impala | 172,078 | 10 | Toyota Prius | 139,682 |

## TOP 10 LIGHT TRUCKS SOLD IN THE U.S.

| | 2010 | | | 2009 | |
|---|---|---|---|---|---|
| Rank | Model | Sales | Rank | Model | Sales |
| 1 | Ford F-Series | 502,125 | 1 | Ford F-Series | 392,112 |
| 2 | Chevrolet Silverado | 370,135 | 2 | Chevrolet Silverado | 316,544 |
| 3 | Honda CR-V | 203,714 | 3 | Honda CR-V | 191,214 |
| 4 | Ram Pickup | 194,175 | 4 | Ram Pickup | 173,066 |
| 5 | Ford Escape | 191,026 | 5 | Ford Escape | 173,044 |
| 6 | Toyota RAV4 | 170,877 | 6 | Toyota RAV4 | 149,088 |
| 7 | Chevrolet Equinox | 149,979 | 7 | GMC Sierra | 111,842 |
| 8 | GMC Sierra | 129,794 | 8 | Toyota Tacoma | 111,824 |
| 9 | Ford Edge | 118,637 | 9 | Honda Odyssey | 100,133 |
| 10 | Chrysler Town & Country | 112,275 | 10 | Lexus RX | 93,379 |

SOURCE: *Ward's AutoInfoBank.*

## AUTOMOTIVE PAINT COLOR POPULARITY BY VEHICLE TYPE, 2010 MODEL YEAR

| Luxury Cars | | Full Size/Intermediate Cars | | Compact/Sports Cars | | Light Trucks | |
|---|---|---|---|---|---|---|---|
| Color | Percent | Color | Percent | Color | Percent | Color | Percent |
| Black/Black Effect | 27% | Silver | 19% | Silver | 19% | White/White Pearl | 35% |
| White/White Pearl | 13% | Gray | 17% | Black/Black Effect | 19% | Black/Black Effect | 18% |
| Gray | 20% | White/White Pearl | 16% | Gray | 19% | Blue | 8% |
| Silver | 14% | Black/Black Effect | 18% | Blue | 14% | Silver | 12% |
| Red | 12% | Blue | 9% | Red | 10% | Red | 12% |
| Blue | 4% | Red | 10% | White/White Pearl | 13% | Gray | 10% |
| Beige/Brown | 9% | Beige/Brown | 6% | Beige/Brown | 4% | Beige/Brown | 2% |
| Yellow/Gold | 1% | Green | 3% | Yellow/Gold | 1% | Green | 2% |
| Green | <1% | Yellow/Gold | 2% | Green | 1% | Yellow/Gold | 2% |
| Other | <1% | Other | <1% | Other | <1% | Other | <1% |

SOURCE: Du Pont Automotive Products.

# Canada Vehicle Sales and Registrations

## CANADA VEHICLE SALES BY SOURCE

| Year | Cars | | | Commercial Vehicles | | | Total Vehicles |
|------|-----------|----------|----------|-----------|----------|----------|-----------|
| | Domestic[1] | Imports | Total | Domestic[1] | Imports | Total | |
| 2010 | 399,330 | 295,019 | 694,349 | 766,826 | 122,213 | 889,039 | 1,583,388 |
| 2009 | 427,930 | 301,093 | 729,023 | 636,568 | 116,641 | 753,209 | 1,482,232 |
| 2008 | 547,321 | 325,399 | 872,720 | 664,145 | 136,657 | 800,802 | 1,673,522 |
| 2007 | 552,838 | 288,747 | 841,585 | 723,401 | 125,359 | 848,760 | 1,690,345 |
| 2006 | 578,491 | 280,335 | 858,826 | 674,514 | 132,668 | 807,182 | 1,666,008 |
| 2005 | 572,202 | 275,234 | 847,436 | 668,342 | 114,364 | 782,706 | 1,630,142 |
| 2004 | 545,767 | 275,783 | 821,550 | 649,525 | 103,728 | 753,253 | 1,574,803 |
| 2003 | 603,444 | 261,545 | 864,989 | 654,112 | 105,949 | 760,061 | 1,625,050 |
| 2002 | 651,703 | 282,354 | 934,057 | 700,427 | 97,339 | 797,766 | 1,731,823 |
| 2001 | 620,162 | 248,026 | 868,188 | 651,952 | 77,735 | 729,687 | 1,597,875 |
| 2000 | 640,916 | 208,216 | 849,132 | 673,631 | 63,320 | 736,951 | 1,586,083 |
| 1999 | 620,233 | 186,207 | 806,440 | 676,107 | 57,832 | 733,939 | 1,540,379 |
| 1998 | 590,041 | 150,775 | 740,816 | 629,720 | 56,056 | 685,776 | 1,426,592 |
| 1997 | 628,739 | 109,816 | 738,555 | 628,124 | 56,315 | 684,439 | 1,422,994 |
| 1996 | 572,001 | 88,803 | 660,804 | 516,288 | 25,302 | 541,590 | 1,202,394 |
| 1995 | 554,878 | 116,103 | 670,981 | 470,147 | 23,470 | 493,617 | 1,164,598 |
| 1994 | 584,985 | 165,343 | 750,328 | 478,826 | 27,828 | 506,654 | 1,256,982 |
| 1993 | 511,611 | 229,257 | 740,868 | 407,864 | 41,850 | 449,714 | 1,190,582 |
| 1992 | 511,220 | 289,107 | 800,327 | 369,896 | 54,155 | 424,051 | 1,224,378 |
| 1991 | 576,480 | 299,308 | 875,788 | 346,332 | 62,529 | 408,861 | 1,284,649 |

(1)  Units produced in the United States, Canada and Mexico.
SOURCE: *Ward's AutoInfoBank.*

## CANADA TOTAL REGISTRATIONS BY PROVINCE, 2009

| Province | Total Vehicle Registrations by Weight | | | |
|----------|-----------|-----------|--------|-----------|
| | less than 9,000 lbs. | over 9,000 lbs. | Buses | Total |
| Alberta | 2,605,008 | 222,468 | 15,201 | 2,842,677 |
| British Columbia | 2,561,329 | 148,027 | 9,557 | 2,718,913 |
| Manitoba | 670,511 | 29,537 | 3,939 | 703,987 |
| New Brunswick | 489,507 | 12,305 | 3,086 | 504,898 |
| Newfoundland | 297,249 | 8,323 | 1,242 | 306,814 |
| Northwest Territories | 21,539 | 2,184 | 142 | 23,865 |
| Nova Scotia | 541,748 | 16,733 | 1,962 | 560,443 |
| Nunavut | 3,752 | 524 | 31 | 4,307 |
| Ontario | 7,243,898 | 216,157 | 28,649 | 7,488,704 |
| Prince Edward Island | 81,699 | 4,241 | 132 | 86,072 |
| Quebec | 4,613,923 | 94,379 | 17,409 | 4,725,711 |
| Saskatchewan | 719,577 | 71,147 | 3,884 | 794,608 |
| Yukon Territory | 27,244 | 3,660 | 341 | 31,245 |
| **Total** | **19,876,984** | **829,685** | **85,575** | **20,792,244** |

SOURCE: Statistics Canada.

## CANADA TOTAL REGISTRATIONS

| Year | Cars (000) | Commercial Vehicles (000) | Total (000) |
|------|-----------|-----------|--------|
| 2009 | 19,877 | 915 | 20,792 |
| 2008 | 19,613 | 907 | 20,520 |
| 2007 | 19,199 | 872 | 20,071 |
| 2006 | 18,739 | 841 | 19,580 |
| 2005 | 18,124 | 786 | 18,910 |
| 2004 | 17,920 | 745 | 18,665 |
| 2003 | 17,755 | 741 | 18,496 |
| 2002 | 17,544 | 723 | 18,267 |
| 2001 | 17,055 | 728 | 17,783 |
| 2000 | 16,832 | 739 | 17,571 |
| 1999 | 16,538 | 2,679 | 19,217 |
| 1998 | 13,887 | 3,694 | 17,581 |
| 1996 | 13,217 | 3,644 | 16,861 |
| 1994 | 13,122 | 3,466 | 16,588 |
| 1992 | 12,781 | 3,413 | 16,194 |
| 1990 | 12,622 | 3,931 | 16,553 |
| 1988 | 12,086 | 3,766 | 15,852 |
| 1986 | 11,586 | 3,213 | 14,799 |

NOTE: Beginning in 2000,  data excludes farm tractors and off-road vehicles. SOURCE: Statistics Canada.

# Canada Vehicle Sales

## CANADA VEHICLE SALES BY MODEL

| Model | 2010 | 2009 | 2008 | 2007 | 2006 |
|---|---|---|---|---|---|
| A3* | 1,322 | 1,245 | 1,351 | 1,175 | 1,531 |
| A4* | 5,211 | 4,224 | 4,480 | 4,334 | 4,655 |
| A5* | 2,309 | 1,520 | 400 | 35 | — |
| A6* | 596 | 579 | 795 | 769 | 1,026 |
| A8* | 132 | 96 | 161 | 234 | 273 |
| R8* | 137 | 152 | 155 | 34 | — |
| TT* | 319 | 406 | 660 | 414 | 111 |
| **AUDI TOTAL** | **10,026** | **8,222** | **8,002** | **6,995** | **7,596** |
| 1-Series* | 1,764 | 2,533 | 2,212 | — | — |
| 3-Series* | 14,009 | 12,610 | 11,754 | 13,102 | 10,721 |
| 5-Series* | 2,382 | 1,619 | 2,042 | 2,651 | 2,577 |
| 6-Series* | 61 | 165 | 286 | 371 | 433 |
| 7-Series* | 741 | 638 | 424 | 467 | 542 |
| Z4 | — | 7 | 249 | 390 | 492 |
| Z4* | 376 | 479 | — | — | — |
| Z8* | — | — | — | — | 1 |
| **BMW Total** | **19,333** | **18,051** | **16,967** | **16,981** | **14,766** |
| Mini Cooper* | 4,501 | 4,251 | 4,905 | 3,703 | 3,410 |
| **BMW TOTAL** | **23,834** | **22,302** | **21,872** | **20,684** | **18,176** |
| 200 Series | 1 | — | — | — | — |
| 300 Series | 4,180 | 5,234 | 7,443 | 10,210 | 13,316 |
| Crossfire* | — | 3 | 119 | 75 | 574 |
| PT Cruiser Convertible | — | — | 19 | 739 | 1,509 |
| Sebring Convertible | 1,180 | 866 | 2,404 | 1,325 | 1,081 |
| Sebring Sedan | 2,160 | 3,966 | 7,600 | 8,250 | 10,165 |
| **Chrysler Total** | **7,521** | **10,069** | **17,585** | **20,599** | **26,645** |
| Avenger | 3,495 | 5,533 | 7,873 | 7,067 | — |
| Caliber | 7,275 | 9,802 | 19,544 | 18,553 | 19,524 |
| Challenger | 3,097 | 2,660 | 1,631 | — | — |
| Charger | 4,662 | 4,861 | 6,675 | 7,858 | 7,440 |
| Magnum | — | 13 | 585 | 2,494 | 4,547 |
| SX 2.0 | — | — | — | — | 1,847 |
| Viper | 54 | 71 | 157 | 27 | 93 |
| **Dodge Total** | **18,583** | **22,940** | **36,465** | **35,999** | **33,451** |
| **CHRYSLER TOTAL** | **26,104** | **33,009** | **54,050** | **56,598** | **60,096** |
| B-Class* | 2,994 | 2,865 | 3,207 | 3,035 | 2,723 |
| C-Class* | 8,151 | 7,589 | 7,966 | 5,066 | 4,603 |
| E-Class* | 3,914 | 2,819 | 2,161 | 2,267 | 1,841 |
| S-Class* | 763 | 748 | 1,026 | 1,320 | 1,205 |
| SL* | 230 | 268 | 398 | 286 | 345 |
| SLK* | 324 | 371 | 519 | — | — |
| SLR* | 7 | 4 | 11 | 11 | 7 |
| SLS* | 111 | — | — | — | — |
| Maybach* | 3 | 3 | 5 | 6 | 8 |
| **Mercedes Total** | **16,497** | **14,667** | **15,293** | **11,991** | **10,732** |
| Smart Fortwo* | 2,019 | 2,667 | 3,749 | 2,433 | 3,023 |
| **DAIMLER TOTAL** | **18,516** | **17,334** | **19,042** | **14,424** | **13,755** |
| Crown Victoria | 2,243 | 2,429 | 2,938 | 2,809 | 3,315 |
| Fiesta | 4,423 | — | — | — | — |
| Five Hundred | — | — | — | 1,045 | 3,659 |
| Focus | 23,452 | 21,831 | 23,654 | 24,013 | 27,718 |
| Ford GT | — | — | — | 95 | 245 |
| Fusion | 19,364 | 16,526 | 13,326 | 15,882 | 17,370 |
| Mustang | 5,232 | 5,200 | 6,261 | 7,987 | 9,150 |
| Taurus | 3,847 | 2,035 | 2,064 | 1,513 | 6,691 |
| **Ford Total** | **58,561** | **48,021** | **48,243** | **53,344** | **68,148** |
| LS | — | — | — | — | 234 |
| MKS | 980 | 1,142 | 615 | — | — |
| MKZ | 1,493 | 1,508 | 1,358 | 1,585 | 527 |
| Town Car | 233 | 447 | 652 | 883 | 1,107 |
| Zephyr | — | — | — | — | 1,205 |
| **Lincoln Total** | **2,706** | **3,097** | **2,625** | **2,468** | **3,073** |
| Grand Marquis | 48 | 126 | 305 | 335 | 336 |
| **Mercury Total** | **48** | **126** | **305** | **335** | **336** |
| **FORD TOTAL** | **61,315** | **51,244** | **51,173** | **56,147** | **71,557** |
| Allure | — | 2,025 | 9,200 | 8,741 | 11,072 |
| Century | — | — | — | — | 5 |
| LaCrosse | 3,947 | 810 | — | — | — |
| LeSabre | — | — | — | — | 25 |
| Lucerne | 2,367 | 1,749 | 2,872 | 2,948 | 4,042 |
| Park Ave | — | — | — | — | 2 |
| Regal | — | — | — | — | 2 |
| Regal* | 820 | — | — | — | — |
| **Buick Total** | **7,134** | **4,584** | **12,072** | **11,689** | **15,148** |
| CTS | 2,974 | 2,488 | 4,223 | 3,839 | 3,946 |
| Deville | — | — | — | 6 | 30 |
| DTS | 278 | 355 | 704 | 959 | 1,308 |

# Canada Vehicle Sales

## CANADA VEHICLE SALES BY MODEL — continued

| Model | 2010 | 2009 | 2008 | 2007 | 2006 |
|---|---|---|---|---|---|
| Seville | — | — | — | — | 3 |
| STS | 46 | 74 | 279 | 505 | 659 |
| XLR | 1 | 16 | 30 | 59 | 81 |
| **Cadillac Total** | **3,299** | **2,933** | **5,236** | **5,368** | **6,027** |
| Aveo | 6,653 | 4,577 | 121 | — | — |
| Aveo* | 305 | 2,909 | 10,532 | 11,082 | 10,315 |
| Camaro | 4,113 | 2,554 | — | — | — |
| Cavalier | — | — | — | — | 4 |
| Cobalt | 25,957 | 14,350 | 33,754 | 32,613 | 31,729 |
| Corvette | 364 | 307 | 596 | 787 | 992 |
| Cruze | 3,184 | — | — | — | — |
| Epica* | — | — | 6 | 46 | 635 |
| Impala | 11,434 | 12,292 | 14,913 | 16,326 | 21,486 |
| Malibu | 13,092 | 12,427 | 17,596 | 9,857 | 18,097 |
| Monte Carlo | — | 2 | 37 | 802 | 1,548 |
| Optra* | — | 1 | 76 | 4,148 | 6,654 |
| **Chevrolet Total** | **65,102** | **49,419** | **77,631** | **75,661** | **91,460** |
| Alero | — | — | — | — | 5 |
| **Oldsmobile Total** | **—** | **—** | **—** | **—** | **5** |
| Bonneville | — | — | — | 1 | 26 |
| G5 | 2,834 | 10,085 | 26,436 | 25,211 | 9,810 |
| G6 | 307 | 3,891 | 13,640 | 11,848 | 18,559 |
| G8* | 1 | 2,171 | 691 | — | — |
| Grand Am | — | — | — | 2 | 17 |
| Grand Prix | — | 12 | 333 | 13,086 | 8,234 |
| Pursuit | — | — | — | — | 15,741 |
| Solstice | 46 | 443 | 899 | 1,816 | 1,889 |
| Vibe | 1,559 | 11,537 | 17,335 | 12,915 | 11,444 |
| Wave | 1,740 | 3,074 | 106 | — | — |
| Wave* | 241 | 2,612 | 8,426 | 8,711 | 8,019 |
| **Pontiac Total** | **6,728** | **33,825** | **67,866** | **73,590** | **73,739** |
| Astra* | 2 | 4,066 | 7,536 | 1 | — |
| Aura | — | 1,156 | 2,587 | 3,165 | 762 |
| Ion | — | 3 | 445 | 13,932 | 12,984 |
| Saturn L | — | — | — | 1 | 1 |
| Sky | — | 169 | 409 | 613 | 360 |
| **Saturn Total** | **2** | **5,394** | **10,977** | **17,712** | **14,107** |
| **GM TOTAL** | **82,265** | **96,155** | **173,782** | **184,020** | **200,486** |
| CSX | 2,064 | 2,526 | 2,998 | 3,729 | 5,186 |
| RL* | 64 | 94 | 157 | 158 | 233 |
| RSX* | — | — | 5 | 12 | 1,755 |
| TL | 2,895 | 3,577 | 4,019 | 3,995 | 4,694 |
| TSX* | 2,297 | 2,020 | 3,118 | 2,104 | 2,816 |
| **Acura Total** | **7,320** | **8,217** | **10,297** | **9,998** | **14,684** |
| Accord | 12,483 | 16,017 | 22,623 | 22,102 | 20,165 |
| Civic | 56,838 | 61,810 | 70,270 | 68,470 | 67,996 |
| Civic* | 663 | 844 | 2,193 | 2,368 | 2,032 |
| CR-Z* | 325 | — | — | — | — |
| Fit* | 7,900 | 9,553 | 14,836 | 13,507 | 10,634 |
| Insight* | 1,136 | 668 | 1 | 2 | 21 |
| S2000* | 21 | 49 | 65 | 123 | 146 |
| **Honda Total** | **79,366** | **88,941** | **109,988** | **106,572** | **100,994** |
| **HONDA TOTAL** | **86,686** | **97,158** | **120,285** | **116,570** | **115,678** |
| Accent* | 24,017 | 25,220 | 29,751 | 16,390 | 17,784 |
| Azera* | 3 | 176 | 369 | 762 | 837 |
| Elantra | 201 | — | — | — | — |
| Elantra* | 34,355 | 30,675 | 11,814 | 14,327 | 12,228 |
| Genesis* | 3,924 | 3,438 | 342 | — | — |
| Sonata | 13,792 | 8,587 | 9,320 | 8,633 | 6,272 |
| Sonata* | 64 | 388 | 978 | 2,401 | 6,194 |
| Tiburon* | 2 | 890 | 1,996 | 1,429 | 1,231 |
| XG350* | — | — | — | — | 95 |
| **HYUNDAI TOTAL** | **76,358** | **69,374** | **54,570** | **43,942** | **44,641** |
| Jaguar S-Type* | — | — | 32 | 132 | 199 |
| Jaguar X-Type* | — | — | 80 | 208 | 351 |
| Jaguar XF* | 449 | 604 | 536 | — | — |
| Jaguar XJ6/8* | 189 | 77 | 133 | 156 | 193 |
| Jaguar XK8* | 117 | 123 | 148 | 242 | 200 |
| **JAGUAR LAND ROVER TOTAL** | **755** | **804** | **929** | **738** | **943** |
| Amanti* | 37 | 111 | 158 | 142 | 710 |
| Forte* | 13,578 | 5,734 | — | — | — |
| Magentis* | 574 | 1,033 | 1,975 | 2,021 | 2,025 |
| Rio* | 7,887 | 10,287 | 9,742 | 7,236 | 7,297 |
| Soul* | 9,857 | 8,489 | — | — | — |
| Spectra* | 13 | 2,027 | 5,030 | 6,602 | 6,677 |
| **KIA TOTAL** | **31,946** | **27,681** | **16,905** | **16,001** | **16,709** |
| Mazda2* | 2,868 | — | — | — | — |

# Canada Vehicle Sales

## CANADA VEHICLE SALES BY MODEL — continued

| Model | 2010 | 2009 | 2008 | 2007 | 2006 |
|---|---|---|---|---|---|
| Mazda3* | 47,740 | 46,943 | 50,317 | 48,236 | 47,933 |
| Mazda6 | 6,092 | 6,614 | 6,561 | 8,451 | 9,971 |
| MX-5 Miata* | 736 | 850 | 1,407 | 1,814 | 1,582 |
| RX-8* | 111 | 310 | 543 | 659 | 1,029 |
| **MAZDA TOTAL** | **57,547** | **54,717** | **58,828** | **59,160** | **60,515** |
| Eclipse | 851 | 802 | 1,675 | 1,951 | 2,097 |
| Galant | 362 | 463 | 902 | 553 | 705 |
| Lancer* | 8,765 | 9,446 | 9,157 | 7,192 | 4,433 |
| **MITSUBISHI TOTAL** | **9,978** | **10,711** | **11,734** | **9,696** | **7,235** |
| G35/37* | 4,408 | 3,998 | 4,286 | 4,908 | 3,992 |
| M35/45* | 550 | 217 | 410 | 550 | 1,083 |
| Q45* | — | — | — | — | 7 |
| **Infiniti Total** | **4,958** | **4,215** | **4,696** | **5,458** | **5,082** |
| 350Z* | 899 | 112 | 311 | 469 | 624 |
| 370Z* | — | 455 | — | — | — |
| Altima | 13,425 | 13,853 | 16,676 | 17,126 | 13,997 |
| Cube* | 2,864 | 2,416 | — | — | — |
| GT-R* | 62 | 133 | 137 | — | — |
| Maxima | 2,266 | 1,642 | 1,475 | 1,304 | 2,940 |
| Sentra | 14,651 | 13,431 | 11,000 | 8,563 | 8,656 |
| Versa | 15,743 | 20,097 | 21,845 | 21,940 | 6,727 |
| **Nissan Total** | **49,910** | **52,139** | **51,444** | **49,402** | **32,944** |
| **NISSAN TOTAL** | **54,868** | **56,354** | **56,140** | **54,860** | **38,026** |
| 911* | 525 | 495 | 463 | 660 | 657 |
| Boxster* | 166 | 208 | 272 | 282 | 347 |
| Carrera GT* | — | — | — | — | 4 |
| Cayman* | 119 | 154 | 169 | 222 | 288 |
| Panamera* | 387 | 114 | — | — | — |
| **PORSCHE TOTAL** | **1,197** | **971** | **904** | **1,164** | **1,296** |
| 9-2X* | — | — | 1 | 19 | 357 |
| 9-3* | 2 | 627 | 1,254 | 1,575 | 1,568 |
| 9-5* | — | 92 | 197 | 327 | 444 |
| **SAAB TOTAL** | **2** | **719** | **1,452** | **1,921** | **2,369** |
| Impreza* | 8,658 | 9,126 | 8,555 | 7,480 | 6,155 |
| Legacy | 3,269 | 2,612 | 4,089 | 4,919 | 5,345 |
| **SUBARU TOTAL** | **11,927** | **11,738** | **12,644** | **12,399** | **11,500** |
| Aerio* | — | 2 | 1 | 303 | 2,186 |
| Kizashi* | 688 | — | — | — | — |
| Swift+* | 473 | 988 | 1,828 | 2,593 | 2,671 |
| SX4* | 4,970 | 7,079 | 7,833 | 4,424 | 1,601 |
| Verona* | — | 15 | — | — | 200 |
| **SUZUKI TOTAL** | **6,131** | **8,084** | **9,662** | **7,320** | **6,658** |
| ES* | 2,688 | 2,999 | 3,634 | 4,251 | 3,104 |
| GS* | 251 | 336 | 511 | 596 | 625 |
| HS* | 746 | 269 | — | — | — |
| IS* | 2,233 | 2,617 | 3,600 | 2,792 | 2,713 |
| LS* | 226 | 256 | 311 | 588 | 269 |
| SC* | 29 | 44 | 80 | 109 | 159 |
| **Lexus Total** | **6,173** | **6,521** | **8,136** | **8,336** | **6,870** |
| tC* | 233 | — | — | — | — |
| xB* | 367 | — | — | — | — |
| xD* | 79 | — | — | — | — |
| **Scion Total** | **679** | **—** | **—** | **—** | **—** |
| Avalon | 502 | 280 | 380 | 1,010 | 1,408 |
| Camry | 12,251 | 15,600 | 24,814 | 28,785 | 27,325 |
| Camry* | — | — | 2 | 173 | 1,740 |
| Celica* | — | — | — | — | 21 |
| Corolla | 38,680 | 53,933 | 57,736 | 40,474 | 44,182 |
| Echo* | — | — | — | — | 381 |
| Matrix | 19,093 | 22,526 | 23,549 | 21,369 | 23,536 |
| Prius* | 2,967 | 4,610 | 4,458 | 2,585 | 2,003 |
| Yaris* | 13,817 | 23,773 | 40,602 | 34,424 | 34,202 |
| **Toyota Total** | **87,310** | **120,722** | **151,541** | **128,820** | **134,798** |
| **TOYOTA TOTAL** | **94,162** | **127,243** | **159,677** | **137,156** | **141,668** |
| Beetle | 395 | 499 | 869 | 928 | 826 |
| Beetle Cabrio | 404 | 438 | 737 | 779 | 778 |
| CC* | 1,620 | 1,577 | 237 | — | — |
| Eos* | 774 | 802 | 1,121 | 1,013 | 376 |
| Golf* | 15,868 | 8,698 | 9,259 | 7,839 | 5,828 |
| GTI* | 2,135 | 1,045 | 1,406 | 1,614 | 1,421 |
| Jetta | 14,758 | 13,970 | 13,915 | 14,665 | 19,251 |
| Passat* | 2,024 | 1,559 | 2,352 | 3,093 | 3,716 |
| Phaeton* | — | — | — | — | 7 |
| Rabbit* | 83 | 4,027 | 7,660 | 6,324 | 2,236 |
| **VOLKSWAGEN TOTAL** | **38,061** | **32,615** | **37,556** | **36,255** | **34,439** |
| 30-Series* | 755 | 906 | 1,142 | 1,143 | — |
| 40-Series* | 818 | 758 | 683 | 1,099 | 1,431 |

# Canada Vehicle Sales

## CANADA VEHICLE SALES BY MODEL — continued

| Model | 2010 | 2009 | 2008 | 2007 | 2006 |
|---|---:|---:|---:|---:|---:|
| 50-Series* | 260 | 264 | 353 | 606 | 717 |
| 60-Series* | 208 | 145 | 541 | 1,425 | 1,978 |
| 70-Series* | 269 | 265 | 551 | 719 | 1,109 |
| 80-Series* | 361 | 250 | 243 | 543 | 248 |
| **VOLVO TOTAL** | **2,671** | **2,588** | **3,513** | **5,535** | **5,483** |
| **TOTAL CARS** | **694,349** | **729,023** | **872,720** | **841,585** | **858,826** |
| Allroad* | — | — | — | — | 7 |
| Q5* | 3,060 | 1,942 | — | — | — |
| Q7* | 1,247 | 1,146 | 1,269 | 1,235 | 618 |
| **AUDI TOTAL** | **4,307** | **3,088** | **1,269** | **1,235** | **625** |
| X3* | 2,840 | 2,236 | 2,296 | 2,975 | 3,096 |
| X5 | 4,012 | 3,410 | 3,255 | 4,075 | 2,158 |
| X6 | 1,017 | 1,027 | 726 | — | — |
| **BMW TOTAL** | **7,869** | **6,673** | **6,277** | **7,050** | **5,254** |
| Aspen | 15 | 411 | 1,719 | 1,535 | 383 |
| Pacifica | — | 2 | 290 | 2,016 | 3,876 |
| PT Cruiser | 1,020 | 2,534 | 2,615 | 5,058 | 8,516 |
| Town & Country | 4,175 | 3,165 | 4,865 | 1,531 | 623 |
| **Chrysler Total** | **5,210** | **6,112** | **9,489** | **10,140** | **13,398** |
| Caravan | 55,306 | 40,283 | 39,780 | 55,041 | 61,901 |
| Durango | 6 | 97 | 1,115 | 1,634 | 3,836 |
| Journey | 23,785 | 15,390 | 11,817 | — | — |
| Nitro | 1,103 | 2,348 | 5,831 | 8,793 | 1,692 |
| **Dodge Total** | **80,200** | **58,118** | **58,543** | **65,468** | **67,429** |
| Commander | 650 | 627 | 793 | 1,147 | 3,359 |
| Compass | 4,610 | 5,176 | 9,423 | 10,229 | 2,504 |
| Grand Cherokee | 7,255 | 5,285 | 7,617 | 8,078 | 7,075 |
| Liberty | 2,993 | 3,824 | 6,904 | 8,776 | 11,286 |
| Patriot | 10,753 | 7,998 | 13,836 | 9,629 | — |
| Wrangler | 11,062 | 7,271 | 12,137 | 9,834 | 5,090 |
| **Jeep Total** | **37,323** | **30,181** | **50,710** | **47,693** | **29,314** |
| Dakota | 1,715 | 3,161 | 4,982 | 8,425 | 8,004 |
| Ram Pickup Light-Duty | 53,386 | 30,621 | 41,320 | 42,296 | 39,837 |
| Sprinter Van* | 136 | 1,161 | 2,486 | 2,068 | 2,475 |
| **Ram Total** | **55,237** | **34,943** | **48,788** | **52,789** | **50,316** |
| **CHRYSLER TOTAL** | **177,970** | **129,354** | **167,530** | **176,090** | **160,457** |
| G-Class* | 37 | 26 | 21 | 83 | 217 |
| GL | 1,400 | 1,117 | 1,135 | 863 | 467 |
| GLK* | 5,852 | 5,012 | — | — | — |
| M-Class | 3,871 | 3,146 | 3,525 | 2,689 | 2,172 |
| R-Class | 408 | 308 | 394 | 488 | 956 |
| Sprinter Van* | 1,567 | — | — | — | — |
| **Mercedes Total** | **13,135** | **9,609** | **5,075** | **4,123** | **3,812** |
| Mitsubishi Fuso Light-Duty* | 14 | 23 | 21 | 2 | 2 |
| Sterling Light-Duty* | 1 | 19 | 14 | — | — |
| **DAIMLER TOTAL** | **13,150** | **9,651** | **5,110** | **4,125** | **3,814** |
| Club Wagon | 718 | 524 | 724 | 861 | 976 |
| Econoline | 8,323 | 5,438 | 7,659 | 8,778 | 10,956 |
| Edge | 17,040 | 12,060 | 11,834 | 10,349 | 161 |
| Escape | 43,038 | 36,980 | 32,898 | 31,643 | 25,542 |
| Expedition | 1,664 | 1,584 | 1,557 | 2,217 | 2,528 |
| Explorer | 4,292 | 4,121 | 4,486 | 7,583 | 9,234 |
| F-Series Light-Duty | 95,446 | 79,411 | 65,430 | 70,406 | 69,501 |
| Flex | 4,803 | 6,047 | 2,134 | — | — |
| Freestar | — | — | — | 883 | 11,692 |
| Freestyle | — | — | — | 2,848 | 5,200 |
| Ranger | 19,653 | 20,715 | 24,211 | 23,386 | 17,198 |
| Taurus X | 8 | 870 | 3,106 | 1,267 | — |
| Transit Connect* | 3,180 | 803 | — | — | — |
| **Ford Total** | **198,165** | **168,553** | **154,039** | **160,221** | **152,988** |
| Mark LT | — | 6 | 493 | 701 | 685 |
| MKT | 922 | 186 | — | — | — |
| MKX | 4,458 | 2,471 | 2,218 | 2,531 | 53 |
| Navigator | 544 | 414 | 384 | 961 | 968 |
| **Lincoln Total** | **5,924** | **3,077** | **3,095** | **4,193** | **1,706** |
| **FORD TOTAL** | **204,089** | **171,630** | **157,134** | **164,414** | **154,694** |
| Enclave | 4,135 | 3,854 | 4,994 | 2,557 | — |
| Rainier | — | — | 5 | 74 | 296 |
| Rendezvous | — | — | 5 | 1,112 | 5,164 |
| Terraza | — | — | 2 | 467 | 1,202 |
| **Buick Total** | **4,135** | **3,854** | **5,006** | **4,210** | **6,662** |
| Escalade | 713 | 512 | 848 | 1,083 | 1,070 |
| Escalade ESV | 264 | 127 | 208 | 303 | 272 |
| Escalade EXT | 204 | 162 | 270 | 336 | 297 |
| SRX | 2,918 | 990 | 1,045 | 1,503 | 1,589 |
| **Cadillac Total** | **4,099** | **1,791** | **2,371** | **3,225** | **3,228** |

# Canada Vehicle Sales

## CANADA VEHICLE SALES BY MODEL — continued

| Model | 2010 | 2009 | 2008 | 2007 | 2006 |
|---|---|---|---|---|---|
| Astro | — | — | — | 3 | 21 |
| Avalanche | 3,670 | 2,775 | 3,875 | 4,958 | 5,371 |
| Colorado | 3,961 | 2,838 | 4,586 | 6,239 | 6,538 |
| Equinox | 19,261 | 11,759 | 11,946 | 13,205 | 15,064 |
| Express | 4,422 | 4,494 | 5,271 | 7,237 | 7,301 |
| HHR | 1,783 | 2,862 | 4,916 | 5,026 | 5,480 |
| S Blazer | — | — | — | — | 3 |
| Silverado | 41,737 | 36,428 | 34,685 | 40,066 | 36,480 |
| SSR | — | — | 7 | 11 | 94 |
| Suburban | 1,492 | 1,059 | 1,118 | 1,460 | 1,246 |
| Tahoe | 1,522 | 1,048 | 1,874 | 2,211 | 1,879 |
| TrailBlazer | 7 | 254 | 2,206 | 2,778 | 3,429 |
| Traverse | 6,307 | 4,351 | 263 | — | — |
| Uplander | 30 | 10,433 | 16,133 | 18,999 | 21,047 |
| Venture | — | — | — | 7 | 33 |
| **Chevrolet Total** | **84,192** | **78,301** | **86,880** | **102,200** | **103,986** |
| Acadia | 5,047 | 4,197 | 5,844 | 6,067 | — |
| Canyon | 3,411 | 2,041 | 3,602 | 4,816 | 5,382 |
| Envoy | 13 | 223 | 2,083 | 1,962 | 3,897 |
| S Jimmy | — | — | — | — | 5 |
| Safari | — | — | — | — | 25 |
| Savana | 4,649 | 4,259 | 4,640 | 7,687 | 7,238 |
| Sierra | 45,457 | 37,316 | 34,555 | 40,606 | 37,834 |
| Terrain | 10,148 | 2,252 | — | — | — |
| W4 Forward* | 12 | 67 | 112 | 410 | 385 |
| Yukon | 1,914 | 1,227 | 1,585 | 2,197 | 2,443 |
| Yukon XL | 1,088 | 664 | 842 | 1,218 | 1,316 |
| **GMC Total** | **71,739** | **52,246** | **53,263** | **64,963** | **58,525** |
| H2 | — | 29 | 131 | 219 | 245 |
| H2 SUT | 2 | 12 | 36 | 58 | 76 |
| H3 | 86 | 178 | 583 | 992 | 1,681 |
| H3T | 80 | 275 | 62 | — | — |
| **Hummer Total** | **168** | **494** | **812** | **1,269** | **2,002** |
| Silhouette | — | — | — | — | 3 |
| **Oldsmobile Total** | **—** | **—** | **—** | **—** | **3** |
| Aztek | — | — | — | — | 5 |
| Montana | — | — | — | 3 | 15 |
| Montana SV6 | 57 | 9,687 | 14,953 | 19,169 | 20,193 |
| Torrent | 16 | 6,112 | 10,465 | 11,799 | 13,890 |
| **Pontiac Total** | **73** | **15,799** | **25,418** | **30,971** | **34,103** |
| Outlook | 1 | 708 | 1,739 | 2,072 | — |
| Relay | — | — | 6 | 227 | 739 |
| Vue | 8 | 2,657 | 6,007 | 5,799 | 6,187 |
| **Saturn Total** | **9** | **3,365** | **7,752** | **8,098** | **6,926** |
| **GM TOTAL** | **164,415** | **155,850** | **181,502** | **214,936** | **215,435** |
| MDX | 5,994 | 5,994 | 5,514 | 6,017 | 4,257 |
| RDX | 3,163 | 2,869 | 3,573 | 4,104 | 1,415 |
| ZDX | 863 | 8 | — | — | — |
| **Acura Total** | **10,020** | **8,871** | **9,087** | **10,121** | **5,672** |
| CR-V | 24,930 | 18,554 | 20,488 | 20,915 | 3,851 |
| CR-V* | — | — | 12 | 65 | 13,970 |
| Crosstour | 2,176 | — | — | — | — |
| Element | 380 | 976 | 1,810 | 1,764 | 3,099 |
| Odyssey | 8,616 | 6,449 | 10,125 | 12,025 | 13,368 |
| Pilot | 5,062 | 4,452 | 5,564 | 4,328 | 5,359 |
| Ridgeline | 3,200 | 3,546 | 3,987 | 4,519 | 4,988 |
| **Honda Total** | **44,364** | **33,977** | **41,986** | **43,616** | **44,635** |
| **HONDA TOTAL** | **54,384** | **42,848** | **51,073** | **53,737** | **50,307** |
| Entourage* | 111 | 380 | 1,400 | 2,383 | 1,779 |
| Santa Fe | 27,882 | 24,676 | 14,401 | 15,389 | 5,038 |
| Santa Fe* | — | — | — | 40 | 6,015 |
| Tucson* | 12,923 | 7,278 | 8,711 | 12,008 | 12,586 |
| Veracruz* | 1,233 | 1,525 | 1,550 | 1,243 | — |
| **HYUNDAI TOTAL** | **42,149** | **33,859** | **26,062** | **31,063** | **25,418** |
| Isuzu Truck Light-Duty | — | 10 | 5 | — | — |
| Isuzu Truck Light-Duty* | 19 | 17 | 2 | — | — |
| **ISUZU TOTAL** | **19** | **27** | **7** | **—** | **—** |
| Land Rover Freelander* | — | — | — | — | 3 |
| Land Rover LR2* | 426 | 549 | 840 | 1,054 | — |
| Land Rover LR3* | — | 254 | 544 | 694 | 1,134 |
| Land Rover LR4* | 522 | 73 | — | — | — |
| Land Rover Range Rover* | 431 | 293 | 244 | 381 | 476 |
| Land Rover Range Rover Sport* | 1,168 | 837 | 665 | 834 | 957 |
| **JAGUAR LAND ROVER TOTAL** | **2,547** | **2,006** | **2,293** | **2,963** | **2,570** |
| Borrego* | 302 | 528 | 187 | — | — |
| Rondo* | 6,307 | 9,835 | 9,906 | 7,682 | 85 |
| Sedona* | 1,615 | 2,135 | 3,615 | 3,171 | 4,085 |
| Sorento | 10,214 | — | — | — | — |
| Sorento* | — | 879 | 1,398 | 1,573 | 2,649 |
| Sportage* | 3,498 | 5,060 | 5,509 | 6,393 | 6,041 |

# Canada Vehicle Sales

## CANADA VEHICLE SALES BY MODEL — continued

| Model | 2010 | 2009 | 2008 | 2007 | 2006 |
|---|---|---|---|---|---|
| **KIA TOTAL** | **21,936** | **18,437** | **20,615** | **18,819** | **12,860** |
| B-Series | 2,545 | 1,638 | 3,464 | 4,297 | 2,811 |
| CX-7* | 4,466 | 2,806 | 3,576 | 4,729 | 3,338 |
| CX-9* | 1,282 | 1,021 | 1,725 | 2,117 | — |
| Mazda5* | 7,532 | 8,638 | 11,944 | 11,690 | 8,694 |
| MPV* | — | — | — | — | 2,272 |
| Tribute | 5,290 | 4,852 | 5,437 | 4,666 | 3,377 |
| **MAZDA TOTAL** | **21,115** | **18,955** | **26,146** | **27,499** | **20,492** |
| Endeavor | 382 | 545 | 398 | 826 | 821 |
| Montero* | — | — | — | 10 | 60 |
| Outlander* | 8,343 | 8,530 | 6,507 | 6,227 | 2,841 |
| RVR* | 801 | — | — | — | — |
| **MITSUBISHI TOTAL** | **9,526** | **9,075** | **6,905** | **7,063** | **3,722** |
| EX* | 1,925 | 1,785 | 2,300 | — | — |
| FX* | 1,085 | 919 | 1,003 | 1,094 | 1,430 |
| QX56 | 211 | 162 | 160 | 204 | 267 |
| QX56* | 54 | — | — | — | — |
| **Infiniti Total** | **3,275** | **2,866** | **3,463** | **1,298** | **1,697** |
| Armada | 413 | 196 | 100 | 153 | 219 |
| Frontier | 2,272 | 1,649 | 1,608 | 2,162 | 2,461 |
| Juke* | 825 | — | — | — | — |
| Murano* | 3,798 | 3,691 | 4,557 | 4,159 | 5,062 |
| Pathfinder | 1,400 | 815 | 1,196 | 1,944 | 3,027 |
| Quest | 20 | 402 | 904 | 1,341 | 1,428 |
| Rogue* | 13,199 | 11,054 | 13,163 | 2,924 | — |
| Titan | 1,903 | 1,377 | 1,520 | 1,894 | 2,441 |
| X-Trail* | — | — | — | 4,579 | 10,211 |
| Xterra | 1,040 | 613 | 800 | 1,469 | 2,183 |
| **Nissan Total** | **24,870** | **19,797** | **23,848** | **20,625** | **27,032** |
| **NISSAN TOTAL** | **28,145** | **22,663** | **27,311** | **21,923** | **28,729** |
| Cayenne* | 839 | 718 | 778 | 823 | 572 |
| **PORSCHE TOTAL** | **839** | **718** | **778** | **823** | **572** |
| 9-7X | — | 58 | 116 | 288 | 271 |
| **SAAB TOTAL** | **—** | **58** | **116** | **288** | **271** |
| Baja | — | — | 1 | 1 | 51 |
| Forester* | 8,941 | 8,638 | 6,322 | 3,303 | 3,737 |
| Outback | 6,401 | 2,070 | — | — | — |
| Tribeca | 536 | 588 | 925 | 801 | 902 |
| **SUBARU TOTAL** | **15,878** | **11,296** | **7,248** | **4,105** | **4,690** |
| Equator | 155 | 294 | 32 | — | — |
| Vitara* | 2,842 | 3,333 | 3,296 | 3,331 | 3,664 |
| XL7 | — | 592 | 452 | 1,336 | 217 |
| XL7* | — | — | — | 14 | 619 |
| **SUZUKI TOTAL** | **2,997** | **4,219** | **3,780** | **4,681** | **4,500** |
| GX* | 513 | 198 | 291 | 342 | 454 |
| LX* | 180 | 255 | 353 | 45 | 54 |
| RX | 4,679 | 5,235 | 2,766 | 2,162 | 2,675 |
| RX* | 2,704 | 3,593 | 3,455 | 2,503 | 1,948 |
| **Lexus Total** | **8,076** | **9,281** | **6,865** | **5,052** | **5,131** |
| 4Runner* | 2,820 | 680 | 725 | 1,530 | 2,213 |
| FJ Cruiser* | 797 | 899 | 2,630 | 4,901 | 4,919 |
| Highlander | 3,344 | 410 | — | — | — |
| Highlander* | 859 | 4,421 | 6,486 | 5,052 | 3,039 |
| Land Cruiser* | 93 | 158 | 261 | 262 | 136 |
| RAV4 | 22,025 | 23,237 | 445 | — | — |
| RAV4* | 785 | 2,547 | 20,077 | 16,329 | 14,804 |
| Sequoia | 912 | 800 | 842 | 195 | 377 |
| Sienna | 9,960 | 6,345 | 7,000 | 9,820 | 11,579 |
| Tacoma | 8,111 | 9,082 | 9,673 | 9,477 | 9,345 |
| Tundra | 7,560 | 7,637 | 9,477 | 11,552 | 2,569 |
| Venza | 12,468 | 12,375 | — | — | — |
| **Toyota Total** | **69,734** | **68,591** | **57,616** | **59,118** | **48,981** |
| **TOYOTA TOTAL** | **77,810** | **77,872** | **64,481** | **64,170** | **54,112** |
| Routan | 1,010 | 1,489 | 355 | — | — |
| Tiguan* | 5,611 | 5,075 | 1,412 | — | — |
| Touareg* | 706 | 880 | 703 | 654 | 684 |
| **VOLKSWAGEN TOTAL** | **7,327** | **7,444** | **2,470** | **654** | **684** |
| XC60* | 1,540 | 1,211 | — | — | — |
| XC70* | 1,145 | 1,287 | 1,492 | 1,416 | 1,859 |
| XC90* | 1,194 | 1,456 | 1,502 | 1,923 | 2,569 |
| **VOLVO TOTAL** | **3,879** | **3,954** | **2,994** | **3,339** | **4,428** |
| **TOTAL LIGHT TRUCKS** | **860,351** | **729,677** | **761,101** | **808,977** | **753,634** |
| **TOTAL LIGHT VEHICLES** | **1,554,700** | **1,458,700** | **1,633,821** | **1,650,562** | **1,612,460** |
| **TOTAL MED./HVY. TRUCKS** | **28,688** | **23,532** | **39,701** | **39,783** | **53,548** |
| **TOTAL VEHICLES** | **1,583,388** | **1,482,232** | **1,673,522** | **1,690,345** | **1,666,008** |

*Units imported from outside North America.
SOURCE: Ward's AutoInfoBank

# Mexico Vehicle Sales

## MEXICO VEHICLE SALES BY MODEL

| Model | 2010 | 2009 | 2008 | 2007 | 2006 |
|---|---|---|---|---|---|
| A1* | 186 | — | — | — | — |
| A3* | 1,368 | 1,365 | 1,726 | 1,609 | 1,590 |
| A4* | 1,622 | 1,292 | 1,724 | 1,529 | 1,738 |
| A5* | 702 | 365 | 349 | 25 | — |
| A6* | 161 | 310 | 331 | 468 | 502 |
| A8* | 22 | 23 | 37 | 48 | 52 |
| R8* | 21 | 26 | 77 | 14 | — |
| TT* | 86 | 183 | 328 | 435 | 140 |
| **AUDI TOTAL** | **4,168** | **3,564** | **4,572** | **4,128** | **4,022** |
| 1-Series* | 922 | 1,055 | 1,168 | 977 | 1,152 |
| 3-Series* | 2,255 | 2,247 | 2,855 | 3,429 | 2,726 |
| 5-Series* | 518 | 382 | 636 | 755 | 871 |
| 6-Series* | 9 | 21 | 33 | 48 | 73 |
| 7-Series* | 72 | 65 | 63 | 71 | 74 |
| Z4 | — | 35 | 145 | 145 | 253 |
| Z4* | 126 | 87 | — | — | — |
| **BMW Total** | **3,902** | **3,892** | **4,900** | **5,425** | **5,149** |
| Mini Cooper* | 2,093 | 1,786 | 2,015 | 2,070 | 1,806 |
| **BMW TOTAL** | **5,995** | **5,678** | **6,915** | **7,495** | **6,955** |
| 300 Series | 218 | 196 | 412 | 660 | 1,085 |
| Cirrus Coupe | 6 | 16 | 47 | 40 | 23 |
| Cirrus Sedan | 344 | 423 | 1,012 | 2,772 | 2,323 |
| Crossfire* | — | — | 96 | 40 | 40 |
| Neon | — | — | — | 7 | 924 |
| PT Cruiser Convertible | — | — | 6 | 54 | 137 |
| **Chrysler Total** | **568** | **635** | **1,573** | **3,573** | **4,532** |
| Atoz* | 6,454 | 6,395 | 8,946 | 12,088 | 14,872 |
| Attitude* | 10,989 | 8,060 | 10,901 | 9,068 | 11,263 |
| Avenger | 4,375 | 4,362 | 8,091 | 7,798 | — |
| Caliber | 764 | 1,869 | 4,811 | 6,993 | 7,906 |
| Challenger | 233 | 270 | 233 | — | — |
| Charger | 687 | 589 | 3,283 | 990 | 2,135 |
| Stratus Sedan | — | 22 | 10 | 3,042 | 12,704 |
| Verna* | — | 4 | 5 | 31 | 877 |
| Viper | 6 | 5 | 13 | 3 | 12 |
| **Dodge Total** | **23,508** | **21,576** | **36,293** | **40,013** | **49,769** |
| **CHRYSLER TOTAL** | **24,076** | **22,211** | **37,866** | **43,586** | **54,301** |
| A-Class* | — | — | — | — | 2 |
| B-Class* | 384 | 304 | 469 | 552 | 637 |
| C-Class* | 2,579 | 2,049 | 2,901 | 2,657 | 1,871 |
| CL* | 1 | 11 | 19 | 34 | 1 |
| CLK* | — | 41 | 79 | 98 | 79 |
| CLS* | 18 | 69 | 114 | 144 | 167 |
| E-Class* | 700 | 617 | 537 | 713 | 717 |
| S-Class* | 48 | 65 | 94 | 147 | 143 |
| SL* | 12 | 19 | 20 | 26 | 27 |
| SLK* | 91 | 168 | 248 | 322 | 327 |
| SLS* | 40 | — | — | — | — |
| **Mercedes Total** | **3,873** | **3,343** | **4,481** | **4,693** | **3,971** |
| Forfour* | — | — | 1 | 39 | 207 |
| Fortwo* | 936 | 678 | 786 | 515 | 388 |
| Roadster* | — | — | — | — | 2 |
| **Smart Total** | **936** | **678** | **787** | **554** | **597** |
| **DAIMLER TOTAL** | **4,809** | **4,021** | **5,268** | **5,247** | **4,568** |
| 500* | 278 | 340 | 124 | — | — |
| Albea* | 306 | 435 | 110 | — | — |
| Bravo* | 17 | 109 | — | — | — |
| Grande Punto* | 9 | 610 | 669 | 605 | 69 |
| Linea* | 10 | — | — | — | — |
| Palio* | 805 | 608 | 648 | 1,460 | 861 |
| Panda* | 179 | 464 | 445 | 330 | — |
| Stilo* | — | 29 | 90 | 116 | 28 |
| **FIAT TOTAL** | **1,604** | **2,595** | **2,086** | **2,511** | **958** |
| Crown Victoria | 82 | 21 | 205 | 140 | 263 |
| Fiesta | 5,280 | — | — | — | — |
| Fiesta* | 5,245 | 7,394 | 13,861 | 18,870 | 30,022 |
| Five Hundred | — | 1 | 53 | 459 | 1,028 |
| Focus | 8,436 | 8,896 | 8,230 | 6,629 | 4,496 |
| Fusion | 3,833 | 3,718 | 5,476 | 5,853 | 4,983 |
| Ikon | — | — | 501 | 6,865 | 6,088 |
| Ka* | — | 3 | 441 | 2,727 | 4,645 |
| Mondeo* | — | — | 115 | 824 | 2,674 |
| Mustang | 1,558 | 1,655 | 1,769 | 2,052 | 2,952 |

# Mexico Vehicle Sales

## MEXICO VEHICLE SALES BY MODEL — continued

| Model | 2010 | 2009 | 2008 | 2007 | 2006 |
|---|---|---|---|---|---|
| **Ford Total** | **24,434** | **21,688** | **30,651** | **44,419** | **57,151** |
| LS | — | — | — | 6 | 67 |
| MKS | 199 | 222 | 261 | — | — |
| MKZ | 300 | 337 | 526 | 491 | 326 |
| Town Car | — | — | 5 | 67 | 117 |
| Zephyr | — | — | — | — | 523 |
| **Lincoln Total** | **499** | **559** | **792** | **564** | **1,033** |
| Milan | 5 | 10 | 357 | 520 | 93 |
| Montego | — | 1 | 15 | 83 | 191 |
| **Mercury Total** | **5** | **11** | **372** | **603** | **284** |
| **FORD TOTAL** | **24,938** | **22,258** | **31,815** | **45,586** | **58,468** |
| LaCrosse | 351 | — | — | — | — |
| **Buick Total** | **351** | **—** | **—** | **—** | **—** |
| BLS* | — | 2 | 152 | 204 | 39 |
| CTS | 238 | 257 | 658 | 323 | 156 |
| STS | 5 | 14 | 31 | 52 | 59 |
| XLR | — | — | — | 1 | 5 |
| **Cadillac Total** | **243** | **273** | **841** | **580** | **259** |
| Astra* | 8 | 250 | 2,384 | 2,654 | 8,504 |
| Aveo | 29,409 | 24,157 | 14,083 | — | — |
| Aveo* | — | 49 | 5,788 | — | — |
| Camaro | 1,079 | 1,263 | — | — | — |
| Chevy | 43,964 | 36,320 | 56,142 | 59,621 | 63,109 |
| Corsa* | — | 6 | 6,277 | 20,800 | 33,745 |
| Corvette | 6 | 10 | 22 | 37 | 37 |
| Cruze* | 10,919 | 2,878 | — | — | — |
| Epica* | 152 | 610 | 106 | — | — |
| Impala | — | — | 1 | 6 | 34 |
| Malibu | 3,123 | 3,073 | 5,691 | 5,988 | 6,996 |
| Meriva* | 1 | 134 | 1,618 | 3,632 | 5,284 |
| Optra* | 2,954 | 10,518 | 16,828 | 21,798 | 10,444 |
| Spark* | 6,129 | — | — | — | — |
| Vectra* | — | 7 | 117 | 589 | 1,380 |
| **Chevrolet Total** | **97,744** | **79,275** | **109,057** | **115,125** | **129,533** |
| G3 | 13 | 2,985 | 1,783 | — | — |
| G3* | 4 | 26 | 5,784 | 7,520 | 4,416 |
| G4 | — | — | — | — | 1,610 |
| G5 | 9 | 768 | 2,426 | 2,592 | 1,038 |
| G6 | 5 | 124 | 557 | 595 | 863 |
| Matiz* | 6,315 | 5,193 | 9,721 | 9,587 | 10,488 |
| Solstice | 25 | 237 | 377 | 458 | 372 |
| Sunfire | — | — | — | — | 1 |
| **Pontiac Total** | **6,371** | **9,333** | **20,648** | **20,752** | **18,788** |
| **GM TOTAL** | **104,709** | **88,881** | **130,546** | **136,457** | **148,580** |
| RL* | 21 | 31 | 57 | 92 | 125 |
| TL | 445 | 656 | 397 | 543 | 755 |
| TSX* | 378 | 366 | 546 | — | — |
| **Acura Total** | **844** | **1,053** | **1,000** | **635** | **880** |
| Accord | 5,339 | 6,466 | 11,828 | 9,572 | 9,002 |
| City* | 5,949 | 2,428 | — | — | — |
| Civic | 5,186 | 6,295 | 13,643 | 13,319 | 12,050 |
| Fit* | 2,658 | 3,466 | 3,327 | 4,745 | 4,075 |
| **Honda Total** | **19,132** | **18,655** | **28,798** | **27,636** | **25,127** |
| **HONDA TOTAL** | **19,976** | **19,708** | **29,798** | **28,271** | **26,007** |
| Jaguar S-Type* | 2 | 6 | 11 | 60 | 105 |
| Jaguar X-Type* | — | — | 21 | 105 | 176 |
| Jaguar XF* | 73 | 131 | 175 | — | — |
| Jaguar XJ* | 17 | 6 | 13 | 8 | 21 |
| Jaguar XK8* | 4 | 16 | 17 | 26 | 30 |
| **JAGUAR LAND ROVER TOTAL** | **96** | **159** | **237** | **199** | **332** |
| Mazda3* | 13,213 | 9,217 | 9,502 | 6,939 | 4,750 |
| Mazda6 | 3,216 | 2,193 | 2,241 | 980 | 1,003 |
| MX-5 Miata* | 149 | 119 | 179 | 261 | 223 |
| **MAZDA TOTAL** | **16,578** | **11,529** | **11,922** | **8,180** | **5,976** |
| Eclipse | 161 | 247 | 326 | 729 | 768 |
| Galant | 4 | 452 | 356 | 572 | 703 |
| Lancer* | 4,277 | 5,585 | 5,525 | 7,253 | 5,092 |
| **MITSUBISHI TOTAL** | **4,442** | **6,284** | **6,207** | **8,554** | **6,563** |
| Q45* | — | 1 | — | 1 | 12 |
| **Infiniti Total** | **—** | **1** | **—** | **1** | **12** |
| 350Z* | — | 4 | 25 | 40 | 50 |
| 370Z* | 44 | 69 | — | — | — |
| Almera* | — | — | — | 1 | 390 |

# Mexico Vehicle Sales

## MEXICO VEHICLE SALES BY MODEL — continued

| Model | 2010 | 2009 | 2008 | 2007 | 2006 |
|---|---|---|---|---|---|
| Altima | 4,207 | 3,003 | 5,213 | 7,127 | 6,586 |
| Aprio* | 4,006 | 4,632 | 12,140 | 6,374 | — |
| Maxima* | 187 | 442 | 367 | 172 | 486 |
| Micra* | — | — | 120 | 501 | 1,403 |
| Platina | 584 | 2,316 | 6,288 | 15,687 | 35,201 |
| Sentra | 19,836 | 14,318 | 17,859 | 22,309 | 33,930 |
| Tiida | 40,091 | 22,982 | 24,030 | 26,424 | 3,377 |
| Tsuru | 61,147 | 54,463 | 68,874 | 63,461 | 66,243 |
| **Nissan Total** | **130,102** | **102,229** | **134,916** | **142,096** | **147,666** |
| **NISSAN TOTAL** | **130,102** | **102,230** | **134,916** | **142,097** | **147,678** |
| 206* | — | 53 | 2,970 | 6,010 | 9,548 |
| 207* | 3,712 | 4,861 | 1,892 | 178 | — |
| 307* | 47 | 394 | 1,525 | 3,255 | 3,086 |
| 308* | 179 | 155 | 129 | — | — |
| 407* | 2 | 65 | 185 | 447 | 612 |
| 607* | — | — | — | 14 | 23 |
| Grand Raid* | 475 | 532 | 1,144 | 1,989 | 863 |
| Partner* | 872 | 816 | 1,463 | 1,694 | 1,936 |
| RCZ* | 22 | — | — | — | — |
| **PEUGEOT TOTAL** | **5,309** | **6,876** | **9,308** | **13,587** | **16,068** |
| 911* | 95 | 116 | 183 | 165 | 132 |
| Boxster* | 51 | 61 | 65 | 74 | 197 |
| Cayman* | 36 | 74 | 93 | 110 | 15 |
| Panamera* | 45 | 22 | — | — | — |
| **PORSCHE TOTAL** | **227** | **273** | **341** | **349** | **344** |
| Clio | 3 | 4,114 | 8,098 | 9,019 | 10,953 |
| Clio* | — | 19 | 411 | 911 | 241 |
| Fluence* | 958 | — | — | — | — |
| Laguna* | — | — | 5 | 24 | 148 |
| Megane* | 65 | 1,723 | 2,948 | 3,429 | 5,472 |
| Safrane* | 776 | 487 | — | — | — |
| Sandero* | 8,979 | — | — | — | — |
| Scala* | 3,018 | — | — | — | — |
| **RENAULT TOTAL** | **13,799** | **6,343** | **11,462** | **13,383** | **16,814** |
| 9-3* | 8 | 93 | 247 | 228 | 349 |
| 9-5* | — | — | 3 | 27 | 48 |
| **SAAB TOTAL** | **8** | **93** | **250** | **255** | **397** |
| Impreza* | 152 | 313 | 333 | 116 | 22 |
| Legacy | 93 | 70 | 133 | 136 | 103 |
| **SUBARU TOTAL** | **245** | **383** | **466** | **252** | **125** |
| Aerio* | — | — | — | 600 | 1,172 |
| Kizashi* | 666 | 48 | — | — | — |
| SX4* | 4,859 | 4,515 | 4,675 | 1,668 | 227 |
| **SUZUKI TOTAL** | **5,525** | **4,563** | **4,675** | **2,268** | **1,399** |
| Avanza* | 3,082 | 3,021 | 2,825 | 1,307 | — |
| Camry | 3,717 | 3,836 | 4,980 | 6,872 | 7,201 |
| Corolla | 8,349 | 9,249 | 9,850 | 9,316 | 7,963 |
| Matrix | 185 | 634 | 1,024 | 1,033 | 1,163 |
| MR2 Spyder* | — | — | — | — | 35 |
| Prius* | 168 | — | — | — | — |
| Yaris* | 5,883 | 8,934 | 13,357 | 11,762 | 9,360 |
| **TOYOTA TOTAL** | **21,384** | **25,674** | **32,036** | **30,290** | **25,722** |
| Altea* | 742 | 391 | 87 | 241 | 157 |
| Cordoba* | — | 3,549 | 3,535 | 4,552 | 5,931 |
| Ibiza* | 11,243 | 10,216 | 8,334 | 9,573 | 12,156 |
| Leon* | 1,395 | 1,428 | 1,077 | 1,119 | 1,435 |
| Toledo* | — | — | 29 | 159 | 168 |
| **SEAT Total** | **13,380** | **15,584** | **13,062** | **15,644** | **19,847** |
| Beetle | 2,445 | 2,552 | 3,657 | 4,365 | 3,692 |
| Beetle Cabrio | 17 | 37 | 47 | 51 | 196 |
| Bora | 16,447 | 20,137 | 23,263 | 25,104 | 20,682 |
| Derby* | — | 90 | 3,008 | 4,207 | 7,045 |
| Eos* | 136 | 74 | — | — | — |
| Gol* | 24,294 | 23,699 | 2,672 | — | — |
| Golf* | 508 | 325 | 728 | 1,129 | 1,259 |
| Jetta | 51,847 | 32,585 | 41,783 | 44,395 | 40,690 |
| Lupo* | — | 99 | 826 | 1,934 | 5,293 |
| Passat* | 1,727 | 2,170 | 1,719 | 2,072 | 2,591 |
| Pointer* | — | 1,829 | 25,279 | 28,300 | 31,962 |
| Polo* | — | — | 33 | 899 | 3,090 |
| Sport Van* | 54 | 1,591 | 2,799 | 3,650 | 2,320 |
| **Volkswagen Total** | **97,475** | **85,188** | **105,814** | **116,106** | **118,820** |

# Mexico Vehicle Sales

## MEXICO VEHICLE SALES BY MODEL — continued

| Model | 2010 | 2009 | 2008 | 2007 | 2006 |
|---|---|---|---|---|---|
| **VOLKSWAGEN TOTAL** | **110,855** | **100,772** | **118,876** | **131,750** | **138,667** |
| 30-Series* | 287 | 154 | 376 | 346 | — |
| 40-Series* | 315 | 361 | 834 | 1,112 | 1,258 |
| 50-Series* | — | — | — | 8 | 23 |
| 60-Series* | 38 | 9 | 50 | 189 | 385 |
| 70-Series* | 38 | 21 | 44 | 106 | 51 |
| 80-Series* | 44 | 39 | 108 | 186 | 17 |
| **VOLVO TOTAL** | **722** | **584** | **1,412** | **1,947** | **1,734** |
| **TOTAL CARS** | **499,567** | **434,679** | **580,974** | **626,392** | **665,678** |
| Q5* | 907 | 877 | — | — | — |
| Q7* | 415 | 429 | 666 | 772 | 183 |
| **AUDI TOTAL** | **1,322** | **1,306** | **666** | **772** | **183** |
| X1* | 526 | — | — | — | — |
| X3* | 191 | 456 | 781 | 1,187 | 1,207 |
| X5 | 759 | 789 | 1,008 | 1,220 | 731 |
| X6 | 354 | 392 | 211 | — | — |
| **BMW TOTAL** | **1,830** | **1,637** | **2,000** | **2,407** | **1,938** |
| Aspen | 4 | 245 | 772 | 982 | 521 |
| Pacifica | — | 6 | 71 | 447 | 779 |
| PT Cruiser | 312 | 887 | 1,571 | 2,478 | 4,277 |
| Town & Country | 2,942 | 2,226 | 3,154 | 2,822 | 3,094 |
| Voyager | — | 8 | 1,394 | 8,505 | 10,715 |
| **Chrysler Total** | **3,258** | **3,372** | **6,962** | **15,234** | **19,386** |
| Durango | 2 | 582 | 2,074 | 2,880 | 3,480 |
| Journey | 12,879 | 13,491 | 10,711 | — | — |
| Nitro | 661 | 1,058 | 3,000 | 6,779 | 2,250 |
| **Dodge Total** | **13,542** | **15,131** | **15,785** | **9,659** | **5,730** |
| Commander | 23 | 79 | 238 | 558 | 1,013 |
| Compass | 1,565 | 2,130 | 2,960 | 4,367 | 1,535 |
| Grand Cherokee | 3,742 | 1,623 | 2,856 | 3,250 | 4,058 |
| Liberty | 2,204 | 2,156 | 3,726 | 6,988 | 12,010 |
| Patriot | 7,066 | 7,676 | 11,516 | 10,950 | — |
| Wrangler | 2,054 | 1,312 | 2,345 | 2,653 | 1,507 |
| **Jeep Total** | **16,654** | **14,976** | **23,641** | **28,766** | **20,123** |
| Dakota | 3,778 | 3,760 | 5,431 | 4,283 | 3,913 |
| H100* | 3,373 | 4,082 | 6,505 | 8,008 | 6,127 |
| Ram 1000* | 9 | 1,236 | 1,115 | 225 | — |
| Ram Pickup | 13,884 | 17,569 | 18,832 | 18,780 | 18,866 |
| **Ram Total** | **21,044** | **26,647** | **31,883** | **31,296** | **28,906** |
| **CHRYSLER TOTAL** | **54,498** | **60,126** | **78,271** | **84,955** | **74,145** |
| Mercedes G-Class* | 46 | 54 | 26 | 4 | 10 |
| Mercedes GL | 149 | 157 | 183 | 263 | 112 |
| Mercedes GLK* | 626 | 675 | 162 | — | — |
| Mercedes M-Class | 433 | 451 | 636 | 729 | 827 |
| Mercedes R-Class | 36 | 21 | 40 | 64 | 68 |
| Mercedes Sprinter Van* | 788 | 498 | 1,515 | 1,844 | 1,374 |
| Mercedes Sprinter Wagon* | 115 | 106 | 175 | 173 | 90 |
| Mercedes Vito Cargo* | 78 | 15 | — | — | — |
| Mercedes Vito Passenger* | 61 | 19 | — | — | — |
| **DAIMLER TOTAL** | **2,332** | **1,996** | **2,737** | **3,077** | **2,481** |
| Ducato* | 352 | 127 | 182 | 1 | — |
| Idea* | 6 | 296 | 507 | 407 | — |
| Strada* | 540 | 490 | 429 | 381 | 78 |
| **FIAT TOTAL** | **898** | **913** | **1,118** | **789** | **78** |
| Courier* | 3,020 | 2,839 | 4,426 | 4,910 | 6,089 |
| Econoline | 972 | 1,130 | 1,785 | 1,800 | 1,894 |
| Ecosport* | 3,774 | 4,599 | 9,446 | 13,909 | 24,215 |
| Edge | 2,817 | 2,405 | 3,103 | 2,710 | 38 |
| Escape | 8,916 | 8,281 | 12,260 | 10,857 | 9,716 |
| Excursion | — | — | — | — | 15 |
| Expedition | 1,653 | 2,112 | 3,135 | 3,535 | 3,957 |
| Explorer | 3,043 | 2,783 | 3,676 | 3,603 | 4,837 |
| F-Series Light-Duty | 20,733 | 24,875 | 37,461 | 40,030 | 46,038 |
| Freestar | — | — | 8 | 160 | 3,307 |
| Ranger | 13,049 | 13,449 | 14,826 | 17,669 | 16,268 |
| Transit* | 2,432 | 2,211 | 1,638 | 215 | — |
| **Ford Total** | **60,409** | **64,684** | **91,764** | **99,398** | **116,374** |
| Aviator | — | — | — | — | 9 |
| Mark LT | 755 | 541 | 1,189 | 1,544 | 2,083 |
| MKX | 375 | 263 | 513 | 677 | — |
| Navigator | 326 | 342 | 465 | 625 | 674 |
| **Lincoln Total** | **1,456** | **1,146** | **2,167** | **2,846** | **2,766** |

# Mexico Vehicle Sales

**MEXICO VEHICLE SALES BY MODEL — continued**

| Model | 2010 | 2009 | 2008 | 2007 | 2006 |
|---|---|---|---|---|---|
| Mariner | 730 | 660 | 921 | 1,024 | 1,104 |
| **Mercury Total** | **730** | **660** | **921** | **1,024** | **1,104** |
| **FORD TOTAL** | **62,595** | **66,490** | **94,852** | **103,268** | **120,244** |
| Enclave | 745 | 57 | — | — | — |
| **Buick Total** | **745** | **57** | **—** | **—** | **—** |
| Escalade | 230 | 178 | 257 | 325 | 329 |
| Escalade ESV | 319 | 252 | 338 | 379 | 357 |
| Escalade EXT | 128 | 133 | 277 | 395 | 300 |
| SRX | 708 | 216 | 2 | 2 | 26 |
| **Cadillac Total** | **1,385** | **779** | **874** | **1,101** | **1,012** |
| Avalanche | 437 | 697 | 1,007 | 1,915 | 1,240 |
| Captiva Sport* | 8,156 | 7,739 | 7,615 | 274 | — |
| Colorado | 2,680 | 2,805 | 4,389 | 4,462 | 4,169 |
| Equinox | 1 | 72 | 1,876 | 5,402 | 6,086 |
| Express | 1,708 | 1,504 | 2,687 | 3,349 | 3,940 |
| HHR | 4 | 147 | 1,132 | 3,254 | 4,092 |
| LUV* | — | — | — | — | 488 |
| Silverado | 16,634 | 17,395 | 27,152 | 28,246 | 29,461 |
| Sonora | — | — | — | 16 | 326 |
| Suburban | 2,413 | 2,114 | 3,583 | 4,431 | 4,140 |
| Tahoe | 1,030 | 1,257 | 2,103 | 3,249 | 1,720 |
| Tornado* | 8,727 | 7,158 | 12,704 | 14,677 | 15,480 |
| Tracker | — | 30 | 2,677 | 5,093 | 5,775 |
| TrailBlazer | — | 2 | 195 | 1,320 | 2,909 |
| Traverse | 2,061 | 1,668 | — | — | — |
| Uplander | 8 | 404 | 2,467 | 3,821 | 5,249 |
| W4 Tiltmaster | — | — | — | — | 6 |
| Zafira* | — | — | 1 | 434 | 876 |
| **Chevrolet Total** | **43,859** | **42,992** | **69,588** | **79,943** | **85,957** |
| Acadia | 1,925 | 1,979 | 2,601 | 2,048 | — |
| Canyon | 605 | 502 | 587 | 618 | 184 |
| Sierra | 1,293 | 828 | 1,678 | 1,739 | 24 |
| Yukon | 647 | 646 | 1,013 | 1,268 | 1,110 |
| **GMC Total** | **4,470** | **3,955** | **5,879** | **5,673** | **1,318** |
| H2 | 3 | 32 | 84 | 132 | 473 |
| H2 SUT | — | 70 | 206 | 262 | — |
| H3 | 153 | 341 | 1,005 | 1,472 | 1,940 |
| H3T | 240 | 739 | 368 | — | — |
| **Hummer Total** | **396** | **1,182** | **1,663** | **1,866** | **2,413** |
| Montana SV6 | — | 15 | 329 | 581 | 802 |
| Torrent | 16 | 491 | 1,340 | 1,969 | 1,768 |
| **Pontiac Total** | **16** | **506** | **1,669** | **2,550** | **2,570** |
| **GM TOTAL** | **50,871** | **49,471** | **79,673** | **91,133** | **93,270** |
| MDX | 719 | 593 | 743 | 761 | 466 |
| RDX | 293 | 296 | 389 | 455 | 285 |
| ZDX | 20 | — | — | — | — |
| **Acura Total** | **1,032** | **889** | **1,132** | **1,216** | **751** |
| CR-V | 12,650 | 11,211 | 16,929 | 3,941 | — |
| CR-V* | — | 5 | 172 | 14,134 | 14,084 |
| Crosstour | 407 | 112 | — | — | — |
| Odyssey | 3,029 | 2,457 | 4,264 | 4,391 | 5,414 |
| Pilot | 2,368 | 2,375 | 3,244 | 1,937 | 2,445 |
| Ridgeline | 404 | 430 | 725 | 912 | 401 |
| **Honda Total** | **18,858** | **16,590** | **25,334** | **25,315** | **22,344** |
| **HONDA TOTAL** | **19,890** | **17,479** | **26,466** | **26,531** | **23,095** |
| Isuzu Truck Light-Duty* | 1,337 | 972 | 787 | 171 | — |
| **ISUZU TOTAL** | **1,337** | **972** | **787** | **171** | **—** |
| Land Rover Defender* | 26 | — | — | — | — |
| Land Rover Freelander* | — | — | — | 4 | 173 |
| Land Rover LR2* | 150 | 170 | 309 | 367 | — |
| Land Rover LR3* | — | 60 | 99 | 179 | 243 |
| Land Rover LR4* | 80 | 18 | — | — | — |
| Land Rover Range Rover* | 34 | 30 | 39 | 82 | 73 |
| Land Rover Range Rover Sport* | 209 | 154 | 279 | 277 | 285 |
| **JAGUAR LAND ROVER TOTAL** | **499** | **432** | **726** | **909** | **774** |
| CX-7* | 5,420 | 5,204 | 7,014 | 6,089 | 868 |
| CX-9* | 2,573 | 1,661 | 2,204 | 1,614 | — |
| Mazda5* | 545 | 520 | 857 | 721 | 651 |
| **MAZDA TOTAL** | **8,538** | **7,385** | **10,075** | **8,424** | **1,519** |
| Endeavor | 1,106 | 934 | 1,219 | 2,039 | 3,160 |
| Grandis* | 55 | 343 | 489 | 579 | 255 |
| L200* | 1,891 | 2,007 | 1,672 | — | — |
| Montero* | 368 | 120 | 400 | 188 | 361 |

# Mexico Vehicle Sales

## MEXICO VEHICLE SALES BY MODEL — continued

| Model | 2010 | 2009 | 2008 | 2007 | 2006 |
|---|---|---|---|---|---|
| Montero Sport* | 536 | 339 | 152 | 518 | 736 |
| Outlander* | 4,135 | 4,293 | 6,665 | 5,788 | 5,676 |
| **MITSUBISHI TOTAL** | **8,091** | **8,036** | **10,597** | **9,112** | **10,188** |
| Armada | 94 | 141 | 321 | 445 | 1,012 |
| Cabstar* | 131 | 988 | 1,696 | 468 | — |
| Frontier | 1,994 | 1,052 | 4,309 | 5,188 | 6,051 |
| Murano* | 605 | 611 | 1,307 | 680 | 1,319 |
| Nissan Chassis | 21,044 | 18,429 | 25,782 | 24,187 | 25,465 |
| Nissan Pickup | 14,837 | 14,324 | 16,365 | 17,092 | 16,827 |
| Pathfinder | 496 | 512 | 826 | 1,345 | 2,175 |
| Quest | 2 | 295 | 1,012 | 1,414 | 1,488 |
| Rogue* | 5,690 | 3,765 | 4,632 | 892 | — |
| Titan | 59 | 118 | 435 | 830 | 974 |
| Urvan* | 8,174 | 8,063 | 11,057 | 9,852 | 9,974 |
| X-Trail* | 6,290 | 5,657 | 9,347 | 9,567 | 15,069 |
| Xterra | — | 1 | 17 | 64 | 283 |
| **NISSAN TOTAL** | **59,416** | **53,956** | **77,106** | **72,024** | **80,637** |
| 3008* | 400 | — | | | |
| Expert* | 177 | 111 | 62 | — | — |
| Manager* | 308 | 257 | 146 | — | — |
| **PEUGEOT TOTAL** | **885** | **368** | **208** | **—** | **—** |
| Cayenne* | 213 | 262 | 414 | 424 | 288 |
| **PORSCHE TOTAL** | **213** | **262** | **414** | **424** | **288** |
| Kangoo* | 1,902 | 2,540 | 3,171 | 4,391 | 3,078 |
| Koleos* | 1,979 | 1,866 | 590 | — | — |
| Scenic* | — | 27 | 134 | 344 | 382 |
| Trafic* | 366 | 724 | 703 | 495 | — |
| **RENAULT TOTAL** | **4,247** | **5,157** | **4,598** | **5,230** | **3,460** |
| Forester* | 165 | 271 | 355 | 207 | 61 |
| Outback | 30 | 7 | 18 | 11 | — |
| Tribeca | 60 | 91 | 237 | 233 | 122 |
| **SUBARU TOTAL** | **255** | **369** | **610** | **451** | **183** |
| Vitara* | 2,407 | 2,482 | 3,114 | 3,220 | 3,014 |
| XL7 | — | 50 | 215 | 212 | — |
| **SUZUKI TOTAL** | **2,407** | **2,532** | **3,329** | **3,432** | **3,014** |
| 4Runner* | — | 14 | 172 | 576 | 1,390 |
| FJ Cruiser* | 596 | 1,234 | 2,824 | 2,032 | — |
| Hiace* | 2,573 | 3,552 | 3,679 | 3,141 | 2,778 |
| Highlander* | 1,767 | 1,354 | 1,493 | 1,293 | — |
| Hilux | 4,779 | 4,146 | 6,162 | 4,914 | 2,908 |
| Land Cruiser* | 65 | 73 | 148 | 147 | 217 |
| RAV4* | 5,323 | 5,958 | 7,491 | 11,948 | 14,848 |
| Rush* | — | 649 | — | — | — |
| Sequoia | 528 | 543 | 267 | — | — |
| Sienna | 5,619 | 3,303 | 4,363 | 6,580 | 6,950 |
| Tacoma | 3,432 | 4,129 | 4,154 | 4,886 | 5,275 |
| Tundra | 703 | 1,362 | 517 | 401 | — |
| **TOYOTA TOTAL** | **25,385** | **26,317** | **31,270** | **35,918** | **34,366** |
| Alhambra* | — | 4 | 4 | 25 | 52 |
| **SEAT Total** | **—** | **—** | **4** | **25** | **52** |
| Amarok* | 581 | | — | — | — |
| Crafter* | 611 | 636 | 688 | 93 | — |
| Crossfox* | 3,251 | 3,074 | 4,953 | 8,294 | 6,920 |
| Eurovan* | 299 | 1,921 | 3,955 | 5,299 | 5,866 |
| Pointer Pickup* | 245 | 3,686 | 2,585 | 2,167 | 1,934 |
| Routan | 501 | 1,139 | 114 | — | — |
| Saveiro* | 3,223 | — | — | — | — |
| Sharan* | — | — | 381 | 593 | 834 |
| Tiguan* | 2,673 | 1,539 | 53 | — | — |
| Touareg* | 249 | 323 | 857 | 688 | 653 |
| Transporter* | 1,224 | — | — | — | — |
| **Volkswagen Total** | **12,857** | **12,318** | **13,586** | **17,134** | **16,207** |
| **VOLKSWAGEN TOTAL** | **12,857** | **12,318** | **13,590** | **17,159** | **16,259** |
| XC60* | 492 | 181 | — | — | — |
| XC70* | — | — | — | 4 | 7 |
| XC90* | 79 | 170 | 425 | 770 | 976 |
| **VOLVO TOTAL** | **571** | **351** | **425** | **774** | **983** |
| **TOTAL LIGHT TRUCKS** | **318,937** | **317,873** | **439,518** | **466,960** | **467,105** |
| **TOTAL LIGHT VEHICLES** | **818,504** | **752,552** | **1,020,492** | **1,093,352** | **1,132,783** |
| **TOTAL MED./HVY. TRUCKS** | **28,377** | **20,833** | **48,244** | **50,953** | **44,317** |
| **TOTAL VEHICLES** | **846,881** | **773,385** | **1,068,736** | **1,144,305** | **1,177,100** |

*Units imported from outside North America.
SOURCE: Ward's AutoInfoBank.

# Car, Truck and Bus Registrations by State

## U.S. TOTAL VEHICLE REGISTRATIONS BY STATE

| State | Cars | | Trucks and Buses | | Total | |
|---|---|---|---|---|---|---|
| | 2009 | 2008 | 2009 | 2008 | 2009 | 2008 |
| Alabama | 2,171,584 | 2,220,095 | 2,439,261 | 2,509,696 | 4,610,845 | 4,729,791 |
| Alaska | 236,223 | 242,650 | 459,059 | 448,106 | 695,282 | 690,756 |
| Arizona | 2,228,172 | 2,234,963 | 2,129,462 | 2,138,269 | 4,357,634 | 4,373,232 |
| Arkansas | 947,406 | 957,446 | 1,089,995 | 1,083,542 | 2,037,401 | 2,040,988 |
| California | 19,972,837 | 19,919,068 | 14,460,369 | 13,563,993 | 34,433,206 | 33,483,061 |
| Colorado | 2,345,502 | 2,386,065 | 2,927,972 | 2,916,384 | 5,273,474 | 5,302,449 |
| Connecticut | 1,983,114 | 2,018,461 | 1,088,461 | 1,075,283 | 3,071,575 | 3,093,744 |
| Delaware | 463,779 | 461,882 | 379,578 | 405,862 | 843,357 | 867,744 |
| Dist. of Columbia | 166,519 | 171,255 | 51,129 | 52,544 | 217,648 | 223,799 |
| Florida | 7,597,789 | 8,180,462 | 7,716,968 | 8,281,463 | 15,314,757 | 16,461,925 |
| Georgia | 4,134,274 | 4,260,495 | 4,373,019 | 4,309,130 | 8,507,293 | 8,569,625 |
| Hawaii | 448,535 | 488,217 | 446,801 | 457,274 | 895,336 | 945,491 |
| Idaho | 563,021 | 534,911 | 811,946 | 783,322 | 1,374,967 | 1,318,233 |
| Illinois | 5,824,074 | 5,779,977 | 4,066,798 | 4,013,844 | 9,890,872 | 9,793,821 |
| Indiana | 3,082,306 | 3,135,611 | 2,722,693 | 2,711,935 | 5,804,999 | 5,847,546 |
| Iowa | 1,736,330 | 1,798,052 | 1,626,778 | 1,632,815 | 3,363,108 | 3,430,867 |
| Kansas | 874,869 | 884,039 | 1,550,394 | 1,564,729 | 2,425,263 | 2,448,768 |
| Kentucky | 1,952,420 | 1,972,534 | 1,632,081 | 1,631,514 | 3,584,501 | 3,604,048 |
| Louisiana | 1,940,586 | 1,957,262 | 2,092,825 | 2,021,926 | 4,033,411 | 3,979,188 |
| Maine | 538,469 | 561,893 | 517,451 | 512,572 | 1,055,920 | 1,074,465 |
| Maryland | 2,597,592 | 2,650,579 | 1,886,006 | 1,874,654 | 4,483,598 | 4,525,233 |
| Massachusetts | 3,128,371 | 3,236,056 | 2,133,432 | 2,092,293 | 5,261,803 | 5,328,349 |
| Michigan | 4,371,772 | 4,388,023 | 3,541,352 | 3,557,448 | 7,913,124 | 7,945,471 |
| Minnesota | 2,506,177 | 2,543,559 | 2,289,918 | 2,239,932 | 4,796,095 | 4,783,491 |
| Mississippi | 1,155,792 | 1,155,133 | 869,898 | 879,774 | 2,025,690 | 2,034,907 |
| Missouri | 2,559,639 | 2,620,559 | 2,344,562 | 2,245,217 | 4,904,201 | 4,865,776 |
| Montana | 370,107 | 375,757 | 554,843 | 551,218 | 924,950 | 926,975 |
| Nebraska | 784,194 | 816,515 | 1,008,829 | 940,113 | 1,793,023 | 1,756,628 |
| Nevada | 706,912 | 699,041 | 690,429 | 718,173 | 1,397,341 | 1,417,214 |
| New Hampshire | 639,635 | 650,130 | 572,858 | 563,825 | 1,212,493 | 1,213,955 |
| New Jersey | 3,705,322 | 3,826,995 | 2,408,485 | 2,420,271 | 6,113,807 | 6,247,266 |
| New Mexico | 698,100 | 692,415 | 922,604 | 877,356 | 1,620,704 | 1,569,771 |
| New York | 8,725,551 | 8,576,151 | 2,519,657 | 2,512,752 | 11,245,208 | 11,088,903 |
| North Carolina | 3,451,087 | 3,572,277 | 2,596,152 | 2,676,552 | 6,047,239 | 6,248,829 |
| North Dakota | 347,356 | 346,622 | 374,715 | 370,599 | 722,071 | 717,221 |
| Ohio | 6,318,803 | 6,413,063 | 4,703,326 | 4,520,106 | 11,022,129 | 10,933,169 |
| Oklahoma | 1,670,353 | 1,654,409 | 1,726,042 | 1,637,561 | 3,396,395 | 3,291,970 |
| Oregon | 1,439,985 | 1,463,189 | 1,606,388 | 1,642,484 | 3,046,373 | 3,105,673 |
| Pennsylvania | 5,818,056 | 6,086,264 | 4,039,255 | 4,280,144 | 9,857,311 | 10,366,408 |
| Rhode Island | 481,905 | 490,628 | 306,718 | 303,752 | 788,623 | 794,380 |
| South Carolina | 1,974,494 | 1,996,617 | 1,639,906 | 1,607,343 | 3,614,400 | 3,603,960 |
| South Dakota | 401,661 | 347,408 | 524,507 | 559,976 | 926,168 | 907,384 |
| Tennessee | 2,854,803 | 2,833,546 | 2,284,859 | 2,264,601 | 5,139,662 | 5,098,147 |
| Texas | 8,680,858 | 8,830,985 | 9,414,100 | 9,376,963 | 18,094,958 | 18,207,948 |
| Utah | 1,217,120 | 1,192,191 | 1,236,759 | 1,246,494 | 2,453,879 | 2,438,685 |
| Vermont | 292,317 | 306,690 | 265,053 | 274,776 | 557,370 | 581,466 |
| Virginia | 3,732,468 | 3,881,087 | 2,569,367 | 2,644,861 | 6,301,835 | 6,525,948 |
| Washington | 3,101,571 | 3,299,259 | 2,479,097 | 2,680,451 | 5,580,668 | 5,979,710 |
| West Virginia | 700,103 | 700,301 | 712,375 | 701,729 | 1,412,478 | 1,402,030 |
| Wisconsin | 2,526,673 | 2,659,162 | 2,347,643 | 2,339,741 | 4,874,316 | 4,998,903 |
| Wyoming | 214,199 | 261,294 | 438,125 | 443,906 | 652,324 | 705,200 |
| **Total** | **136,380,785** | **138,731,243** | **113,590,300** | **113,159,268** | **249,971,085** | **251,890,511** |

NOTE: Registrations include both privately and publicly owned motor vehicles, except those owned by the military.
SOURCE: U.S. Department of Transportation, Federal Highway Administration.

# Truck Registrations by State and Type

## U.S. TOTAL TRUCK REGISTRATIONS BY STATE AND TYPE, 2009

| State | Pickups | Vans | Sport Utilities | Other Light | Truck Tractors | Other Med./Hvy. | Total |
|---|---|---|---|---|---|---|---|
| Alabama | 1,237,499 | 252,272 | 774,044 | — | 92,757 | 73,805 | 2,430,377 |
| Alaska | 209,512 | 50,011 | 173,161 | 3,838 | 4,301 | 15,538 | 456,361 |
| Arizona | 855,606 | 304,884 | 850,673 | 9,453 | 26,778 | 77,039 | 2,124,433 |
| Arkansas | 571,666 | 122,751 | 360,931 | 4,576 | 21,826 | 409 | 1,082,159 |
| California | 4,913,332 | 2,340,917 | 5,541,919 | 56,040 | 91,749 | 1,456,877 | 14,400,834 |
| Colorado[1] | 952,323 | 316,694 | 1,377,475 | 6,099 | 16,067 | 253,575 | 2,922,233 |
| Connecticut | 297,218 | 207,642 | 531,116 | 5,526 | 2,413 | 33,641 | 1,077,556 |
| Delaware | 46,773 | 24,800 | 63,295 | 2,402 | 1,490 | 238,564 | 377,324 |
| Dist. of Columbia | 5,153 | 8,792 | 22,723 | 342 | 225 | 10,994 | 48,229 |
| Florida | 1,998,333 | 1,147,575 | 2,713,470 | 25,247 | 240,567 | 1,540,186 | 7,665,378 |
| Georgia | 1,694,515 | 609,110 | 1,650,235 | 20,174 | 86,026 | 289,395 | 4,349,455 |
| Hawaii | 177,934 | 73,585 | 174,718 | 2,349 | 1,160 | 12,450 | 442,196 |
| Idaho | 408,455 | 77,716 | 229,983 | 3,776 | 14,082 | 74,039 | 808,051 |
| Illinois | 1,144,282 | 912,673 | 1,744,531 | 15,110 | 71,338 | 160,667 | 4,048,601 |
| Indiana[1] | 1,021,447 | 534,540 | 868,254 | 10,756 | 54,176 | 200,087 | 2,689,260 |
| Iowa | 713,792 | 276,005 | 424,759 | 5,598 | 53,892 | 145,809 | 1,619,855 |
| Kansas | 635,900 | 329,589 | 378,730 | 8,528 | 28,221 | 165,515 | 1,546,483 |
| Kentucky | 776,684 | 230,917 | 502,847 | 6,380 | 27,894 | 72,768 | 1,617,490 |
| Louisiana | 1,058,865 | 206,441 | 685,055 | 7,207 | 41,780 | 70,080 | 2,069,428 |
| Maine | 234,476 | 70,713 | 173,768 | 2,048 | 3,793 | 29,067 | 513,865 |
| Maryland | 525,194 | 390,552 | 888,752 | 9,489 | 17,260 | 42,709 | 1,873,956 |
| Massachusetts | 556,377 | 415,548 | 1,064,747 | 10,775 | 13,077 | 61,122 | 2,121,646 |
| Michigan | 1,164,241 | 781,480 | 1,411,389 | 11,089 | 18,370 | 128,293 | 3,514,862 |
| Minnesota | 814,290 | 431,088 | 735,176 | 11,385 | 35,289 | 244,189 | 2,271,417 |
| Mississippi | 467,797 | 89,231 | 258,967 | 3,980 | 8,761 | 31,571 | 860,307 |
| Missouri | 997,212 | 382,763 | 792,150 | 9,216 | 48,373 | 104,307 | 2,334,021 |
| Montana | 257,877 | 49,054 | 146,585 | 2,007 | 19,661 | 77,263 | 552,447 |
| Nebraska | 382,258 | 135,240 | 291,674 | 3,439 | 37,108 | 151,568 | 1,001,287 |
| Nevada | 236,087 | 74,671 | 272,851 | 2,252 | 8,070 | 93,732 | 687,663 |
| New Hampshire | 217,344 | 88,216 | 231,606 | 3,218 | 5,831 | 24,609 | 570,824 |
| New Jersey | 461,758 | 522,351 | 1,261,477 | 14,961 | 13,927 | 110,023 | 2,384,497 |
| New Mexico | 428,676 | 91,442 | 289,490 | 3,479 | 13,068 | 93,051 | 919,206 |
| New York | 513,437 | 529,661 | 1,137,408 | 14,417 | 7,476 | 245,819 | 2,448,218 |
| North Carolina | 990,756 | 379,703 | 912,289 | 11,125 | 48,585 | 218,362 | 2,560,820 |
| North Dakota | 167,608 | 45,266 | 88,453 | 1,258 | 9,652 | 60,014 | 372,251 |
| Ohio | 1,568,740 | 999,677 | 1,723,852 | 16,064 | 41,897 | 303,731 | 4,653,961 |
| Oklahoma | 822,046 | 182,806 | 458,266 | 6,844 | 13,241 | 223,166 | 1,706,369 |
| Oregon | 657,679 | 229,758 | 548,701 | 7,645 | 21,662 | 125,105 | 1,590,550 |
| Pennsylvania | 1,159,552 | 737,117 | 1,736,786 | 15,343 | 70,517 | 287,006 | 4,006,321 |
| Rhode Island | 85,791 | 59,644 | 139,740 | 1,205 | 3,656 | 14,965 | 305,001 |
| South Carolina | 677,869 | 231,535 | 623,873 | 7,397 | 21,487 | 58,540 | 1,620,701 |
| South Dakota | 216,331 | 65,996 | 133,926 | 1,965 | 21,242 | 82,478 | 521,938 |
| Tennessee | 1,005,779 | 314,574 | 803,676 | 7,903 | 61,218 | 71,017 | 2,264,167 |
| Texas[1] | 4,157,769 | 1,051,668 | 3,522,131 | 30,214 | 169,474 | 390,205 | 9,321,461 |
| Utah | 490,145 | 157,643 | 460,281 | 5,554 | 53,986 | 67,811 | 1,235,420 |
| Vermont | 109,380 | 35,119 | 102,748 | 959 | 2,956 | 11,941 | 263,103 |
| Virginia | 866,243 | 445,540 | 1,083,907 | 10,576 | 42,028 | 104,514 | 2,552,808 |
| Washington | 989,824 | 386,850 | 902,165 | 12,447 | 36,633 | 138,319 | 2,466,238 |
| West Virginia | 326,319 | 80,588 | 238,956 | 2,069 | 11,383 | 50,349 | 709,664 |
| Wisconsin | 813,191 | 479,362 | 788,355 | 8,299 | 40,983 | 202,706 | 2,332,896 |
| Wyoming | 230,200 | 33,045 | 131,610 | 1,944 | 4,186 | 33,690 | 434,675 |
| **Total** | **41,311,535** | **17,994,815** | **42,423,674** | **443,967** | **1,801,592** | **8,772,680** | **112,748,263** |

(1) Adjusted to compensate for partial data reporting by state.
NOTE: The registrations given in this table are as reported by the states in most instances, but have been supplemented in some cases by estimates by USDOT based on data from other sources.
SOURCE: U.S. Department of Transportation, Federal Highway Administration.

# Bus Registrations by State

## U.S. TOTAL BUS REGISTRATIONS BY STATE, 2009

| State | Private and Commercial | | Publicly Owned | | Total Privately and Publicly Owned | | |
|---|---|---|---|---|---|---|---|
| | Commercial Buses[1] | School and Other[2] | Federal | School[3] | Commercial and Federal | School | Total Buses |
| Alabama | 2,227 | 229 | 45 | 6,383 | 2,272 | 6,612 | 8,884 |
| Alaska | 1,628 | 589 | 86 | 395 | 1,714 | 984 | 2,698 |
| Arizona | 1,195 | 240 | 430 | 3,164 | 1,625 | 3,404 | 5,029 |
| Arkansas | 52 | 1,605 | 33 | 6,146 | 85 | 7,751 | 7,836 |
| California | 30,684 | 10,746 | 532 | 17,573 | 31,216 | 28,319 | 59,535 |
| Colorado | 635 | 1,033 | 49 | 4,022 | 684 | 5,055 | 5,739 |
| Connecticut | 3,097 | 6,889 | 14 | 905 | 3,111 | 7,794 | 10,905 |
| Delaware | 473 | 1,095 | 6 | 680 | 479 | 1,775 | 2,254 |
| District of Columbia | 2,346 | 123 | 313 | 118 | 2,659 | 241 | 2,900 |
| Florida | 3,773 | 1,245 | 236 | 46,336 | 4,009 | 47,581 | 51,590 |
| Georgia | 1,780 | 3,640 | 120 | 18,024 | 1,900 | 21,664 | 23,564 |
| Hawaii | 2,257 | 859 | 32 | 1,457 | 2,289 | 2,316 | 4,605 |
| Idaho | 652 | 692 | 170 | 2,381 | 822 | 3,073 | 3,895 |
| Illinois | 5,547 | 12,275 | 97 | 278 | 5,644 | 12,553 | 18,197 |
| Indiana (4) | 4,410 | 5,165 | 63 | 23,795 | 4,473 | 28,960 | 33,433 |
| Iowa | 1,307 | 301 | 15 | 5,300 | 1,322 | 5,601 | 6,923 |
| Kansas | 350 | 1,013 | 14 | 2,534 | 364 | 3,547 | 3,911 |
| Kentucky | 572 | 817 | 180 | 13,022 | 752 | 13,839 | 14,591 |
| Louisiana | 1,232 | 15,275 | 28 | 6,862 | 1,260 | 22,137 | 23,397 |
| Maine | 159 | 354 | 14 | 3,059 | 173 | 3,413 | 3,586 |
| Maryland | 2,803 | 3,887 | 172 | 5,188 | 2,975 | 9,075 | 12,050 |
| Massachusetts | 3,692 | 7,401 | 94 | 599 | 3,786 | 8,000 | 11,786 |
| Michigan | 2,194 | 7,525 | 88 | 16,683 | 2,282 | 24,208 | 26,490 |
| Minnesota | 2,283 | 5,189 | 8 | 11,021 | 2,291 | 16,210 | 18,501 |
| Mississippi | 916 | 2,678 | 89 | 5,908 | 1,005 | 8,586 | 9,591 |
| Missouri | 806 | 2,916 | 41 | 6,778 | 847 | 9,694 | 10,541 |
| Montana | 391 | 585 | 22 | 1,398 | 413 | 1,983 | 2,396 |
| Nebraska | 648 | 823 | 11 | 6,060 | 659 | 6,883 | 7,542 |
| Nevada | 2,291 | 181 | 161 | 133 | 2,452 | 314 | 2,766 |
| New Hampshire | 375 | 1,269 | 3 | 387 | 378 | 1,656 | 2,034 |
| New Jersey | 4,758 | 14,563 | 65 | 4,602 | 4,823 | 19,165 | 23,988 |
| New Mexico | 405 | 1,791 | 351 | 851 | 756 | 2,642 | 3,398 |
| New York | 17,030 | 10,476 | 252 | 43,681 | 17,282 | 54,157 | 71,439 |
| North Carolina | 2,778 | 7,960 | 63 | 24,531 | 2,841 | 32,491 | 35,332 |
| North Dakota | 171 | 653 | 75 | 1,565 | 246 | 2,218 | 2,464 |
| Ohio | 21,593 | 2,781 | 96 | 24,895 | 21,689 | 27,676 | 49,365 |
| Oklahoma | 396 | 1,821 | 156 | 17,300 | 552 | 19,121 | 19,673 |
| Oregon | 1,820 | 3,118 | 79 | 10,821 | 1,899 | 13,939 | 15,838 |
| Pennsylvania | 10,336 | 20,078 | 140 | 2,380 | 10,476 | 22,458 | 32,934 |
| Rhode Island | 341 | 1,363 | 6 | 7 | 347 | 1,370 | 1,717 |
| South Carolina | 1,152 | 4,543 | 37 | 13,473 | 1,189 | 18,016 | 19,205 |
| South Dakota | 437 | 439 | 135 | 1,558 | 572 | 1,997 | 2,569 |
| Tennessee | 2,654 | 1,565 | 91 | 16,382 | 2,745 | 17,947 | 20,692 |
| Texas | 3,707 | 16,061 | 286 | 72,585 | 3,993 | 88,646 | 92,639 |
| Utah | 365 | 130 | 43 | 801 | 408 | 931 | 1,339 |
| Vermont | 97 | 555 | 5 | 1,293 | 102 | 1,848 | 1,950 |
| Virginia | 2,196 | 243 | 278 | 13,842 | 2,474 | 14,085 | 16,559 |
| Washington | 1,202 | 2,439 | 225 | 8,993 | 1,427 | 11,432 | 12,859 |
| West Virginia | 715 | 63 | 51 | 1,882 | 766 | 1,945 | 2,711 |
| Wisconsin | 1,499 | 8,540 | 27 | 4,681 | 1,526 | 13,221 | 14,747 |
| Wyoming | 888 | 125 | 11 | 2,426 | 899 | 2,551 | 3,450 |
| **Total** | **155,315** | **195,946** | **5,638** | **485,138** | **160,953** | **681,084** | **842,037** |

SOURCE: U.S. Department of Transportation, Federal Highway Administration.
(1) Includes municipally owned transit buses.
(2) In some instances church, industrial and other private buses are included here; and in other instances privately-owned school buses could not be segregated from commercial buses, and are included with the latter.
(3) This column consists primarily of publicly owned school buses but includes a few privately owned school, institutional, and industrial buses registered free or at a reduced rate.
(4) Adjusted to compensate for partial data reporting by state.

# School Bus Ownership and Usage by State

## U.S. SCHOOL BUS OWNERSHIP AND USAGE BY STATE, 2008-2009 SCHOOL YEAR

| | Pupils Transported at Public Expense | Bus Ownership | | | Total Miles of Service | Total Expenditures for Pupil Transportation |
|---|---|---|---|---|---|---|
| | | Publicly Owned | Contractor | Total | | |
| Alabama | 376,650 | 7,233 | 108 | 7,341 | 82,306,440 | 245,100,957 |
| Alaska | NA | 256 | 827 | 1,083 | NA | NA |
| Arizona | 361,306 | 8,096 | — | 8,096 | 81,848,953 | NA |
| Arkansas | 257,604 | 4,473 | 206 | 4,679 | 47,929,860 | — |
| California | 866,237 | 15,362 | 7,524 | 22,886 | 277,317,718 | NA |
| Colorado | 348,713 | 5,900 | 300 | 6,200 | 54,312,359 | 48,769,106 |
| Connecticut | 467,168 | NA | NA | NA | NA | NA |
| Delaware | 107,700 | — | 1,189 | 1,189 | 23,000,000 | 84,000,000 |
| Florida | 1,024,726 | 14,344 | 1,153 | 15,497 | 272,654,664 | NA |
| Georgia | 992,488 | 17,551 | 94 | 17,645 | 160,673,760 | NA |
| Hawaii | 40,000 | NA | 830 | 830 | 30,000 | NA |
| Idaho | 107,604 | 1,524 | 570 | 2,094 | 24,508,509 | 69,947,754 |
| Illinois | 1,177,833 | NA | NA | NA | 246,755,921 | NA |
| Indiana | NA | 13,528 | 2,276 | 15,804 | NA | 507,910,901 |
| Iowa | 233,977 | 5,378 | 670 | 6,048 | 41,656,125 | NA |
| Kansas | 206,211 | 2,920 | 1,555 | 4,475 | 62,343,802 | — |
| Kentucky | 407,952 | 9,840 | — | 9,840 | 111,000,000 | 172,858,100 |
| Louisiana | 416,143 | 4,421 | 2,372 | 6,793 | 425,162 | NA |
| Maine | 160,984 | 2,099 | 614 | 2,713 | 34,672,583 | NA |
| Maryland | 618,742 | 3,888 | 3,312 | 7,200 | 123,274,416 | NA |
| Massachusetts | NA | NA | NA | NA | NA | NA |
| Michigan | 774,935 | 15,315 | 1,282 | 16,597 | 174,697,731 | NA |
| Minnesota | 778,185 | 4,231 | 6,826 | 11,057 | NA | NA |
| Mississippi | 457,439 | 5,195 | 324 | 5,519 | 47,669,244 | NA |
| Missouri | 560,582 | 7,539 | 4,600 | 12,139 | 107,183,278 | NA |
| Montana | 602,153 | 1,234 | 1,525 | 2,759 | 17,911,845 | — |
| Nebraska | 77,885 | 2,107 | 1,128 | 3,235 | 28,724,458 | NA |
| Nevada | 128,299 | 2,378 | — | 2,378 | 29,339,458 | NA |
| New Hampshire | 136,541 | 482 | 2,181 | 2,663 | NA | NA |
| New Jersey | 747,763 | NA | NA | NA | NA | NA |
| New Mexico | 322,956 | 667 | 1,557 | 2,224 | 34,384,871 | 86,343,110 |
| New York | 1,942,503 | 24,439 | 20,000 | 44,439 | 215,321,369 | NA |
| North Carolina | 794,950 | 14,104 | 125 | 14,229 | 181,285,181 | 370,060,543 |
| North Dakota | 93,715 | 970 | 335 | 1,305 | 19,020,047 | 20,716,355 |
| Ohio | 873,687 | 13,629 | 1,322 | 14,951 | 162,463,140 | 366,904,820 |
| Oklahoma | 372,049 | NA | NA | NA | 49,303 | NA |
| Oregon | 270,728 | 3,405 | 2,224 | 5,629 | 66,861,662 | NA |
| Pennsylvania | 1,379,907 | 5,083 | 16,407 | 21,490 | 401,416,449 | 556,180,345 |
| Rhode Island | 156,454 | 335 | 1,356 | 1,691 | NA | NA |
| South Carolina | 356,848 | 130 | 70 | 200 | 80,683,034 | 129,032,372 |
| South Dakota | 43,036 | NA | NA | NA | 13,738,992 | — |
| Tennessee | 525,601 | 6,745 | 1,953 | 8,698 | NA | NA |
| Texas | 1,400,000 | NA | NA | — | 352,000,000 | 309,000,000 |
| Utah | 175,439 | 2,461 | 41 | 2,502 | 26,097,749 | 63,062,465 |
| Vermont | NA | NA | NA | NA | NA | NA |
| Virginia | 944,823 | 13,649 | 143 | 13,792 | 195,099,608 | NA |
| Washington | 486,078 | 8,793 | 1,312 | 10,105 | 92,400,000 | 266,161,061 |
| West Virginia | 233,901 | 2,855 | — | 2,855 | 498,208 | 48,615,000 |
| Wisconsin | 554,000 | 2,000 | 8,000 | 10,000 | NA | NA |
| Wyoming | 35,185 | 1,480 | — | 1,480 | 14,018,984 | 58,440,479 |
| **Total** | **23,397,680** | **256,039** | **96,311** | **352,350** | **3,905,574,883** | **3,403,103,368** |

NOTE: NA Not available.
SOURCE: Bobit Publishing Company, School Bus Fleet Fact Book.

# Government Ownership of Vehicles by State

## U.S. GOVERNMENT OWNERSHIP OF VEHICLES BY STATE, 2009

| State | Federal[1] | | | | State, County and Municipal[2] | | | | Total Government Owned Vehicles |
|---|---|---|---|---|---|---|---|---|---|
| | Cars | Trucks | Buses | Total | Cars | Trucks | Buses | Total | |
| Alabama | 1,703 | 5,427 | 45 | 7,175 | 15,634 | 22,623 | 6,383 | 44,640 | 51,815 |
| Alaska | 515 | 3,504 | 86 | 4,105 | 2,297 | 7,151 | 395 | 9,843 | 13,948 |
| Arizona | 2,278 | 10,180 | 430 | 12,888 | 15,739 | 9,760 | 3,164 | 28,663 | 41,551 |
| Arkansas | 950 | 3,037 | 33 | 4,020 | 8,986 | 8,786 | 6,146 | 23,918 | 27,938 |
| California | 12,953 | 49,298 | 532 | 62,783 | 201,036 | 272,973 | 17,573 | 491,582 | 554,365 |
| Colorado | 1,781 | 9,685 | 49 | 11,515 | 8,307 | 18,127 | 3,994 | 30,428 | 41,943 |
| Connecticut | 903 | 4,829 | 14 | 5,746 | 10,956 | 25,338 | 905 | 37,199 | 42,945 |
| Delaware | 278 | 852 | 6 | 1,136 | 7,340 | 2,414 | 680 | 10,434 | 11,570 |
| Dist. of Columbia | 2,596 | 4,139 | 313 | 7,048 | 1,775 | 2,870 | 118 | 4,763 | 11,811 |
| Florida | 4,830 | 16,508 | 236 | 21,574 | 114,144 | 157,232 | 46,336 | 317,712 | 339,286 |
| Georgia | 2,541 | 8,036 | 120 | 10,697 | 29,438 | 73,099 | 18,024 | 120,561 | 131,258 |
| Hawaii | 524 | 1,903 | 32 | 2,459 | 6,742 | 7,315 | 1,457 | 15,514 | 17,973 |
| Idaho | 676 | 5,421 | 170 | 6,267 | 5,973 | 9,656 | 2,381 | 18,010 | 24,277 |
| Illinois | 3,580 | 11,726 | 97 | 15,403 | 73,711 | 1,616 | 278 | 75,605 | 91,008 |
| Indiana | 1,408 | 4,892 | 63 | 6,363 | 22,899 | 41,935 | 23,628 | 88,462 | 94,825 |
| Iowa | 704 | 3,626 | 15 | 4,345 | 9,000 | 21,700 | 5,300 | 36,000 | 40,345 |
| Kansas | 812 | 3,492 | 14 | 4,318 | 7,268 | 16,309 | 2,534 | 26,111 | 30,429 |
| Kentucky | 1,614 | 4,813 | 180 | 6,607 | 25,390 | 4,166 | 13,022 | 42,578 | 49,185 |
| Louisiana | 1,655 | 5,327 | 28 | 7,010 | 58,362 | 22,307 | 6,862 | 87,531 | 94,541 |
| Maine | 437 | 1,333 | 14 | 1,784 | 5,916 | 13,326 | 3,059 | 22,301 | 24,085 |
| Maryland | 2,621 | 7,557 | 172 | 10,350 | 11,710 | 17,198 | 5,188 | 34,096 | 44,446 |
| Massachusetts | 2,708 | 7,542 | 94 | 10,344 | 19,164 | 40,125 | 599 | 59,888 | 70,232 |
| Michigan | 2,661 | 9,625 | 88 | 12,374 | 48,560 | 73,586 | 16,683 | 138,829 | 151,203 |
| Minnesota | 1,527 | 6,020 | 8 | 7,555 | 12,018 | 24,928 | 11,021 | 47,967 | 55,522 |
| Mississippi | 1,356 | 3,830 | 89 | 5,275 | 11,748 | 8,116 | 5,908 | 25,772 | 31,047 |
| Missouri | 3,098 | 5,193 | 41 | 8,332 | 4,837 | 13,289 | 6,778 | 24,904 | 33,236 |
| Montana | 894 | 5,434 | 22 | 6,350 | 5,743 | 14,753 | 1,398 | 21,894 | 28,244 |
| Nebraska | 1,090 | 3,010 | 11 | 4,111 | 14,320 | 20,567 | 6,060 | 40,947 | 45,058 |
| Nevada | 1,161 | 6,994 | 161 | 8,316 | 9,029 | 8,155 | 133 | 17,317 | 25,633 |
| New Hampshire | 601 | 1,199 | 3 | 1,803 | 3,913 | 11,725 | 387 | 16,025 | 17,828 |
| New Jersey | 2,231 | 11,157 | 65 | 13,453 | 39,853 | 97,528 | 4,602 | 141,983 | 155,436 |
| New Mexico | 1,374 | 7,362 | 351 | 9,087 | 14,997 | 18,002 | 851 | 33,850 | 42,937 |
| New York | 8,479 | 19,739 | 252 | 28,470 | 72,963 | 78,388 | 43,681 | 195,032 | 223,502 |
| North Carolina | 1,833 | 5,840 | 63 | 7,736 | 31,314 | 48,209 | 24,531 | 104,054 | 111,790 |
| North Dakota | 603 | 2,081 | 75 | 2,759 | 3,677 | 6,765 | 1,565 | 12,007 | 14,766 |
| Ohio | 3,129 | 9,777 | 96 | 13,002 | 68,654 | 81,529 | 24,895 | 175,078 | 188,080 |
| Oklahoma | 1,522 | 5,272 | 156 | 6,950 | 12,336 | 50,821 | 17,300 | 80,457 | 87,407 |
| Oregon | 1,385 | 9,778 | 79 | 11,242 | 29,383 | 25,276 | 10,821 | 65,480 | 76,722 |
| Pennsylvania | 5,104 | 13,761 | 140 | 19,005 | 38,903 | 57,507 | 2,380 | 98,790 | 117,795 |
| Rhode Island | 241 | 1,201 | 6 | 1,448 | 4,741 | 4,414 | 7 | 9,162 | 10,610 |
| South Carolina | 1,596 | 5,305 | 37 | 6,938 | 10,371 | 23,839 | 13,473 | 47,683 | 54,621 |
| South Dakota | 566 | 2,871 | 135 | 3,572 | 3,988 | 12,737 | 1,558 | 18,283 | 21,855 |
| Tennessee | 3,382 | 10,341 | 91 | 13,814 | 19,877 | 54,282 | 16,382 | 90,541 | 104,355 |
| Texas | 6,346 | 25,070 | 286 | 31,702 | 106,619 | 227,908 | 72,077 | 406,604 | 438,306 |
| Utah | 935 | 4,806 | 43 | 5,784 | 11,213 | 12,701 | 801 | 24,715 | 30,499 |
| Vermont | 335 | 519 | 5 | 859 | 2,866 | 6,107 | 1,293 | 10,266 | 11,125 |
| Virginia | 2,560 | 9,557 | 278 | 12,395 | 29,676 | 24,542 | 13,842 | 68,060 | 80,455 |
| Washington | 2,820 | 13,578 | 225 | 16,623 | 18,365 | 28,999 | 8,993 | 56,357 | 72,980 |
| West Virginia | 885 | 2,163 | 51 | 3,099 | 12,257 | 23,755 | 1,882 | 37,894 | 40,993 |
| Wisconsin | 1,113 | 5,152 | 27 | 6,292 | 15,588 | 43,483 | 4,681 | 63,752 | 70,044 |
| Wyoming | 390 | 3,139 | 11 | 3,540 | 6,283 | 12,852 | 2,426 | 21,561 | 25,101 |
| **Total** | **107,284** | **382,901** | **5,638** | **495,823** | **1,325,879** | **1,910,789** | **484,435** | **3,721,103** | **4,216,926** |

(1) Vehicles of the civilian branches of the federal government are given in this table. Vehicles of the military services are not included. Distribution by state is estimated by the Federal Highway Administration.

(2) This information, compiled chiefly from reports of state authorities, is incomplete in many cases. Some states give state owned vehicles only; others exclude certain classes, such as fire apparatus and police vehicles. For the states not reporting state, county and municipal vehicles separately from private and commercial vehicles and those reporting unsegregated totals only, classification by vehicle type has been estimated on the basis of other available data.

SOURCE: U.S. Department of Transportation, Federal Highway Administration.

# Vehicles in Operation by Year

## U.S. VEHICLES IN OPERATION BY YEAR

| Year | Cars | Trucks | Total | % Change | Truck % of Total |
|------|------|--------|-------|----------|------------------|
| 2010[1] | 118,946,744 | 120,865,240 | 239,811,984 | 0.3 | 50.4 |
| 2009[1] | 119,291,910 | 119,770,033 | 239,061,943 | -4.5 | 50.1 |
| 2008 | 135,882,003 | 114,356,659 | 250,238,662 | 0.6 | 45.7 |
| 2007 | 135,222,259 | 113,478,738 | 248,700,997 | 1.7 | 45.6 |
| 2006 | 135,046,706 | 109,595,904 | 244,642,610 | 2.6 | 44.8 |
| 2005 | 132,908,828 | 105,475,340 | 238,384,168 | 2.7 | 44.2 |
| 2004 | 132,469,269 | 99,697,867 | 232,167,136 | 2.8 | 42.9 |
| 2003 | 131,072,466 | 94,809,637 | 225,882,103 | 2.2 | 42.0 |
| 2002 | 129,906,797 | 91,120,324 | 221,027,121 | 2.0 | 41.2 |
| 2001 | 128,714,022 | 87,968,915 | 216,682,937 | 1.6 | 40.6 |
| 2000 | 127,720,809 | 85,578,504 | 213,299,313 | 1.8 | 40.1 |
| 1999 | 126,868,744 | 82,640,417 | 209,509,161 | 2.2 | 39.4 |
| 1998 | 125,965,709 | 79,076,930 | 205,042,639 | 2.0 | 38.6 |
| 1997 | 124,672,920 | 76,397,477 | 201,070,397 | 1.4 | 38.0 |
| 1996 | 124,612,787 | 73,680,672 | 198,293,459 | 2.5 | 37.2 |
| 1995 | 123,241,881 | 70,198,512 | 193,440,393 | 2.5 | 36.3 |
| 1994 | 121,996,580 | 66,717,417 | 188,713,997 | 1.3 | 35.4 |
| 1993 | 121,055,398 | 65,260,066 | 186,315,464 | 2.6 | 35.0 |
| 1992 | 120,346,746 | 61,172,404 | 181,519,150 | — | 33.7 |
| 1991 | 123,327,046 | 58,178,883 | 181,505,929 | 1.2 | 32.1 |
| 1990 | 123,276,268 | 56,022,934 | 179,299,202 | 1.9 | 31.2 |
| 1989 | 122,758,378 | 53,201,657 | 175,960,035 | 2.5 | 30.2 |
| 1988 | 121,519,074 | 50,221,502 | 171,740,576 | 2.7 | 29.2 |
| 1987 | 119,848,769 | 47,344,319 | 167,193,088 | 3.1 | 28.3 |
| 1986 | 117,268,071 | 44,825,523 | 162,093,594 | 3.2 | 27.7 |
| 1985 | 114,662,333 | 42,386,882 | 157,049,215 | 3.2 | 27.0 |
| 1984 | 112,018,640 | 40,142,872 | 152,161,512 | 3.4 | 26.4 |
| 1983 | 108,961,215 | 38,143,304 | 147,104,519 | 2.3 | 25.9 |
| 1982 | 106,867,108 | 36,986,537 | 143,853,645 | 1.4 | 25.7 |
| 1981 | 105,838,582 | 36,069,197 | 141,907,779 | 1.5 | 25.4 |
| 1980 | 104,563,781 | 35,267,535 | 139,831,316 | 1.9 | 25.2 |
| 1979 | 104,676,507 | 32,582,991 | 137,259,498 | 2.8 | 23.7 |
| 1978 | 102,956,713 | 30,564,701 | 133,521,414 | 4.2 | 22.9 |
| 1977 | 99,903,594 | 28,221,661 | 128,125,255 | 3.0 | 22.0 |
| 1976 | 97,818,221 | 26,560,296 | 124,378,517 | 3.6 | 21.4 |
| 1975 | 95,240,602 | 24,812,843 | 120,053,445 | 3.6 | 20.7 |
| 1974 | 92,607,551 | 23,312,245 | 115,919,796 | 4.2 | 20.1 |
| 1973 | 89,805,159 | 21,411,931 | 111,217,090 | 4.7 | 19.3 |
| 1972 | 86,438,957 | 19,772,938 | 106,211,895 | 4.5 | 18.6 |
| 1971 | 83,137,324 | 18,462,287 | 101,599,611 | 3.5 | 18.2 |
| 1970 | 80,448,463 | 17,687,505 | 98,135,968 | 3.2 | 18.0 |
| 1969 | 78,494,938 | 16,586,368 | 95,081,306 | 4.4 | 17.4 |
| 1968 | 75,358,034 | 15,684,917 | 91,042,951 | 3.5 | 17.2 |
| 1967 | 72,967,686 | 14,988,491 | 87,956,177 | 2.7 | 17.0 |
| 1966 | 71,263,738 | 14,356,591 | 85,620,329 | 4.3 | 16.8 |
| 1965 | 68,939,770 | 13,126,579 | 82,066,349 | 4.5 | 16.0 |
| 1964 | 66,051,415 | 12,444,964 | 78,496,379 | 4.1 | 15.8 |
| 1963 | 63,493,277 | 11,902,039 | 75,395,316 | 4.2 | 15.8 |
| 1962 | 60,919,579 | 11,463,381 | 72,382,960 | 3.6 | 15.8 |
| 1961 | 58,854,380 | 11,042,770 | 69,897,150 | 2.9 | 15.8 |
| 1960 | 57,102,676 | 10,802,959 | 67,905,635 | 3.5 | 15.9 |
| 1959 | 55,086,761 | 10,532,145 | 65,618,906 | 4.9 | 16.1 |
| 1958 | 52,492,509 | 10,056,567 | 62,549,076 | 2.2 | 16.1 |
| 1957 | 51,432,460 | 9,775,950 | 61,208,410 | 3.1 | 16.0 |

(1) 2009 and 2010 not comparable to prior years, for these years truck data is light truck only.
SOURCE: R.L. Polk Company for 2008 data and prior. 2009 and 2010 data from Experian.

# U.S. Market Used Vehicle Sales and Consumer Leases

## USED VEHICLE SALES (in Thousands)

| Year | Franchised Dealers | Independent Dealers | Casual | Total |
|------|------|------|------|------|
| 2010 | 12,816 | 13,010 | 11,057 | 36,883 |
| 2009 | 12,820 | 11,712 | 10,960 | 35,492 |
| 2008 | 13,190 | 11,742 | 11,599 | 36,531 |
| 2007 | 14,285 | 13,077 | 14,056 | 41,418 |
| 2006 | 14,319 | 13,710 | 14,536 | 42,565 |
| 2005 | 16,450 | 14,210 | 13,478 | 44,138 |
| 2004 | 15,953 | 14,751 | 11,841 | 42,545 |
| 2003 | 16,171 | 13,732 | 13,668 | 43,571 |
| 2002 | 16,470 | 13,078 | 13,478 | 43,026 |
| 2001 | 15,945 | 14,416 | 12,263 | 42,624 |
| 2000 | 16,178 | 13,559 | 11,883 | 41,620 |
| 1999 | 16,504 | 12,786 | 11,448 | 40,738 |
| 1998 | 15,684 | 13,182 | 11,976 | 40,842 |
| 1997 | 15,796 | 12,685 | 12,757 | 41,238 |
| 1996 | 15,713 | 13,247 | 11,871 | 40,831 |
| 1995 | 15,679 | 14,124 | 11,958 | 41,761 |

SOURCE: CNW Marketing Research, Inc.

## AVERAGE USED VEHICLE TRANSACTION PRICES

| Year | Franchised Dealers | Independent Dealers | Casual | Total |
|------|------|------|------|------|
| 2010 | $10,345 | $8,875 | $6,874 | $8,715 |
| 2009 | $10,243 | $8,459 | $6,451 | $8,483 |
| 2008 | $9,643 | $8,358 | $5,725 | $7,986 |
| 2007 | $10,100 | $8,650 | $5,810 | $8,186 |
| 2006 | $9,750 | $8,492 | $5,838 | $8,009 |
| 2005 | $10,516 | $8,545 | $4,471 | $8,036 |
| 2004 | $11,414 | $8,490 | $4,263 | $8,410 |
| 2003 | $12,177 | $7,632 | $4,002 | $8,180 |
| 2002 | $12,537 | $7,157 | $3,688 | $8,130 |
| 2001 | $12,238 | $8,275 | $4,316 | $8,618 |
| 2000 | $12,748 | $7,613 | $4,539 | $8,896 |
| 1999 | $12,630 | $7,590 | $4,505 | $8,828 |
| 1998 | $12,165 | $7,172 | $4,190 | $8,341 |
| 1997 | $12,350 | $7,155 | $4,164 | $8,399 |
| 1996 | $12,256 | $7,076 | $4,283 | $8,257 |
| 1995 | $11,585 | $7,413 | $4,316 | $8,093 |

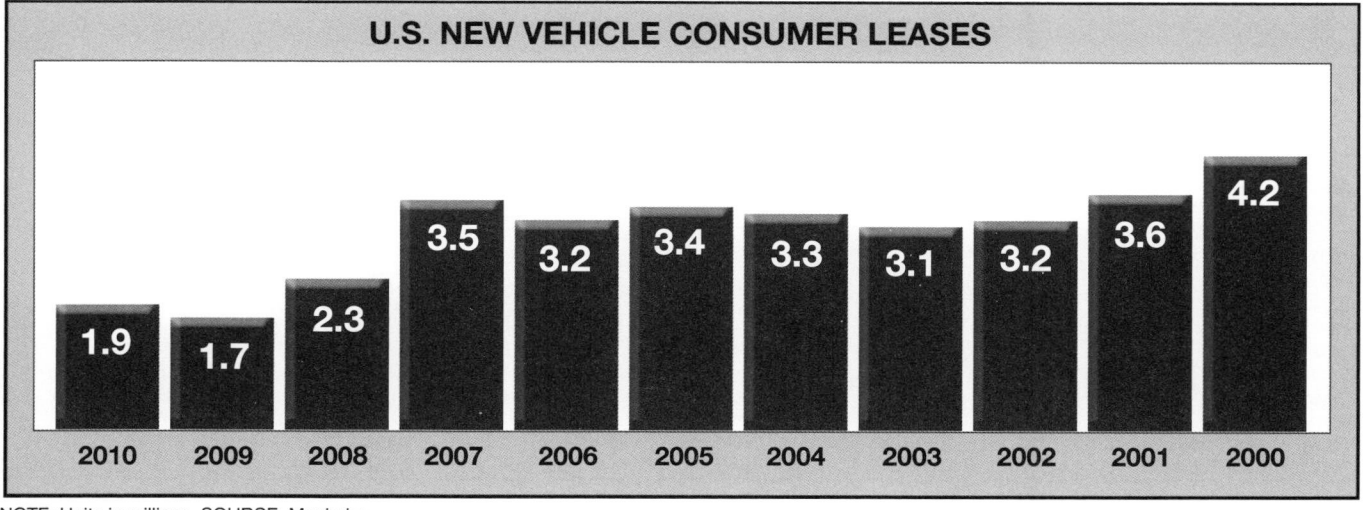

**U.S. NEW VEHICLE CONSUMER LEASES**

| 2010 | 2009 | 2008 | 2007 | 2006 | 2005 | 2004 | 2003 | 2002 | 2001 | 2000 |
|------|------|------|------|------|------|------|------|------|------|------|
| 1.9 | 1.7 | 2.3 | 3.5 | 3.2 | 3.4 | 3.3 | 3.1 | 3.2 | 3.6 | 4.2 |

NOTE: Units in millions. SOURCE: Manheim.

# Light Vehicle Fleet Registrations

## LIGHT VEHICLE FLEET REGISTRATIONS BY MODEL YEAR, 2010

| Make | Commercial | Rental | Government | Total Fleet | Total Sales | Fleet % of Total Sales |
|------|-----------:|-------:|-----------:|------------:|------------:|-----------------------:|
| Audi | 2,655 | 341 | 27 | 3,023 | 66,233 | 4.6 |
| BMW/Mini | 3,394 | 886 | 69 | 4,349 | 191,657 | 2.3 |
| Buick | 2,139 | 12,308 | 363 | 14,810 | 90,761 | 16.3 |
| Cadillac | 1,749 | 16,510 | 19 | 18,278 | 65,372 | 28.0 |
| Chevrolet | 26,296 | 226,135 | 15,819 | 268,250 | 628,940 | 42.7 |
| Chrysler | 2,393 | 54,555 | 90 | 57,038 | 82,025 | 69.5 |
| Dodge | 3,093 | 117,334 | 13,648 | 134,075 | 209,872 | 63.9 |
| Ford | 58,090 | 97,870 | 42,166 | 198,126 | 553,644 | 35.8 |
| Honda/Acura | 5,608 | 16,099 | 484 | 22,191 | 686,253 | 3.2 |
| Hyundai/Kia | 2,598 | 111,640 | 130 | 114,368 | 489,181 | 23.4 |
| Jaguar | 278 | 396 | 2 | 676 | 11,068 | 6.1 |
| Lincoln/Mercury | 3,575 | 41,249 | 121 | 44,945 | 105,808 | 42.5 |
| Mazda | 1,546 | 15,407 | 150 | 17,103 | 145,463 | 11.8 |
| Mercedes-Benz | 3,126 | 4,530 | 70 | 7,726 | 135,647 | 5.7 |
| Mitsubishi | 74 | 8,474 | 24 | 8,572 | 36,663 | 23.4 |
| Nissan/Infiniti | 9,737 | 86,041 | 295 | 96,073 | 532,692 | 18.0 |
| Pontiac | 347 | 12,771 | 860 | 13,978 | 28,242 | 49.5 |
| Porsche | 370 | 27 | 3 | 400 | 14,128 | 2.8 |
| Saab | 101 | — | 3 | 104 | 4,319 | 2.4 |
| Saturn | 60 | 16 | 14 | 90 | 7,906 | 1.1 |
| Scion | 69 | 23 | 3 | 95 | 22,817 | 0.4 |
| Subaru | 4,850 | 10,074 | 64 | 14,988 | 162,953 | 9.2 |
| Suzuki | 127 | 940 | 8 | 1,075 | 13,315 | 8.1 |
| Toyota/Lexus | 22,634 | 118,741 | 2,021 | 143,396 | 934,069 | 15.4 |
| Volkswagen | 2,355 | 12,937 | 86 | 15,378 | 199,716 | 7.7 |
| Volvo | 2,409 | 2,800 | 18 | 5,227 | 31,757 | 16.5 |
| Other | 494 | 706 | 251 | 1,451 | 14,290 | 10.2 |
| **Total Cars** | **160,167** | **968,810** | **76,808** | **1,205,785** | **5,464,791** | **22.1** |
| Audi | 1,440 | 25 | 26 | 1,491 | 26,931 | 5.5 |
| BMW | 1,420 | 42 | 35 | 1,497 | 43,108 | 3.5 |
| Buick | 892 | 6,467 | 13 | 7,372 | 50,667 | 14.5 |
| Cadillac | 1,953 | 8,064 | 17 | 10,034 | 73,804 | 13.6 |
| Chevrolet | 88,709 | 147,080 | 31,135 | 266,924 | 875,811 | 30.5 |
| Chrysler | 2,178 | 50,531 | 93 | 52,802 | 118,267 | 44.6 |
| Dodge | 33,343 | 72,334 | 13,252 | 118,929 | 357,118 | 33.3 |
| Ford | 164,372 | 112,702 | 59,228 | 336,302 | 1,063,707 | 31.6 |
| Freightliner | 776 | 379 | 137 | 1,292 | 2,418 | 53.4 |
| GMC | 17,164 | 23,199 | 2,660 | 43,023 | 302,867 | 14.2 |
| Honda/Acura | 5,803 | 260 | 344 | 6,407 | 475,975 | 1.3 |
| Hummer | 122 | 856 | 2 | 980 | 4,299 | 22.8 |
| Hyundai/Kia | 2,380 | 53,451 | 91 | 55,922 | 322,428 | 17.3 |
| International | 4 | — | — | 4 | 4 | 100.0 |
| Isuzu | 1 | — | — | 1 | 21 | 4.8 |
| Jeep | 7,853 | 49,383 | 1,246 | 58,482 | 251,780 | 23.2 |
| Land Rover | 1,119 | 167 | 10 | 1,296 | 26,622 | 4.9 |
| Lincoln/Mercury | 4,763 | 4,517 | 56 | 9,336 | 68,791 | 13.6 |
| Mazda | 732 | 5,523 | 90 | 6,345 | 73,051 | 8.7 |
| Mercedes-Benz | 2,574 | 1,208 | 62 | 3,844 | 69,558 | 5.5 |
| Mitsubishi | 75 | 1,354 | 15 | 1,444 | 15,017 | 9.6 |
| Nissan/Infiniti | 3,890 | 14,499 | 228 | 18,617 | 310,555 | 6.0 |
| Pontiac | 4 | — | 1 | 5 | 623 | 0.8 |
| Porsche | 335 | 15 | 8 | 358 | 5,613 | 6.4 |
| Saab | — | — | — | — | 263 | — |
| Saturn | 43 | 6,523 | 5 | 6,571 | 11,585 | 56.7 |
| Scion | 636 | 77 | 17 | 730 | 20,124 | 3.6 |
| Subaru | 2,474 | 4,733 | 38 | 7,245 | 81,932 | 8.8 |
| Suzuki | 93 | 282 | 2 | 377 | 8,694 | 4.3 |
| Toyota/Lexus | 21,928 | 16,970 | 976 | 39,874 | 751,536 | 5.3 |
| Volkswagen | 472 | 349 | 54 | 875 | 34,345 | 2.5 |
| Volvo Truck | 454 | 103 | 31 | 588 | 22,410 | 2.6 |
| **Total Light Trucks** | **368,002** | **581,093** | **109,872** | **1,058,967** | **5,469,924** | **19.4** |
| **Total Light Vehicles** | **528,169** | **1,549,903** | **186,680** | **2,264,752** | **10,934,715** | **20.7** |

NOTE: Total sales includes fleet plus retail.
SOURCE: Bobit Business Media, Automotive Fleet Fact Book 2011.

# Total Vehicle Registrations by Country

## VEHICLES IN OPERATION BY COUNTRY

| Country | 2009 Cars | 2009 Commercial Vehicles | 2009 Total | Population (000) | Persons Per Car | 2008 Cars | 2008 Commercial Vehicles | 2008 Total |
|---|---|---|---|---|---|---|---|---|
| **AFRICA** | | | | | | | | |
| Algeria | 2,593,310 | 1,253,953 | 3,847,263 | 34,178 | 13.2 | 2,300,000 | 1,150,000 | 3,450,000 |
| Angola | 50,000 | 68,000 | 118,000 | 12,799 | 256.0 | 49,000 | 67,500 | 116,500 |
| Benin | 11,250 | 18,100 | 29,350 | 8,792 | 781.5 | 11,000 | 17,900 | 28,900 |
| Botswana | 127,634 | 117,805 | 245,439 | 1,991 | 15.6 | 120,783 | 114,760 | 235,543 |
| Burkina Faso | 110,931 | 48,994 | 159,925 | 15,746 | 141.9 | 103,623 | 46,223 | 149,846 |
| Burundi | 30,000 | 25,750 | 55,750 | 9,511 | 317.0 | 29,500 | 25,500 | 55,000 |
| Cameroon | 210,000 | 68,900 | 278,900 | 18,879 | 89.9 | 201,900 | 66,600 | 268,500 |
| Central African Republic | 2,250 | 2,000 | 4,250 | 4,742 | 2,107.6 | 2,100 | 1,950 | 4,050 |
| Congo | 43,500 | 19,500 | 63,000 | 4,013 | 92.3 | 42,800 | 18,600 | 61,400 |
| Congo, Democratic Republic of | 916,750 | 709,000 | 1,625,750 | 68,016 | 74.2 | 914,200 | 707,900 | 1,622,100 |
| Egypt | 2,437,543 | 995,020 | 3,432,563 | 78,867 | 32.4 | 2,206,823 | 931,406 | 3,138,229 |
| Ethiopia | 76,000 | 57,000 | 133,000 | 85,237 | 1,121.5 | 75,000 | 56,250 | 131,250 |
| Ghana | 113,750 | 60,500 | 174,250 | 23,888 | 210.0 | 113,000 | 60,000 | 173,000 |
| Ivory Coast | 22,000 | 96,500 | 118,500 | 21,504 | 977.5 | 21,750 | 95,600 | 117,350 |
| Kenya | 299,000 | 132,500 | 431,500 | 39,003 | 130.4 | 297,000 | 131,000 | 428,000 |
| Liberia | 13,500 | 37,900 | 51,400 | 3,583 | 265.4 | 13,000 | 37,500 | 50,500 |
| Libya | 441,000 | 400,000 | 841,000 | 6,324 | 14.3 | 435,000 | 390,000 | 825,000 |
| Madagascar | 77,500 | 53,000 | 130,500 | 20,654 | 266.5 | 76,900 | 52,500 | 129,400 |
| Malawi | 13,000 | 17,250 | 30,250 | 15,029 | 1,156.1 | 12,800 | 17,000 | 29,800 |
| Mali | 10,000 | 12,800 | 22,800 | 13,443 | 1,344.3 | 9,750 | 12,500 | 22,250 |
| Mauritania | 13,400 | 9,100 | 22,500 | 3,129 | 233.5 | 13,100 | 8,900 | 22,000 |
| Mauritius | 117,890 | 88,521 | 206,411 | 1,284 | 10.9 | 109,507 | 86,843 | 196,350 |
| Morocco | 1,395,600 | 445,000 | 1,840,600 | 31,285 | 22.4 | 1,364,900 | 432,100 | 1,797,000 |
| Mozambique | 34,000 | 31,750 | 65,750 | 21,922 | 644.8 | 33,500 | 31,200 | 64,700 |
| Namibia | 83,000 | 90,750 | 173,750 | 2,109 | 25.4 | 82,100 | 90,100 | 172,200 |
| Niger | 93,118 | 25,968 | 119,086 | 15,306 | 164.4 | 84,675 | 23,503 | 108,178 |
| Nigeria | 763,500 | 476,000 | 1,239,500 | 149,229 | 195.5 | 760,000 | 475,000 | 1,235,000 |
| Reunion | 237,750 | 96,250 | 334,000 | 843 | 3.5 | 236,500 | 95,500 | 332,000 |
| Sierra Leone | 20,650 | 9,550 | 30,200 | 5,132 | 248.5 | 20,400 | 9,400 | 29,800 |
| South Africa | 5,050,364 | 2,771,394 | 7,821,758 | 49,052 | 9.7 | 5,039,596 | 2,757,688 | 7,797,284 |
| Sudan | 41,000 | 51,500 | 92,500 | 42,811 | 1,044.2 | 40,000 | 50,000 | 90,000 |
| Tanzania | 24,000 | 52,500 | 76,500 | 41,049 | 1,710.4 | 23,750 | 51,750 | 75,500 |
| Togo | 106,000 | 49,000 | 155,000 | 6,405 | 60.4 | 105,000 | 48,500 | 153,500 |
| Tunisia | 660,000 | 322,500 | 982,500 | 10,421 | 15.8 | 655,000 | 320,000 | 975,000 |
| Uganda | 56,900 | 46,500 | 103,400 | 32,370 | 568.9 | 56,500 | 46,000 | 102,500 |
| Zambia | 171,350 | 99,500 | 270,850 | 13,061 | 76.2 | 167,055 | 97,450 | 264,505 |
| Zimbabwe | 394,000 | 68,000 | 462,000 | 11,393 | 28.9 | 390,500 | 67,000 | 457,500 |
| **Total Africa** | **16,861,440** | **8,928,255** | **25,789,695** | **923,000** | **54.7** | **16,218,012** | **8,691,623** | **24,909,635** |
| **AMERICA, Caribbean** | | | | | | | | |
| Bahamas | 91,200 | 31,300 | 122,500 | 308 | 3.4 | 90,750 | 31,000 | 121,750 |

# Total Vehicle Registrations by Country

## VEHICLES IN OPERATION BY COUNTRY — continued

| Country | 2009 Cars | 2009 Commercial Vehicles | 2009 Total | Population (000) | Persons Per Car | 2008 Cars | 2008 Commercial Vehicles | 2008 Total |
|---|---|---|---|---|---|---|---|---|
| Barbados | 79,750 | 17,900 | 97,650 | 285 | 3.6 | 78,800 | 17,500 | 96,300 |
| Bermuda | 22,626 | 4,802 | 27,428 | 68 | 3.0 | 22,730 | 4,955 | 27,685 |
| Cuba | 205,500 | 221,500 | 427,000 | 11,110 | 54.1 | 202,000 | 219,500 | 421,500 |
| Dominican Republic | 645,158 | 629,394 | 1,274,552 | 9,691 | 15.0 | 630,090 | 596,555 | 1,226,645 |
| Haiti | 35,000 | 35,000 | 70,000 | 9,778 | 279.4 | 36,800 | 36,500 | 73,300 |
| Jamaica | 134,500 | 35,750 | 170,250 | 2,826 | 21.0 | 133,000 | 35,500 | 168,500 |
| Netherlands Antilles | 109,000 | 26,500 | 135,500 | 227 | 2.1 | 100,163 | 25,264 | 125,427 |
| Puerto Rico | 1,065,000 | 458,500 | 1,523,500 | 3,967 | 3.7 | 1,054,200 | 453,300 | 1,507,500 |
| Trinidad and Tobago | 317,000 | 41,000 | 358,000 | 1,230 | 3.9 | 313,800 | 40,500 | 354,300 |
| Virgin Islands (US) | 36,500 | 20,000 | 56,500 | 110 | 3.0 | 36,000 | 19,500 | 55,500 |
| **Total Caribbean** | **2,741,234** | **1,521,646** | **4,262,880** | **39,598** | **14.4** | **2,698,333** | **1,480,074** | **4,178,407** |
| **AMERICA, Central & South** | | | | | | | | |
| Argentina | 6,706,101 | 2,248,774 | 8,954,875 | 40,914 | 6.1 | 6,243,879 | 2,215,848 | 8,459,727 |
| Belize | 13,100 | 15,650 | 28,750 | 308 | 23.5 | 13,000 | 15,500 | 28,500 |
| Bolivia | 217,900 | 307,500 | 525,400 | 9,775 | 44.9 | 215,500 | 305,200 | 520,700 |
| Brazil | 23,612,000 | 6,031,000 | 29,643,000 | 198,739 | 8.4 | 21,884,000 | 5,597,000 | 27,481,000 |
| Chile | 1,816,143 | 1,018,496 | 2,834,639 | 16,602 | 9.1 | 1,599,152 | 984,545 | 2,583,697 |
| Colombia | 1,018,000 | 624,000 | 1,642,000 | 43,677 | 42.9 | 1,010,500 | 621,000 | 1,631,500 |
| Costa Rica | 565,364 | 185,150 | 750,514 | 4,455 | 7.9 | 551,885 | 183,059 | 734,944 |
| Ecuador | 329,184 | 440,341 | 769,525 | 14,573 | 44.3 | 371,241 | 483,100 | 854,341 |
| El Salvador | 86,000 | 113,500 | 199,500 | 6,031 | 70.1 | 85,000 | 112,500 | 197,500 |
| Guatemala | 146,500 | 154,000 | 300,500 | 13,277 | 90.6 | 145,000 | 152,500 | 297,500 |
| Guyana | 31,500 | 15,250 | 46,750 | 753 | 23.9 | 31,000 | 15,000 | 46,000 |
| Honduras | 31,600 | 93,000 | 124,600 | 7,834 | 247.9 | 31,000 | 92,500 | 123,500 |
| Nicaragua | 75,000 | 113,000 | 188,000 | 5,541 | 73.9 | 73,500 | 112,000 | 185,500 |
| Panama | 283,000 | 183,000 | 466,000 | 3,360 | 11.9 | 279,000 | 181,000 | 460,000 |
| Paraguay | 95,500 | 91,500 | 187,000 | 6,291 | 65.9 | 94,000 | 91,000 | 185,000 |
| Peru | 766,742 | 694,541 | 1,461,283 | 28,647 | 37.4 | 735,314 | 661,056 | 1,396,370 |
| Suriname | 77,000 | 33,000 | 110,000 | 481 | 6.2 | 76,600 | 32,500 | 109,100 |
| Uruguay | 611,000 | 122,500 | 733,500 | 3,294 | 5.4 | 573,354 | 72,031 | 645,385 |
| Venezuela | 1,840,000 | 1,260,000 | 3,100,000 | 26,815 | 14.6 | 1,800,000 | 1,240,000 | 3,040,000 |
| **Total Central & S. America** | **38,321,634** | **13,744,202** | **52,065,836** | **431,367** | **11.3** | **35,812,925** | **13,167,339** | **48,980,264** |
| **AMERICA, North** | | | | | | | | |
| Canada | 19,876,990 | 915,274 | 20,792,264 | 33,487 | 1.7 | 19,612,930 | 907,166 | 20,520,096 |
| Mexico | 20,523,704 | 9,179,909 | 29,703,613 | 111,212 | 5.4 | 19,420,942 | 8,786,888 | 28,207,830 |
| United States | 132,424,003 | 116,035,659 | 248,459,662 | 307,007 | 2.3 | 135,882,003 | 114,356,659 | 250,238,662 |
| **Total North America** | **172,824,697** | **126,130,842** | **298,955,539** | **451,706** | **2.6** | **174,915,875** | **124,050,713** | **298,966,588** |
| **ASIA, Far East** | | | | | | | | |
| Afghanistan | 558,495 | 221,940 | 780,435 | 28,396 | 50.8 | 517,601 | 193,495 | 711,096 |
| Bangladesh | 40,000 | 73,500 | 113,500 | 153,700 | 3,842.5 | 39,750 | 73,000 | 112,750 |
| Brunei | 88,500 | 20,000 | 108,500 | 388 | 4.4 | 88,000 | 19,500 | 107,500 |

# Total Vehicle Registrations by Country

## VEHICLES IN OPERATION BY COUNTRY — continued

| Country | 2009 | | | Population (000) | Persons Per Car | 2008 | | |
|---|---|---|---|---|---|---|---|---|
| | Cars | Commercial Vehicles | Total | | | Cars | Commercial Vehicles | Total |
| Burma | 9,250 | 18,750 | 28,000 | 52,826 | 5,710.9 | 9,000 | 18,500 | 27,500 |
| China, Peoples Republic of | 25,300,500 | 35,875,000 | 61,175,500 | 1,323,592 | 52.3 | 18,270,000 | 28,750,000 | 47,020,000 |
| Hong Kong | 394,000 | 151,000 | 545,000 | 7,055 | 17.9 | 383,000 | 153,000 | 536,000 |
| India | 10,400,000 | 6,250,000 | 16,650,000 | 1,156,898 | 111.2 | 9,400,000 | 5,610,000 | 15,010,000 |
| Indonesia | 10,364,125 | 7,917,312 | 18,281,437 | 240,272 | 23.2 | 9,859,926 | 7,729,844 | 17,589,770 |
| Japan | 58,019,853 | 15,789,222 | 73,809,075 | 127,079 | 2.2 | 57,864,972 | 16,127,183 | 73,992,155 |
| Korea, South | 13,023,803 | 4,301,407 | 17,325,210 | 48,509 | 3.7 | 12,483,809 | 4,310,478 | 16,794,287 |
| Malaysia | 8,506,080 | 1,098,531 | 9,604,611 | 27,818 | 3.3 | 7,966,525 | 1,063,767 | 9,030,292 |
| Pakistan | 1,657,860 | 512,570 | 2,170,430 | 181,457 | 109.5 | 1,549,854 | 494,372 | 2,044,226 |
| Philippines | 780,252 | 2,210,473 | 2,990,725 | 97,977 | 125.6 | 761,919 | 2,119,680 | 2,881,599 |
| Singapore | 566,608 | 198,932 | 765,540 | 4,658 | 8.2 | 540,455 | 195,716 | 736,171 |
| Sri Lanka | 353,000 | 409,000 | 762,000 | 20,879 | 59.1 | 352,000 | 407,500 | 759,500 |
| Taiwan | 5,704,312 | 1,014,434 | 6,718,746 | 22,974 | 4.0 | 5,530,314 | 1,001,010 | 6,531,324 |
| Thailand | 4,462,231 | 5,721,804 | 10,184,035 | 65,940 | 14.8 | 4,188,292 | 5,550,657 | 9,738,949 |
| Vietnam | 160,100 | 178,500 | 338,600 | 88,577 | 553.3 | 158,500 | 176,000 | 334,500 |
| **Total Far East** | **140,388,969** | **81,962,375** | **222,351,344** | **3,648,993** | **26.0** | **129,963,917** | **73,993,702** | **203,957,619** |
| **ASIA, Middle East** | | | | | | | | |
| Azerbaijan | 759,203 | 147,363 | 906,566 | 8,239 | 10.9 | 700,080 | 142,428 | 842,508 |
| Bahrain | 317,000 | 141,000 | 458,000 | 1,144 | 3.6 | 312,000 | 138,000 | 450,000 |
| Cyprus | 447,605 | 162,357 | 609,962 | 1,085 | 2.4 | 443,517 | 160,000 | 603,517 |
| Iran | 3,065,000 | 794,000 | 3,859,000 | 75,968 | 24.8 | 3,010,000 | 784,000 | 3,794,000 |
| Iraq | 878,000 | 156,500 | 1,034,500 | 28,946 | 33.0 | 871,700 | 155,300 | 1,027,000 |
| Israel | 1,946,749 | 402,420 | 2,349,169 | 7,234 | 3.7 | 1,875,765 | 411,396 | 2,287,161 |
| Jordan | 391,000 | 136,000 | 527,000 | 6,269 | 16.0 | 378,900 | 134,000 | 512,900 |
| Kuwait | 925,000 | 237,000 | 1,162,000 | 2,489 | 2.7 | 909,300 | 233,000 | 1,142,300 |
| Lebanon | 445,000 | 94,000 | 539,000 | 4,099 | 9.2 | 440,000 | 92,000 | 532,000 |
| Oman | 309,500 | 125,500 | 435,000 | 2,910 | 9.4 | 305,500 | 124,000 | 429,500 |
| Qatar | 187,500 | 97,000 | 284,500 | 833 | 4.4 | 185,000 | 95,000 | 280,000 |
| Saudi Arabia | 3,400,000 | 1,920,000 | 5,320,000 | 25,329 | 7.4 | 3,340,000 | 1,890,000 | 5,230,000 |
| Syria | 249,000 | 346,000 | 595,000 | 21,763 | 87.4 | 551,858 | 607,932 | 1,159,790 |
| Turkey | 7,093,964 | 3,517,339 | 10,611,303 | 76,806 | 10.8 | 6,796,629 | 3,393,706 | 10,190,335 |
| United Arab Emirates | 322,000 | 93,500 | 415,500 | 4,798 | 14.9 | 315,000 | 91,000 | 406,000 |
| Yemen | 302,000 | 341,000 | 643,000 | 22,858 | 75.7 | 299,500 | 338,000 | 637,500 |
| **Total Middle East** | **21,038,521** | **8,710,979** | **29,749,500** | **290,769** | **13.8** | **20,734,749** | **8,789,762** | **29,524,511** |
| **EUROPE, East** | | | | | | | | |
| Belarus | 2,339,800 | 132,863 | 2,472,663 | 9,649 | 4.1 | 2,121,300 | 118,350 | 2,239,650 |
| Bulgaria | 2,900,000 | 372,000 | 3,272,000 | 7,205 | 2.5 | 2,875,000 | 368,500 | 3,243,500 |
| Croatia | 1,532,549 | 169,832 | 1,702,381 | 4,489 | 2.9 | 1,535,280 | 185,400 | 1,720,680 |
| Czech Republic | 4,435,052 | 704,863 | 5,139,915 | 10,212 | 2.3 | 4,423,370 | 711,300 | 5,134,670 |
| Hungary | 3,013,719 | 437,136 | 3,450,855 | 10,007 | 3.3 | 3,055,427 | 442,440 | 3,497,867 |
| Poland | 16,494,650 | 2,892,182 | 19,386,832 | 38,483 | 2.3 | 16,079,533 | 2,802,098 | 18,881,631 |
| Romania | 4,245,000 | 703,000 | 4,948,000 | 22,012 | 5.2 | 4,027,000 | 687,000 | 4,714,000 |

# Total Vehicle Registrations by Country

## VEHICLES IN OPERATION BY COUNTRY — continued

| Country | 2009 | | | | | 2008 | | |
| --- | --- | --- | --- | --- | --- | --- | --- | --- |
| | Cars | Commercial Vehicles | Total | Population (000) | Persons Per Car | Cars | Commercial Vehicles | Total |
| Russian Federation | 33,186,915 | 6,322,625 | 39,509,540 | 140,041 | 4.2 | 32,020,998 | 6,242,845 | 38,263,843 |
| Serbia & Montenegro | 1,650,477 | 180,660 | 1,831,137 | 7,379 | 4.5 | 1,499,800 | 172,000 | 1,671,800 |
| Slovak Republic | 1,615,855 | 297,675 | 1,913,530 | 5,463 | 3.4 | 1,599,851 | 291,033 | 1,890,884 |
| Slovenia | 1,065,927 | 77,143 | 1,143,070 | 2,006 | 1.9 | 1,051,836 | 76,616 | 1,128,452 |
| Ukraine | 7,684,500 | 1,538,000 | 9,222,500 | 45,700 | 5.9 | 7,526,900 | 1,523,981 | 9,050,881 |
| **Total Eastern Europe** | **80,164,444** | **13,827,979** | **93,992,423** | **302,646** | **3.8** | **77,816,295** | **13,621,563** | **91,437,858** |
| **EUROPE, West** | | | | | | | | |
| Austria | 4,359,944 | 397,571 | 4,757,515 | 8,210 | 1.9 | 4,284,919 | 390,706 | 4,675,625 |
| Belgium | 5,160,257 | 792,706 | 5,952,963 | 10,414 | 2.0 | 5,086,756 | 777,960 | 5,864,716 |
| Denmark | 2,120,322 | 522,370 | 2,642,692 | 5,501 | 2.6 | 2,099,090 | 545,855 | 2,644,945 |
| Finland | 2,758,291 | 452,574 | 3,210,865 | 5,250 | 1.9 | 2,682,831 | 432,611 | 3,115,442 |
| France | 31,050,000 | 6,388,000 | 37,438,000 | 64,420 | 2.1 | 30,850,000 | 6,362,000 | 37,212,000 |
| Germany | 41,737,627 | 2,895,281 | 44,632,908 | 81,838 | 2.0 | 41,321,171 | 2,859,348 | 44,180,519 |
| Greece | 5,131,960 | 1,329,754 | 6,461,714 | 10,737 | 2.1 | 5,023,944 | 1,316,711 | 6,340,655 |
| Iceland | 207,226 | 32,811 | 240,037 | 307 | 1.5 | 209,740 | 33,774 | 243,514 |
| Ireland | 1,888,000 | 396,000 | 2,284,000 | 4,580 | 2.4 | 1,873,000 | 392,000 | 2,265,000 |
| Italy | 36,477,025 | 4,845,878 | 41,322,903 | 60,462 | 1.7 | 36,105,183 | 4,789,308 | 40,894,491 |
| Latvia | 904,308 | 130,258 | 1,034,566 | 2,232 | 2.5 | 932,828 | 140,348 | 1,073,176 |
| Luxembourg | 331,513 | 39,138 | 370,651 | 492 | 1.5 | 329,038 | 38,468 | 367,506 |
| Malta | 227,264 | 48,646 | 275,910 | 405 | 1.8 | 222,189 | 49,217 | 271,406 |
| Netherlands | 7,800,123 | 1,120,094 | 8,920,217 | 16,716 | 2.1 | 7,777,751 | 1,130,015 | 8,907,766 |
| Norway | 2,241,119 | 559,920 | 2,801,039 | 4,661 | 2.1 | 2,196,107 | 547,331 | 2,743,438 |
| Portugal | 4,457,000 | 1,352,500 | 5,809,500 | 10,708 | 2.4 | 4,408,000 | 1,349,400 | 5,757,400 |
| Spain | 22,199,602 | 5,432,996 | 27,632,598 | 46,295 | 2.1 | 22,145,364 | 5,467,781 | 27,613,145 |
| Sweden | 4,300,752 | 527,983 | 4,828,735 | 9,060 | 2.1 | 4,278,995 | 523,673 | 4,802,668 |
| Switzerland | 4,009,602 | 378,483 | 4,388,085 | 7,604 | 1.9 | 3,989,811 | 374,768 | 4,364,579 |
| United Kingdom | 31,035,791 | 4,181,519 | 35,217,310 | 61,997 | 2.0 | 31,252,476 | 4,285,206 | 35,537,682 |
| **Total Western Europe** | **208,397,726** | **31,824,482** | **240,222,208** | **411,888** | **2.0** | **207,069,193** | **31,806,480** | **238,875,673** |
| **PACIFIC** | | | | | | | | |
| Australia | 12,023,098 | 2,980,713 | 15,003,811 | 21,263 | 1.8 | 11,803,536 | 2,880,647 | 14,684,183 |
| Fiji | 87,249 | 57,404 | 144,653 | 868 | 9.9 | 85,186 | 56,593 | 141,779 |
| French Polynesia | 44,600 | 23,750 | 68,350 | 287 | 6.4 | 44,200 | 23,500 | 67,700 |
| Guam | 140,100 | 54,650 | 194,750 | 178 | 1.3 | 139,000 | 54,000 | 193,000 |
| New Caledonia | 65,000 | 29,300 | 94,300 | 248 | 3.8 | 64,500 | 29,000 | 93,500 |
| New Zealand | 2,574,589 | 498,217 | 3,072,806 | 4,213 | 1.6 | 2,584,337 | 500,748 | 3,085,085 |
| Papua New Guinea | 38,000 | 92,500 | 130,500 | 5,941 | 156.3 | 37,800 | 92,000 | 129,800 |
| Samoa (American) | 7,300 | 7,550 | 14,850 | 66 | 9.0 | 7,250 | 7,500 | 14,750 |
| Vanuatu | 9,100 | 5,050 | 14,150 | 219 | 24.1 | 9,000 | 5,000 | 14,000 |
| **Total Pacific** | **14,989,036** | **3,749,134** | **18,738,170** | **33,283** | **2.2** | **14,774,809** | **3,648,988** | **18,423,797** |
| **WORLD TOTAL** | **695,727,701** | **290,399,894** | **986,127,595** | **6,533,251** | **9.4** | **680,004,108** | **279,250,244** | **959,254,352** |

SOURCE: International Road Federation, VDA, World Bank and Ward's estimates.

# U.S. Vehicle Exports by Country of Destination and Vehicle Type

## U.S. EXPORTS BY COUNTRY OF DESTINATION AND VEHICLE TYPE, 2010

| COUNTRY | Cars Units | Cars Value ($000) | Trucks Units | Trucks Value ($000) | Buses Units | Buses Value ($000) | Total Units | Total Value ($000) |
|---|---|---|---|---|---|---|---|---|
| Afghanistan | 390 | 8,374 | 3,034 | 540,558 | 17 | 311 | 3,441 | 549,243 |
| Algeria | 101 | 1,592 | 134 | 7,900 | — | — | 235 | 9,492 |
| Angola | 583 | 14,476 | 153 | 6,547 | 26 | 680 | 762 | 21,703 |
| Anguilla | 39 | 846 | 1 | 24 | — | — | 40 | 870 |
| Antigua Barbuda | 17 | 371 | 18 | 752 | 1 | 27 | 36 | 1,150 |
| Argentina | 2,322 | 57,261 | 131 | 4,818 | — | — | 2,453 | 62,079 |
| Armenia | 2 | 45 | — | — | — | — | 2 | 45 |
| Aruba | 162 | 3,373 | 37 | 1,804 | — | — | 199 | 5,177 |
| Australia | 16,217 | 461,039 | 1,914 | 161,683 | 21 | 501 | 18,152 | 623,223 |
| Austria | 415 | 9,666 | 4 | 404 | 1 | 93 | 420 | 10,163 |
| Azerbaijan | 70 | 1,578 | — | — | — | — | 70 | 1,578 |
| Bahamas | 595 | 11,760 | 388 | 6,274 | 8 | 227 | 991 | 18,261 |
| Bahrain | 4,804 | 112,597 | 216 | 6,785 | 1 | 31 | 5,021 | 119,413 |
| Barbados | 61 | 1,118 | 18 | 984 | 2 | 53 | 81 | 2,155 |
| Belarus | 58 | 1,108 | 2 | 24 | — | — | 60 | 1,132 |
| Belgium | 1,681 | 38,398 | 125 | 7,121 | 34 | 840 | 1,840 | 46,359 |
| Belize | 66 | 1,425 | 221 | 7,451 | — | — | 287 | 8,876 |
| Benin | 3,477 | 45,097 | 69 | 1,391 | 2 | 91 | 3,548 | 46,579 |
| Bermuda | 49 | 1,008 | 17 | 1,989 | — | — | 66 | 2,997 |
| Bolivia | 263 | 5,896 | 270 | 7,156 | 19 | 507 | 552 | 13,559 |
| Bosnia-Hercegovina | 4 | 65 | — | — | — | — | 4 | 65 |
| Brazil | 7,580 | 167,609 | 459 | 15,804 | 7 | 282 | 8,046 | 183,695 |
| British Virgin Islands | 319 | 5,603 | 32 | 1,521 | — | — | 351 | 7,124 |
| Bulgaria | 22 | 567 | — | — | 1 | 11 | 23 | 578 |
| Cambodia | 50 | 1,263 | 52 | 2,025 | — | — | 102 | 3,288 |
| Cameroon | 73 | 1,260 | 13 | 492 | 2 | 57 | 88 | 1,809 |
| Canada | 444,254 | 10,201,319 | 320,476 | 9,953,032 | 15,662 | 601,390 | 780,392 | 20,755,741 |
| Cayman Islands | 289 | 6,122 | 66 | 2,993 | — | — | 355 | 9,115 |
| Chile | 11,207 | 238,561 | 6,871 | 254,480 | 25 | 671 | 18,103 | 493,712 |
| China | 89,451 | 2,608,402 | 547 | 66,308 | 58 | 2,288 | 90,056 | 2,676,998 |
| Colombia | 3,858 | 78,062 | 1,323 | 75,297 | 9 | 386 | 5,190 | 153,745 |
| Congo (ROC) | 82 | 1,693 | 58 | 1,291 | 2 | 50 | 142 | 3,034 |
| Costa Rica | 1,039 | 26,538 | 878 | 16,804 | 41 | 811 | 1,958 | 44,153 |
| Cote d'Ivoire | 133 | 2,463 | 13 | 242 | 1 | 15 | 147 | 2,720 |
| Croatia | 45 | 828 | 3 | 259 | — | — | 48 | 1,087 |
| Cyprus | 1 | 43 | 2 | 213 | — | — | 3 | 256 |
| Czech Republic | 163 | 3,988 | 1 | 28 | — | — | 164 | 4,016 |
| Denmark | 34 | 697 | 213 | 5,801 | 1 | 40 | 248 | 6,538 |
| Djibouti | 8 | 191 | 10 | 846 | — | — | 18 | 1,037 |
| Dominica Islands | 19 | 430 | 13 | 390 | — | — | 32 | 820 |
| Dominican Republic | 7,461 | 133,569 | 599 | 17,575 | 95 | 2,031 | 8,155 | 153,175 |
| Ecuador | 3,604 | 98,261 | 4,277 | 104,428 | 14 | 410 | 7,895 | 203,099 |

# U.S. Vehicle Exports by Country of Destination and Vehicle Type

## U.S. EXPORTS BY COUNTRY OF DESTINATION AND VEHICLE TYPE, 2010 — continued

| | Cars | | Trucks | | Buses | | Total | |
|---|---|---|---|---|---|---|---|---|
| COUNTRY | Units | Value ($000) | Units | Value ($000) | Units | Value ($000) | Units | Value ($000) |
| Egypt | 785 | 37,342 | 547 | 30,524 | 3 | 79 | 1,335 | 67,945 |
| El Salvador | 157 | 3,443 | 914 | 6,350 | 3 | 42 | 1,074 | 9,835 |
| Eq Guinea | 84 | 1,647 | 6 | 198 | 5 | 65 | 95 | 1,910 |
| Estonia | 33 | 580 | 114 | 2,903 | — | — | 147 | 3,483 |
| Ethiopia | 1 | 34 | 20 | 1,145 | 10 | 296 | 31 | 1,475 |
| Fed. States Micronesia | 2 | 46 | 7 | 271 | 16 | 360 | 25 | 677 |
| Finland | 439 | 13,572 | 104 | 3,236 | — | — | 543 | 16,808 |
| France | 1,718 | 38,442 | 33 | 3,027 | — | — | 1,751 | 41,469 |
| French Polynesia | 176 | 3,297 | 58 | 1,567 | — | — | 234 | 4,864 |
| Gabon | 95 | 2,235 | 19 | 1,165 | 23 | 571 | 137 | 3,971 |
| Gambia | 32 | 489 | 11 | 120 | — | — | 43 | 609 |
| Georgia | 1,289 | 22,556 | 55 | 3,638 | — | — | 1,344 | 26,194 |
| Germany | 96,734 | 3,569,078 | 1,263 | 61,926 | 32 | 814 | 98,029 | 3,631,818 |
| Ghana | 1,986 | 28,269 | 178 | 3,838 | 9 | 214 | 2,173 | 32,321 |
| Greece | 474 | 7,801 | 3 | 691 | 13 | 342 | 490 | 8,834 |
| Grenada | 12 | 262 | 6 | 165 | — | — | 18 | 427 |
| Guadeloupe | 3 | 76 | — | — | — | — | 3 | 76 |
| Guatemala | 1,167 | 30,242 | 2,687 | 24,253 | 3 | 55 | 3,857 | 54,550 |
| Guinea | 106 | 1,890 | 31 | 477 | 1 | 21 | 138 | 2,388 |
| Guyana | 68 | 1,210 | 68 | 1,461 | 4 | 73 | 140 | 2,744 |
| Haiti | 48 | 1,459 | 392 | 16,757 | 13 | 784 | 453 | 19,000 |
| Honduras | 509 | 13,202 | 1,155 | 15,515 | 4 | 66 | 1,668 | 28,783 |
| Hong Kong | 2,572 | 91,850 | 20 | 1,433 | 19 | 608 | 2,611 | 93,891 |
| Hungary | 4 | 172 | 18 | 810 | — | — | 22 | 982 |
| Iceland | 19 | 408 | 1 | 33 | 1 | 13 | 21 | 454 |
| India | 603 | 22,285 | 115 | 9,433 | — | — | 718 | 31,718 |
| Indonesia | 130 | 4,309 | 14 | 2,746 | — | — | 144 | 7,055 |
| Iraq | 1,046 | 21,577 | 335 | 57,230 | — | — | 1,381 | 78,807 |
| Ireland | 5 | 176 | 2 | 269 | — | — | 7 | 445 |
| Israel | 5,489 | 130,538 | 932 | 37,916 | 33 | 1,021 | 6,454 | 169,475 |
| Italy | 2,802 | 61,485 | 27 | 4,920 | 3 | 72 | 2,832 | 66,477 |
| Jamaica | 175 | 5,461 | 61 | 1,613 | — | — | 236 | 7,074 |
| Japan | 6,674 | 175,799 | 651 | 28,167 | 13 | 356 | 7,338 | 204,322 |
| Jordan | 1,792 | 33,529 | 263 | 10,403 | 12 | 285 | 2,067 | 44,217 |
| Kazakhstan | 106 | 3,601 | 52 | 8,769 | — | — | 158 | 12,370 |
| Kenya | 31 | 481 | 46 | 1,723 | — | — | 77 | 2,204 |
| Korea | 12,247 | 283,828 | 1,094 | 32,182 | 116 | 3,043 | 13,457 | 319,053 |
| Kuwait | 19,402 | 478,034 | 3,815 | 76,681 | 39 | 1,198 | 23,256 | 555,913 |
| Laos | 14 | 309 | 1 | 13 | — | — | 15 | 322 |
| Latvia | 38 | 987 | 2 | 360 | — | — | 40 | 1,347 |
| Lebanon | 4,446 | 88,185 | 93 | 5,381 | — | — | 4,539 | 93,566 |
| Liberia | 110 | 1,726 | 6 | 116 | 8 | 232 | 124 | 2,074 |

# U.S. Vehicle Exports by Country of Destination and Vehicle Type

## U.S. EXPORTS BY COUNTRY OF DESTINATION AND VEHICLE TYPE, 2010 — continued

| COUNTRY | Cars Units | Cars Value ($000) | Trucks Units | Trucks Value ($000) | Buses Units | Buses Value ($000) | Total Units | Total Value ($000) |
|---|---|---|---|---|---|---|---|---|
| Libya | 1,906 | 25,035 | 127 | 11,543 | 1 | 13 | 2,034 | 36,591 |
| Lithuania | 30 | 713 | — | — | 1 | 54 | 31 | 767 |
| Luxembourg | 35 | 913 | 18 | 448 | — | — | 53 | 1,361 |
| Macao | 120 | 2,510 | — | — | 5 | 120 | 125 | 2,630 |
| Malawi | — | — | 17 | 317 | — | — | 17 | 317 |
| Malaysia | 10 | 176 | 18 | 9,739 | — | — | 28 | 9,915 |
| Mali | 7 | 114 | 9 | 313 | 3 | 68 | 19 | 495 |
| Malta & Gozo | 2 | 41 | — | — | — | — | 2 | 41 |
| Marshall Islands | — | — | 1 | 19 | 1 | 34 | 2 | 53 |
| Mexico | 116,459 | 2,404,116 | 16,001 | 387,878 | 1,380 | 37,450 | 133,840 | 2,829,444 |
| Monaco | 1 | 65 | — | — | — | — | 1 | 65 |
| Mongolia | 67 | 2,172 | 14 | 876 | 30 | 879 | 111 | 3,927 |
| Montserrat | 3 | 48 | — | — | — | — | 3 | 48 |
| Morocco | 360 | 8,252 | 627 | 41,905 | — | — | 987 | 50,157 |
| Mozambique | 1 | 60 | 1,032 | 16,977 | 1 | 15 | 1,034 | 17,052 |
| Namibia | 35 | 871 | 769 | 9,903 | 4 | 91 | 808 | 10,865 |
| Netherlands | 1,045 | 25,090 | 404 | 7,143 | 1 | 60 | 1,450 | 32,293 |
| Netherlands Antilles | 614 | 12,483 | 135 | 5,944 | 24 | 563 | 773 | 18,990 |
| New Zealand | 1,275 | 35,188 | 462 | 18,157 | — | — | 1,737 | 53,345 |
| Nicaragua | 169 | 3,808 | 224 | 2,634 | 6 | 107 | 399 | 6,549 |
| Niger | 7 | 121 | 15 | 305 | — | — | 22 | 426 |
| Nigeria | 5,704 | 97,149 | 5,429 | 105,213 | 241 | 4,197 | 11,374 | 206,559 |
| Norway | 133 | 4,110 | 23 | 926 | — | — | 156 | 5,036 |
| Oman | 7,112 | 178,046 | 371 | 38,633 | 2 | 64 | 7,485 | 216,743 |
| Pakistan | 424 | 5,159 | 42 | 14,415 | — | — | 466 | 19,574 |
| Panama | 2,346 | 62,327 | 1,120 | 37,390 | 96 | 1,892 | 3,562 | 101,609 |
| Paraguay | 603 | 15,455 | 32 | 1,746 | — | — | 635 | 17,201 |
| Peru | 4,372 | 91,424 | 679 | 55,449 | 5 | 113 | 5,056 | 146,986 |
| Philippines | 1,246 | 31,227 | 76 | 4,382 | 19 | 551 | 1,341 | 36,160 |
| Poland | 432 | 8,389 | 57 | 902 | 1 | 20 | 490 | 9,311 |
| Portugal | 635 | 14,669 | 2 | 419 | — | — | 637 | 15,088 |
| Qatar | 6,344 | 182,715 | 791 | 22,486 | 38 | 1,283 | 7,173 | 206,484 |
| Romania | 6 | 113 | 2 | 136 | — | — | 8 | 249 |
| Russia | 2,413 | 73,545 | 340 | 17,789 | 1 | 38 | 2,754 | 91,372 |
| Saudi Arabia | 85,033 | 2,333,365 | 6,704 | 179,520 | 133 | 3,750 | 91,870 | 2,516,635 |
| Senegal | 344 | 6,311 | 84 | 2,330 | — | — | 428 | 8,641 |
| Sierra Leone | 92 | 1,717 | 18 | 651 | 1 | 40 | 111 | 2,408 |
| Singapore | 156 | 4,783 | 254 | 18,349 | 12 | 301 | 422 | 23,433 |
| Slovak Republic | 16 | 512 | 7 | 249 | — | — | 23 | 761 |
| Slovenia | 7 | 192 | — | — | — | — | 7 | 192 |
| South Africa | 6,851 | 172,540 | 1,405 | 107,897 | 4 | 62 | 8,260 | 280,499 |
| Spain | 3,231 | 90,908 | 23 | 1,361 | 12 | 314 | 3,266 | 92,583 |
| St. Kitts-Nevis | 34 | 599 | 9 | 258 | 1 | 19 | 44 | 876 |
| St. Lucia Islands | 15 | 221 | 8 | 497 | — | — | 23 | 718 |

# U.S. Vehicle Exports by Country of Destination and Vehicle Type

## U.S. EXPORTS BY COUNTRY OF DESTINATION AND VEHICLE TYPE, 2010 — continued

| | Cars | | Trucks | | Buses | | Total | |
|---|---|---|---|---|---|---|---|---|
| COUNTRY | Units | Value ($000) | Units | Value ($000) | Units | Value ($000) | Units | Value ($000) |
| St. Vincent & Grenadines | 19 | 370 | 3 | 88 | — | — | 22 | 458 |
| Suriname | 47 | 1,200 | 19 | 727 | 3 | 74 | 69 | 2,001 |
| Sweden | 903 | 17,525 | 61 | 2,876 | 8 | 200 | 972 | 20,601 |
| Switzerland | 962 | 24,035 | 604 | 17,470 | — | — | 1,566 | 41,505 |
| Taiwan | 4,080 | 65,768 | 56 | 2,765 | 9 | 256 | 4,145 | 68,789 |
| Tanzania | 8 | 158 | 1 | 15 | 1 | 15 | 10 | 188 |
| Thailand | 172 | 5,058 | 42 | 2,531 | — | — | 214 | 7,589 |
| Togo | 527 | 7,145 | 36 | 1,076 | 4 | 50 | 567 | 8,271 |
| Trinidad & Tobago | 47 | 1,668 | 150 | 10,011 | — | — | 197 | 11,679 |
| Tunisia | 14 | 385 | — | — | 1 | 30 | 15 | 415 |
| Turkey | 798 | 18,195 | 134 | 11,158 | 1 | 73 | 933 | 29,426 |
| Turks & Caicos Islands | 126 | 2,392 | 5 | 125 | — | — | 131 | 2,517 |
| Uganda | 3 | 92 | 1 | 14 | — | — | 4 | 106 |
| Ukraine | 126 | 3,764 | 19 | 2,250 | — | — | 145 | 6,014 |
| United Arab Emirates | 34,254 | 903,146 | 2,818 | 103,987 | 239 | 6,462 | 37,311 | 1,013,595 |
| United Kingdom | 21,238 | 789,036 | 355 | 30,144 | 22 | 522 | 21,615 | 819,702 |
| Uruguay | 164 | 4,354 | 36 | 884 | — | — | 200 | 5,238 |
| Uzbekistan | 13 | 283 | 31 | 1,953 | — | — | 44 | 2,236 |
| Venezuela | 538 | 13,745 | 905 | 46,538 | 11 | 387 | 1,454 | 60,670 |
| Vietnam | 1,224 | 43,316 | 935 | 25,684 | 1 | 40 | 2,160 | 69,040 |
| Yemen | 894 | 15,563 | 26 | 1,557 | — | — | 920 | 17,120 |
| Zambia | 6 | 229 | 65 | 943 | — | — | 71 | 1,172 |
| Zimbabwe | 19 | 603 | 207 | 3,290 | 1 | 25 | 227 | 3,918 |
| Other | 413 | 8,836 | 368 | 20,145 | 34 | 2,839 | 815 | 31,820 |
| **Total** | **1,080,981** | **27,360,592** | **402,103** | **13,154,249** | **18,791** | **685,484** | **1,501,875** | **41,200,325** |

SOURCE: Compiled from official statistics of the U.S. Department of Commerce.

## U.S. EXPORTS OF CARS BY COUNTRY OF DESTINATION

| Year | Canada | France | Germany | Japan | Kuwait | Mexico | Saudi Arabia | Taiwan | Other Countries | Total Exports |
|---|---|---|---|---|---|---|---|---|---|---|
| 2010 | 780,392 | 1,751 | 98,029 | 7,338 | 23,256 | 133,840 | 91,870 | 4,145 | 361,254 | 1,501,875 |
| 2009 | 620,735 | 774 | 112,364 | 6,370 | 15,095 | 104,766 | 44,266 | 501 | 202,107 | 1,106,978 |
| 2008 | 1,006,832 | 5,281 | 182,336 | 15,297 | 27,344 | 233,152 | 88,310 | 452 | 407,168 | 1,966,172 |
| 2007 | 969,484 | 11,841 | 173,863 | 18,683 | 25,497 | 307,509 | 101,187 | 1,166 | 786,337 | 2,395,567 |
| 2006 | 905,284 | 5,757 | 145,997 | 17,889 | 26,929 | 304,580 | 100,556 | 1,506 | 546,194 | 2,054,692 |
| 2005 | 892,368 | 3,154 | 120,585 | 26,285 | 38,986 | 348,980 | 127,836 | 9,287 | 496,718 | 2,064,199 |
| 2004 | 851,630 | 3,456 | 129,931 | 27,044 | 26,372 | 314,308 | 79,928 | 3,734 | 357,242 | 1,793,645 |
| 2003 | 851,034 | 2,213 | 131,186 | 25,734 | 22,654 | 266,099 | 49,832 | 3,151 | 262,036 | 1,613,939 |
| 2002 | 938,455 | 1,669 | 97,433 | 25,619 | 16,893 | 301,008 | 58,099 | 3,079 | 216,267 | 1,658,522 |
| 2001 | 822,280 | 5,958 | 77,628 | 29,159 | 8,384 | 266,534 | 36,755 | 4,742 | 210,898 | 1,462,338 |
| 2000 | 844,977 | 3,166 | 49,635 | 34,809 | 4,432 | 214,886 | 14,762 | 11,126 | 120,382 | 1,298,175 |
| 1999 | 817,527 | 3,307 | 43,210 | 40,670 | 2,789 | 140,117 | 9,648 | 8,398 | 153,511 | 1,219,177 |
| 1998 | 772,766 | 3,174 | 46,618 | 50,202 | 4,750 | 127,488 | 19,098 | 9,893 | 213,825 | 1,247,814 |
| 1997 | 921,174 | 2,986 | 62,604 | 81,961 | 5,389 | 152,114 | 20,316 | 25,510 | 318,939 | 1,590,993 |
| 1996 | 693,429 | 4,312 | 65,997 | 119,959 | 11,578 | 78,627 | 28,735 | 35,506 | 251,412 | 1,289,555 |

NOTE: Data include used vehicles prior to 2008.
SOURCE: Compiled from official statistics of the U.S. Department of Commerce.

# U.S. Vehicle Imports by Country of Origin and Vehicle Type

## U.S. IMPORTS BY COUNTRY OF ORIGIN AND VEHICLE TYPE, 2010

| Country of Origin | Cars Units | Cars Value ($000) | Trucks Units | Trucks Value ($000) | Buses Units | Buses Value ($000) | Total Units | Total Value ($000) |
|---|---|---|---|---|---|---|---|---|
| Australia | 79 | 3,494 | 40 | 1,549 | — | — | 119 | 5,044 |
| Austria | 8,373 | 286,728 | — | — | 4 | 16 | 8,377 | 286,744 |
| Belgium | 22,505 | 558,837 | 2 | 123 | 194 | 82,210 | 22,701 | 641,169 |
| Brazil | 219 | 3,698 | 398 | 10,921 | 18 | 1,824 | 635 | 16,444 |
| Canada | 1,737,543 | 35,740,295 | 11,652 | 673,723 | 1,410 | 272,635 | 1,750,605 | 36,686,653 |
| China | 67,410 | 38,286 | 424 | 1,733 | 32 | 3,530 | 67,866 | 43,550 |
| Finland | 2,529 | 109,260 | 14 | 3,876 | — | — | 2,543 | 113,136 |
| France | 2,928 | 12,690 | 9 | 2,899 | — | — | 2,937 | 15,589 |
| Germany | 624,913 | 18,234,962 | 1,454 | 43,431 | 69 | 22,568 | 626,436 | 18,300,961 |
| Hungary | 1,438 | 46,041 | — | — | 17 | 2,076 | 1,455 | 48,117 |
| Italy | 4,065 | 578,775 | 86 | 3,386 | — | — | 4,151 | 582,161 |
| Japan | 2,433,340 | 32,735,358 | 12,848 | 367,608 | 10 | 21,430 | 2,446,198 | 33,124,395 |
| Korea, South | 800,474 | 6,938,041 | 5 | 716 | — | — | 800,479 | 6,938,757 |
| Mexico | 890,100 | 14,342,677 | 420,559 | 13,243,237 | 210 | 36,418 | 1,310,869 | 27,622,331 |
| Netherlands | 8 | 494 | 6 | 827 | 2 | 9 | 16 | 1,330 |
| Slovak Republic | 13,076 | 500,286 | — | — | — | — | 13,076 | 500,286 |
| South Africa | 56,405 | 1,529,411 | — | — | — | — | 56,405 | 1,529,411 |
| Spain | 100 | 1,899 | 64 | 1,532 | — | — | 164 | 3,431 |
| Sweden | 38,150 | 1,065,967 | 2 | 235 | — | — | 38,152 | 1,066,202 |
| Taiwan | 84 | 381 | — | — | 1 | 14 | 85 | 395 |
| United Kingdom | 96,738 | 3,396,843 | 149 | 1,481 | 26 | 1,830 | 96,913 | 3,400,154 |
| Other | 27,746 | 468,520 | 200 | 12,546 | 53 | 15,478 | 27,999 | 496,544 |
| **Total** | **6,828,223** | **116,592,946** | **447,912** | **14,369,821** | **2,046** | **460,037** | **7,278,181** | **131,422,804** |

SOURCE: Compiled from official statistics of the U.S. Department of Commerce.

## U.S. IMPORTS OF NEW ASSEMBLED CARS BY COUNTRY OF ORIGIN

| Year | Canada | Germany | Japan | South Korea | Mexico | Sweden | United Kingdom | Other | Total Imports |
|---|---|---|---|---|---|---|---|---|---|
| 2010 | 1,737,543 | 624,913 | 2,433,340 | 800,474 | 890,100 | 38,150 | 96,738 | 206,965 | 6,828,223 |
| 2009 | 1,161,188 | 526,570 | 2,029,754 | 730,848 | 641,089 | 26,691 | 77,973 | 172,290 | 5,366,403 |
| 2008 | 1,598,115 | 679,624 | 3,119,746 | 800,447 | 912,841 | 59,172 | 111,880 | 254,744 | 7,536,569 |
| 2007 | 1,907,775 | 753,898 | 3,504,443 | 891,237 | 875,417 | 91,788 | 112,399 | 302,423 | 8,439,380 |
| 2006 | 1,927,382 | 695,364 | 3,693,385 | 888,256 | 945,726 | 80,380 | 147,403 | 254,459 | 8,632,355 |
| 2005 | 1,955,072 | 544,971 | 1,628,313 | 730,431 | 692,659 | 92,617 | 184,138 | 144,056 | 5,972,257 |
| 2004 | 2,004,890 | 545,634 | 1,538,805 | 860,057 | 650,400 | 97,992 | 185,059 | 190,114 | 6,072,951 |
| 2003 | 1,751,958 | 560,381 | 1,575,599 | 690,885 | 677,771 | 119,833 | 205,937 | 174,990 | 5,757,354 |
| 2002 | 1,815,323 | 571,164 | 1,827,434 | 623,810 | 838,829 | 89,347 | 156,258 | 157,992 | 6,080,157 |
| 2001 | 1,809,236 | 492,177 | 1,616,950 | 631,945 | 853,264 | 89,412 | 81,261 | 178,380 | 5,752,625 |
| 2000 | 2,076,181 | 489,086 | 1,661,906 | 560,728 | 927,574 | 85,713 | 79,639 | 125,007 | 6,005,834 |
| 1999 | 2,125,876 | 456,246 | 1,560,857 | 369,264 | 637,486 | 82,808 | 67,689 | 99,590 | 5,399,816 |
| 1995 | 1,678,276 | 206,892 | 1,387,193 | 216,618 | 463,305 | 82,634 | 42,176 | 36,823 | 4,113,917 |
| 1990 | 1,220,221 | 245,286 | 1,867,794 | 201,475 | 215,986 | 93,084 | 27,271 | 73,485 | 3,944,602 |
| 1985 | 1,144,805 | 473,110 | 2,527,467 | — | 13,647 | 142,640 | 24,474 | 71,536 | 4,397,679 |
| 1980 | 594,770 | 338,711 | 1,991,502 | — | — | 61,496 | 32,517 | 97,451 | 3,116,448 |
| 1975 | 733,766 | 370,012 | 695,573 | — | — | 51,993 | 67,106 | 156,203 | 2,074,653 |
| 1970 | 692,783 | 674,945 | 381,338 | — | — | 57,844 | 76,257 | 130,253 | 2,013,420 |
| 1965 | 33,378 | 376,950 | 25,538 | — | — | 26,010 | 66,565 | 35,232 | 563,673 |

NOTE: Figures include imports into Puerto Rico and do not include automobiles assembled in U.S. foreign trade zones.
SOURCE: Compiled from official statistics of the U.S. Department of Commerce.

# World Trade in Vehicles

## EXPORTS AND IMPORTS OF VEHICLES FOR SELECTED COUNTRIES, 2010

| Country | Exports Cars | Commercial Vehicles | Total | Imports Cars | Commercial Vehicles | Total |
|---|---|---|---|---|---|---|
| Argentina | 320,609 | 127,344 | 447,953 | 28,300 | 18,775 | 47,075 |
| Austria | 85,642 | 18,268 | 103,910 | 314,509 | 44,456 | 358,965 |
| Belgium | 480,684 | 24,200 | 504,884 | NA | NA | NA |
| Brazil | 374,705 | 127,855 | 502,560 | 460,448 | 219,670 | 680,118 |
| Czech Republic | 1,005,500 | 5,626 | 1,011,126 | NA | NA | NA |
| Finland | — | — | — | 111,956 | 14,428 | 126,384 |
| France | 4,305,065 | 480,430 | 4,785,495 | 1,024,984 | 166,535 | 1,191,519 |
| Germany | 4,238,759 | 242,147 | 4,480,906 | 1,590,977 | 170,728 | 1,761,705 |
| Italy | 231,557 | 205,120 | 436,677 | 1,365,542 | 89,245 | 1,454,787 |
| Japan | 3,859,497 | 511,269 | 4,370,766 | 213,283 | 11,800 | 225,083 |
| Korea, South | 2,610,949 | 161,158 | 2,772,107 | 92,373 | 4,161 | 96,534 |
| Mexico | 1,176,502 | 745,669 | 1,922,171 | 228,516 | 223,655 | 452,171 |
| Portugal | 113,113 | 41,478 | 154,591 | NA | NA | NA |
| Romania | 289,855 | 24,806 | 314,661 | 71,928 | 10,711 | 82,639 |
| Spain | 1,658,341 | 421,441 | 2,079,782 | NA | NA | NA |
| Switzerland | — | — | — | 294,239 | 30,540 | 324,779 |
| Turkey | 439,999 | 314,470 | 754,469 | 354,150 | 111,258 | 465,408 |
| United Kingdom | 961,420 | 85,547 | 1,046,967 | NA | NA | NA |
| United States | 1,080,981 | 420,894 | 1,501,875 | 6,828,223 | 449,958 | 7,278,181 |
| Total | 23,233,178 | 3,957,722 | 27,190,900 | 14,406,313 | 2,097,019 | 16,503,332 |

NA - Not available.
SOURCE: Compiled by *Ward's* Automotive Group from various sources.

## WORLD VEHICLE EXPORTS

### Vehicle Exports by Country of Origin (In Thousands)

| Year | World Total[1] | Belgium | Canada | France | Germany | Italy | Japan | Sweden | United Kingdom | United States |
|---|---|---|---|---|---|---|---|---|---|---|
| 2010 | 27,190.9 | 504.9 | NA | 4,785.5 | 4,480.9 | 436.7 | 4,370.8 | NA | 1,047.0 | 1,501.9 |
| 2009 | 22,106.2 | 505.1 | NA | 3,885.5 | 3,583.7 | 382.6 | 3,616.2 | 367.7 | 838.6 | 1,107.0 |
| 2008 | 30,034.1 | 652.9 | NA | 4,322.2 | 4,500.8 | 561.0 | 6,727.1 | 558.9 | 1,256.4 | 1,966.2 |
| 2007 | 31,496.6 | 758.3 | NA | 4,696.7 | 4,664.3 | 650.5 | 6,550.2 | 750.8 | 1,317.0 | 2,395.6 |
| 2006 | 27,821.9 | 848.2 | NA | 3,126.0 | 4,182.7 | 596.0 | 5,966.7 | 643.9 | 1,242.2 | 2,054.7 |
| 2005 | 27,533.7 | 868.8 | NA | 4,319.4 | 4,080.6 | 497.6 | 5,053.1 | 628.4 | 1,316.5 | 2,064.2 |
| 2004 | 26,962.8 | 870.8 | NA | 4,268.9 | 3,924.1 | 595.7 | 4,957.7 | 648.4 | 1,307.4 | 1,793.6 |
| 2003 | 24,999.7 | 871.9 | NA | 4,045.6 | 3,935.9 | 703.6 | 4,756.3 | 565.3 | 1,246.7 | 1,613.9 |
| 2002 | 26,765.7 | 1,014.6 | 2,373.0 | 3,916.7 | 3,875.1 | 733.7 | 4,698.2 | 546.3 | 1,161.0 | 1,658.5 |
| 2001 | 25,577.3 | 1,140.8 | 2,023.3 | 3,734.7 | 3,915.8 | 813.7 | 4,166.2 | 575.4 | 991.8 | 1,462.3 |
| 2000 | 25,886.6 | 993.7 | 2,323.0 | 3,619.0 | 3,722.8 | 911.6 | 4,454.9 | 453.5 | 1,127.9 | 1,298.2 |
| 1999 | 24,241.3 | 983.0 | 2,331.8 | 3,255.5 | 3,675.8 | 797.8 | 4,408.9 | 221.0 | 1,213.5 | 1,219.2 |
| 1998 | 24,145.6 | 1,026.3 | 2,220.5 | 3,122.8 | 3,510.9 | 812.4 | 4,528.9 | 425.9 | 1,123.6 | 1,247.8 |
| 1997 | 23,620.8 | 1,050.7 | 2,220.5 | 2,822.5 | 3,035.6 | 739.3 | 4,553.2 | 416.6 | 1,065.3 | 1,591.0 |
| 1996 | 21,691.1 | 1,192.7 | 2,134.8 | 2,272.0 | 2,841.8 | 799.2 | 3,711.7 | 194.5 | 1,073.3 | 1,289.6 |
| 1995 | 20,142.7 | 1,218.8 | 1,908.6 | 2,261.2 | 2,639.5 | 806.5 | 3,790.8 | 206.3 | 837.0 | 1,243.6 |
| 1994 | 19,795.6 | 1,215.7 | 1,852.0 | 2,428.5 | 2,410.3 | 669.6 | 4,460.3 | 192.8 | 718.2 | 1,293.2 |

### Percent of World Vehicle Exports

| Year | | Belgium | Canada | France | Germany | Italy | Japan | Sweden | United Kingdom | United States |
|---|---|---|---|---|---|---|---|---|---|---|
| 2010 | 100.0 | 1.9 | NA | 17.6 | 16.5 | 1.6 | 16.1 | NA | 3.9 | 5.5 |
| 2009 | 100.0 | 2.3 | NA | 17.6 | 16.2 | 1.7 | 16.4 | 1.7 | 3.8 | 5.0 |
| 2008 | 100.0 | 2.2 | NA | 14.4 | 15.0 | 1.9 | 22.4 | 1.9 | 4.2 | 6.5 |
| 2007 | 100.0 | 2.4 | NA | 14.9 | 14.8 | 2.1 | 20.8 | 2.4 | 4.2 | 7.6 |
| 2006 | 100.0 | 3.0 | NA | 11.2 | 15.0 | 2.1 | 21.4 | 2.3 | 4.5 | 7.4 |
| 2005 | 100.0 | 3.2 | NA | 15.7 | 14.8 | 1.8 | 18.4 | 2.3 | 4.8 | 7.5 |
| 2004 | 100.0 | 3.2 | NA | 15.8 | 14.6 | 2.2 | 18.4 | 2.4 | 4.9 | 6.7 |
| 2003 | 100.0 | 3.5 | NA | 16.2 | 15.7 | 2.8 | 19.0 | 2.3 | 5.0 | 6.5 |
| 2002 | 100.0 | 3.8 | 8.9 | 14.6 | 14.5 | 2.7 | 17.6 | 2.0 | 4.3 | 6.2 |
| 2001 | 100.0 | 4.5 | 7.9 | 14.6 | 15.3 | 3.2 | 16.3 | 2.2 | 3.9 | 5.7 |
| 2000 | 100.0 | 3.8 | 9.0 | 14.0 | 14.4 | 3.5 | 17.2 | 1.8 | 4.4 | 5.0 |
| 1999 | 100.0 | 4.1 | 9.6 | 13.4 | 15.2 | 3.3 | 18.2 | 1.0 | 5.0 | 5.4 |
| 1998 | 100.0 | 4.3 | 9.2 | 12.9 | 14.5 | 3.4 | 18.8 | 1.8 | 4.7 | 5.2 |
| 1997 | 100.0 | 4.4 | 9.4 | 11.9 | 12.9 | 3.1 | 19.3 | 1.8 | 4.5 | 6.7 |
| 1996 | 100.0 | 5.5 | 9.8 | 10.5 | 13.1 | 3.7 | 17.1 | 0.9 | 4.9 | 5.9 |
| 1995 | 100.0 | 6.1 | 9.5 | 11.2 | 13.1 | 4.0 | 18.8 | 1.0 | 4.2 | 6.2 |
| 1994 | 100.0 | 6.1 | 9.4 | 12.3 | 12.2 | 3.4 | 22.5 | 1.0 | 3.6 | 6.5 |

(1) World total includes countries with vehicle exports not shown separately. NA - Not available.
SOURCE: Compiled by *Ward's* Data Group from various sources.

# MATERIAL CONSUMPTION

## Material Usage by the Automotive Industry

### AUTOMOTIVE CONSUMPTION OF MATERIALS BY TYPE

| Material | U.S. Total Consumption | Automotive Consumption | Automotive Percentage | Material | U.S. Total Consumption | Automotive Consumption | Automotive Percentage |
|---|---|---|---|---|---|---|---|
| **COPPER AND COPPER ALLOY (Thousands of Pounds)** | | | | **ALUMINUM (Thousands of Pounds)** | | | |
| 2010 | 5,460,000 | 688,622 | 12.6 | 2010 | 13,950,000 | 3,350,000 | 24.0 |
| 2009 | 4,565,000 | 578,440 | 12.7 | 2009 | 14,750,000 | 3,317,000 | 22.5 |
| 2008 | 5,855,000 | 637,000 | 10.9 | 2008 | 18,595,000 | 4,473,000 | 24.1 |
| 2007 | 6,617,000 | 737,000 | 11.1 | 2007 | 21,415,000 | 5,923,000 | 27.7 |
| 2006 | 7,279,000 | 778,000 | 10.7 | 2006 | 23,151,000 | 6,397,000 | 27.6 |
| 2005 | 7,786,000 | 794,400 | 10.2 | 2005 | 23,113,000 | 6,529,000 | 28.2 |
| 2004 | 7,755,900 | 835,700 | 10.8 | 2004 | 22,904,000 | 6,585,000 | 28.8 |
| **GRAY IRON (Tons)** | | | | **ALLOY STEEL (Tons)** | | | |
| 2010 | 2,700,000 | 411,000 | 15.2 | 2010 | 3,542,538 | 467,615 | 13.2 |
| 2009 | 3,357,000 | 594,000 | 17.7 | 2009 | 2,592,638 | 339,630 | 13.1 |
| 2008 | 4,158,000 | 793,000 | 19.1 | 2008 | 5,403,008 | 694,867 | 12.9 |
| 2007 | 4,440,000 | 915,000 | 20.6 | 2007 | 5,159,400 | 670,722 | 13.0 |
| 2006 | 4,650,000 | 1,065,000 | 22.9 | 2006 | 5,501,615 | 698,705 | 12.7 |
| 2005 | 4,700,000 | 1,010,000 | 21.5 | 2005 | 5,182,650 | 647,831 | 12.5 |
| 2004 | 4,850,000 | 1,085,000 | 22.4 | 2004 | 5,032,638 | 634,112 | 12.6 |
| **DUCTILE IRON (Tons)** | | | | **STAINLESS STEEL (Tons)** | | | |
| 2010 | 2,850,000 | 571,000 | 20.0 | 2010 | 1,661,971 | 358,985 | 21.6 |
| 2009 | 3,262,000 | 667,000 | 20.4 | 2009 | 1,620,125 | 340,225 | 21.0 |
| 2008 | 3,994,000 | 839,000 | 21.0 | 2008 | 1,876,668 | 401,320 | 21.4 |
| 2007 | 4,440,000 | 1,005,000 | 22.6 | 2007 | 2,275,823 | 455,164 | 20.0 |
| 2006 | 4,500,000 | 1,015,000 | 22.6 | 2006 | 2,524,434 | 499,838 | 19.8 |
| 2005 | 4,400,000 | 1,136,000 | 25.8 | 2005 | 2,361,300 | 448,647 | 19.0 |
| 2004 | 4,271,000 | 1,077,000 | 25.2 | 2004 | 2,521,850 | 484,195 | 19.2 |
| **TOTAL IRON (Tons)** | | | | **TOTAL STEEL (Tons)** | | | |
| 2010 | 5,550,000 | 982,000 | 17.7 | 2010 | 83,444,000 | 10,602,000 | 12.7 |
| 2009 | 6,619,000 | 1,261,000 | 19.1 | 2009 | 62,165,938 | 8,043,253 | 12.9 |
| 2008 | 8,152,000 | 1,632,000 | 20.0 | 2008 | 101,964,789 | 12,842,000 | 12.6 |
| 2007 | 8,880,000 | 1,920,000 | 21.6 | 2007 | 110,169,806 | 13,631,755 | 12.4 |
| 2006 | 9,150,000 | 2,080,000 | 22.7 | 2006 | 109,501,703 | 15,528,000 | 14.2 |
| 2005 | 9,100,000 | 2,146,000 | 23.6 | 2005 | 104,970,522 | 14,477,000 | 13.8 |
| 2004 | 9,291,000 | 2,240,000 | 24.1 | 2004 | 111,385,462 | 13,857,470 | 12.4 |
| **LEAD (Metric Tons)** | | | | **ZINC (Tons)** | | | |
| 2010 | 1,400,000 | 1,023,400 | 73.1 | 2010 | 919,000 | 212,289 | 23.1 |
| 2009 | 1,430,000 | 1,040,600 | 72.8 | 2009 | 891,000 | 201,900 | 22.7 |
| 2008 | 1,470,000 | 1,109,400 | 75.5 | 2008 | 1,000,000 | 230,000 | 23.0 |
| 2007 | 1,590,000 | 1,162,800 | 73.1 | 2007 | 1,110,000 | 244,200 | 22.0 |
| 2006 | 1,510,000 | 1,132,500 | 75.0 | 2006 | 1,130,000 | 248,600 | 22.0 |
| 2005 | 1,510,000 | 1,126,400 | 74.6 | 2005 | 939,000 | 206,580 | 22.0 |
| 2004 | 1,520,000 | 1,135,200 | 74.7 | 2004 | 1,160,000 | 261,000 | 22.5 |

NOTE: For most materials listed, automotive consumption includes materials used for cars, trucks, buses and replacement parts.
SOURCE: Ward's Automotive Group from various sources.

# Material Usage, Vehicles Retired From Use and Vehicle Recycling

## AVERAGE MATERIALS CONTENT OF NORTH AMERICAN LIGHT VEHICLES

| Material | 2009 Pounds | 2009 Percent | 2008 Pounds | 2008 Percent | 2000 Pounds | 2000 Percent | 1995 Pounds | 1995 Percent |
|---|---|---|---|---|---|---|---|---|
| Regular Steel | 1,501 | 38.3 | 1,629 | 40.0 | 1,655 | 42.4 | 1,630 | 44.1 |
| High and Medium Strength Steel | 524 | 13.4 | 523 | 12.9 | 408 | 10.5 | 324 | 8.8 |
| Stainless Steel | 69 | 1.8 | 75 | 1.8 | 62 | 1.6 | 51 | 1.4 |
| Other Steels | 31 | 0.8 | 34 | 0.8 | 26 | 0.7 | 46 | 1.2 |
| Iron Castings | 206 | 5.3 | 301 | 7.4 | 432 | 11.1 | 466 | 12.6 |
| Aluminum | 324 | 8.3 | 315 | 7.7 | 268 | 6.9 | 231 | 6.3 |
| Magnesium Castings | 12 | 0.3 | 11 | 0.3 | 8 | 0.2 | 4 | 0.1 |
| Copper and Brass | 63 | 1.6 | 64 | 1.6 | 52 | 1.3 | 50 | 1.4 |
| Lead | 45 | 1.1 | 45 | 1.1 | 36 | 0.9 | 33 | 0.9 |
| Zinc Castings | 9 | 0.2 | 10 | 0.2 | 13 | 0.3 | 19 | 0.5 |
| Powder Metal | 41 | 1.0 | 43 | 1.1 | 36 | 0.9 | 29 | 0.8 |
| Other Metals | 5 | 0.1 | 5 | 0.1 | 4 | 0.1 | 4 | 0.1 |
| Plastics and Plastic Composites | 384 | 9.8 | 343 | 8.4 | 286 | 7.3 | 240 | 6.5 |
| Rubber | 212 | 5.4 | 185 | 4.5 | 166 | 4.3 | 149 | 4.0 |
| Coatings | 34 | 0.9 | 28 | 0.7 | 25 | 0.6 | 23 | 0.6 |
| Textiles | 53 | 1.4 | 48 | 1.2 | 44 | 1.1 | 42 | 1.1 |
| Fluids and Lubricants | 219 | 5.6 | 214 | 5.3 | 207 | 5.3 | 192 | 5.2 |
| Glass | 93 | 2.4 | 106 | 2.6 | 103 | 2.6 | 97 | 2.6 |
| Other Materials | 90 | 2.3 | 91 | 2.2 | 71 | 1.9 | 64 | 1.7 |
| **Total** | **3,915** | **100.0** | **4,070** | **100.0** | **3,902** | **100.0** | **3,694** | **100.0** |

SOURCE: American Chemistry Council. Data reflects Light Vehicles built in North America.

## VEHICLES RETIRED FROM USE
### (in Thousands)

| Year Ending June 30 | Cars | Trucks & Buses | Total |
|---|---|---|---|
| 2010 | 6,304 | 4,230 | 10,534 |
| 2009 | 10,462 | 4,917 | 15,379 |
| 2008 | 6,896 | 7,149 | 14,045 |
| 2007 | 7,008 | 5,699 | 12,707 |
| 2006 | 6,750 | 5,258 | 12,008 |
| 2005 | 6,478 | 3,511 | 9,989 |
| 2004 | 5,524 | 6,379 | 11,903 |
| 2003 | 6,864 | 5,226 | 12,090 |
| 2002 | 7,310 | 5,986 | 13,296 |
| 2001 | 7,650 | 6,472 | 14,122 |
| 2000 | 8,085 | 6,214 | 14,299 |
| 1999 | 7,216 | 4,447 | 11,663 |
| 1998 | 6,819 | 4,846 | 11,665 |
| 1997 | 8,244 | 4,265 | 12,509 |
| 1996 | 7,527 | 3,284 | 10,811 |
| 1995 | 7,414 | 2,918 | 10,332 |
| 1994 | 7,824 | 4,545 | 12,369 |
| 1993 | 7,366 | 1,048 | 8,414 |
| 1992 | 11,194 | 1,587 | 12,781 |
| 1991 | 8,565 | 2,284 | 10,849 |
| 1989 | 8,981 | 2,189 | 11,170 |
| 1987 | 8,103 | 2,364 | 10,467 |
| 1985 | 7,729 | 2,100 | 9,829 |
| 1983 | 6,243 | 1,491 | 7,734 |
| 1981 | 7,542 | 1,519 | 9,061 |
| 1979 | 9,312 | 1,916 | 11,228 |
| 1977 | 8,234 | 1,668 | 9,902 |
| 1975 | 5,669 | 908 | 6,577 |
| 1973 | 7,987 | 1,208 | 9,195 |
| 1971 | 6,021 | 1,044 | 7,065 |

NOTE: Data as of July 1 each calendar year except 2009, which is Oct. 1. Beginning in 2010, data as of Dec. 31. Car and truck splits are estimated. Figures represent vehicles which are not re-registered.
SOURCE: The Polk Company. Permission for further use must be obtained from The Polk Company.

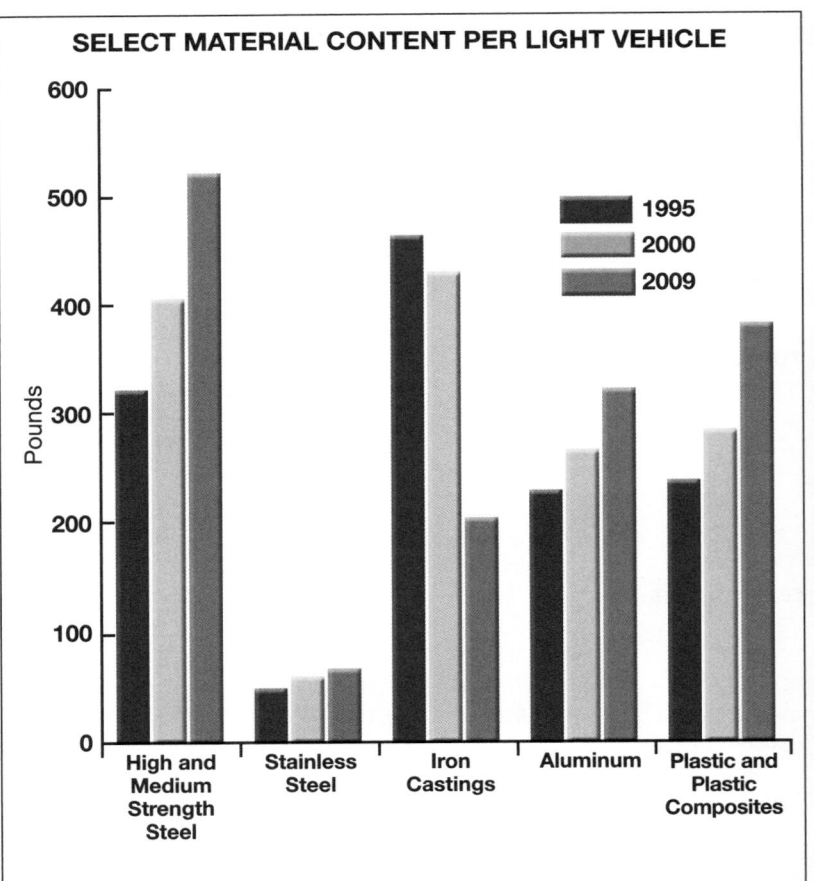

**SELECT MATERIAL CONTENT PER LIGHT VEHICLE**

Legend: 1995, 2000, 2009. Y-axis: Pounds (0–600). Categories: High and Medium Strength Steel, Stainless Steel, Iron Castings, Aluminum, Plastic and Plastic Composites.

# Licensed Drivers by Age Group, Gender and State

## LICENSED DRIVERS BY STATE, 2009

| State | Male (000) | Female (000) | Total (000) |
|---|---|---|---|
| Alabama | 1,849 | 1,933 | 3,782 |
| Alaska | 270 | 238 | 508 |
| Arizona | 2,215 | 2,188 | 4,403 |
| Arkansas | 1,017 | 1,048 | 2,065 |
| California | 12,065 | 11,616 | 23,681 |
| Colorado | 1,896 | 1,808 | 3,704 |
| Connecticut | 1,447 | 1,469 | 2,916 |
| Delaware | 342 | 358 | 700 |
| Dist. of Columbia | 185 | 191 | 376 |
| Florida | 6,835 | 7,170 | 14,005 |
| Georgia | 3,024 | 3,291 | 6,315 |
| Hawaii | 466 | 424 | 890 |
| Idaho | 531 | 524 | 1,055 |
| Illinois | 4,087 | 4,214 | 8,301 |
| Indiana | 2,785 | 2,765 | 5,550 |
| Iowa | 1,055 | 1,090 | 2,145 |
| Kansas | 1,015 | 1,031 | 2,046 |
| Kentucky | 1,452 | 1,488 | 2,940 |
| Louisiana | 1,494 | 1,592 | 3,086 |
| Maine | 502 | 511 | 1,013 |
| Maryland | 1,918 | 1,987 | 3,905 |
| Massachusetts | 2,296 | 2,333 | 4,629 |
| Michigan | 3,469 | 3,614 | 7,083 |
| Minnesota | 1,634 | 1,612 | 3,246 |
| Mississippi | 919 | 1,011 | 1,930 |
| Missouri | 2,074 | 2,144 | 4,218 |
| Montana | 375 | 363 | 738 |
| Nebraska | 677 | 673 | 1,350 |
| Nevada | 874 | 817 | 1,691 |
| New Hampshire | 518 | 516 | 1,034 |
| New Jersey | 2,910 | 3,013 | 5,923 |
| New Mexico | 684 | 694 | 1,378 |
| New York | 5,841 | 5,489 | 11,330 |
| North Carolina | 3,188 | 3,316 | 6,504 |
| North Dakota | 241 | 235 | 476 |
| Ohio | 3,836 | 4,102 | 7,938 |
| Oklahoma | 1,060 | 1,260 | 2,320 |
| Oregon | 1,426 | 1,416 | 2,842 |
| Pennsylvania | 4,316 | 4,371 | 8,687 |
| Rhode Island | 367 | 379 | 746 |
| South Carolina | 1,700 | 1,568 | 3,268 |
| South Dakota | 302 | 301 | 603 |
| Tennessee | 2,166 | 2,311 | 4,477 |
| Texas | 7,690 | 7,684 | 15,374 |
| Utah | 865 | 855 | 1,720 |
| Vermont | 253 | 254 | 507 |
| Virginia | 2,595 | 2,753 | 5,348 |
| Washington | 2,603 | 2,424 | 5,027 |
| West Virginia | 662 | 667 | 1,329 |
| Wisconsin | 2,059 | 2,047 | 4,106 |
| Wyoming | 212 | 199 | 411 |
| **Total** | **104,262** | **105,357** | **209,619** |

SOURCE: U.S. Department of Transportation, Federal Highway Administration.

## DRIVERS BY AGE GROUP AND GENDER, 2009

| Age (in Years) | Male (000) | Female (000) | Total (000) |
|---|---|---|---|
| Under 16 | 206 | 204 | 410 |
| 16 | 662 | 654 | 1,316 |
| 17 | 1,074 | 1,038 | 2,112 |
| 18 | 1,455 | 1,372 | 2,827 |
| 19 | 1,682 | 1,587 | 3,269 |
| 20 | 1,725 | 1,665 | 3,390 |
| 21 | 1,737 | 1,701 | 3,438 |
| 22 | 1,748 | 1,721 | 3,469 |
| 23 | 1,784 | 1,756 | 3,540 |
| 24 | 1,809 | 1,797 | 3,606 |
| 25-29 | 9,221 | 9,260 | 18,481 |
| 30-34 | 8,921 | 8,925 | 17,846 |
| 35-39 | 9,425 | 9,366 | 18,791 |
| 40-44 | 9,729 | 9,638 | 19,367 |
| 45-49 | 10,577 | 10,612 | 21,189 |
| 50-54 | 10,177 | 10,300 | 20,477 |
| 55-59 | 8,925 | 9,082 | 18,007 |
| 60-64 | 7,513 | 7,637 | 15,150 |
| 65-69 | 5,470 | 5,618 | 11,088 |
| 70-74 | 3,939 | 4,098 | 8,037 |
| 75-79 | 2,943 | 3,173 | 6,116 |
| 80-84 | 2,060 | 2,354 | 4,414 |
| 85 and over | 1,480 | 1,799 | 3,279 |
| **Total** | **104,262** | **105,357** | **209,619** |

SOURCE: U.S. Department of Transportation, Federal Highway Administration.

## DRIVERS BY GENDER

| Year | Male (000) | Percent Male | Female (000) | Percent Female | Total (000) |
|---|---|---|---|---|---|
| 2009 | 104,262 | 49.74 | 105,357 | 50.26 | 209,619 |
| 2008 | 103,622 | 49.74 | 104,704 | 50.26 | 208,326 |
| 2007 | 102,465 | 49.80 | 103,277 | 50.20 | 205,742 |
| 2006 | 101,116 | 49.86 | 101,694 | 50.14 | 202,810 |
| 2005 | 100,252 | 49.99 | 100,297 | 50.01 | 200,549 |
| 2004 | 99,571 | 50.06 | 99,318 | 49.94 | 198,889 |
| 2003 | 98,228 | 50.07 | 97,937 | 49.93 | 196,165 |
| 2002 | 97,461 | 50.16 | 96,834 | 49.84 | 194,295 |
| 2001 | 95,792 | 50.08 | 95,483 | 49.92 | 191,275 |
| 2000 | 95,796 | 50.30 | 94,829 | 49.70 | 190,625 |
| 1999 | 94,166 | 50.31 | 93,004 | 49.69 | 187,170 |
| 1998 | 93,105 | 50.33 | 91,875 | 49.67 | 184,980 |
| 1997 | 91,905 | 50.30 | 90,804 | 49.70 | 182,709 |
| 1996 | 90,519 | 50.42 | 89,021 | 49.58 | 179,540 |
| 1995 | 89,214 | 50.51 | 87,414 | 49.49 | 176,628 |
| 1994 | 89,194 | 50.85 | 86,209 | 49.15 | 175,403 |
| 1993 | 87,993 | 50.82 | 85,156 | 49.18 | 173,149 |
| 1992 | 88,387 | 51.05 | 84,738 | 48.95 | 173,125 |
| 1991 | 86,665 | 51.28 | 82,330 | 48.72 | 168,995 |
| 1990 | 85,792 | 51.37 | 81,223 | 48.63 | 167,015 |
| 1989 | 85,378 | 51.57 | 80,177 | 48.43 | 165,555 |
| 1988 | 85,230 | 51.91 | 78,967 | 48.09 | 164,197 |
| 1987 | 84,084 | 51.91 | 77,891 | 48.09 | 161,975 |
| 1986 | 82,494 | 52.02 | 76,100 | 47.98 | 158,594 |
| 1985 | 81,592 | 52.01 | 75,276 | 47.99 | 156,868 |
| 1984 | 80,977 | 52.10 | 74,447 | 47.90 | 155,424 |
| 1983 | 80,894 | 52.40 | 73,495 | 47.60 | 154,389 |
| 1982 | 78,553 | 52.29 | 71,681 | 47.71 | 150,234 |
| 1981 | 77,888 | 52.96 | 69,187 | 47.04 | 147,075 |
| 1980 | 77,187 | 53.12 | 68,108 | 46.88 | 145,295 |

SOURCE: U.S. Department of Transportation, Federal Highway Administration.

# Demographics of New Vehicle Buyers and Initial Vehicle Quality

## DEMOGRAPHICS OF NEW VEHICLE BUYERS AND INITIAL VEHICLE QUALITY, 2011 MODEL YEAR

| Characteristic | New Passenger Car Buyers | | | | New Light Trucks Buyers | | | | New CUV Buyers | | | |
|---|---|---|---|---|---|---|---|---|---|---|---|---|
| | Domestic[1] | European[2] | Asian[2] | Total | Domestic[1] | European[2] | Asian[2] | Total | Domestic[1] | European[2] | Asian[2] | Total |
| **Gender** | | | | | | | | | | | | |
| Male | 60.6% | 63.6% | 55.1% | 58.2% | 82.9% | 62.3% | 69.2% | 77.2% | 52.0% | 58.0% | 48.8% | 50.8% |
| Female | 39.4 | 36.4 | 44.9 | 41.8 | 17.1 | 37.7 | 30.8 | 22.8 | 48.0 | 42.0 | 51.2 | 49.2 |
| Total | 100.0 | 100.0 | 100.0 | 100.0 | 100.0 | 100.0 | 100.0 | 100.0 | 100.0 | 100.0 | 100.0 | 100.0 |
| **Age of Principal Purchaser (In Years)** | | | | | | | | | | | | |
| Under 25 | 2.7% | 1.6% | 3.7% | 3.0% | 1.0% | 0.5% | 0.8% | 0.9% | 1.1% | 0.9% | 1.5% | 1.3% |
| 25-29 | 3.7 | 5.0 | 5.8 | 5.1 | 3.0 | 1.8 | 3.2 | 3.0 | 2.7 | 2.6 | 4.0 | 3.4 |
| 30-34 | 3.9 | 6.3 | 5.0 | 4.9 | 4.7 | 6.7 | 7.3 | 5.7 | 5.0 | 6.4 | 6.3 | 5.8 |
| 35-39 | 4.1 | 7.7 | 5.5 | 5.5 | 6.0 | 11.4 | 10.9 | 8.0 | 5.6 | 9.1 | 5.9 | 6.1 |
| 40-44 | 5.6 | 8.8 | 6.8 | 6.8 | 7.9 | 17.1 | 12.3 | 9.8 | 7.3 | 12.0 | 7.2 | 7.6 |
| 45-49 | 9.0 | 10.6 | 8.7 | 9.1 | 9.9 | 19.0 | 12.0 | 10.9 | 8.8 | 12.9 | 8.9 | 9.2 |
| 50-54 | 11.1 | 12.1 | 11.2 | 11.3 | 12.9 | 13.5 | 10.6 | 12.0 | 11.1 | 13.0 | 11.8 | 11.7 |
| 55-59 | 11.9 | 13.9 | 12.0 | 12.3 | 14.6 | 9.9 | 10.0 | 12.8 | 13.1 | 12.6 | 14.2 | 13.6 |
| 60-64 | 12.5 | 12.8 | 12.5 | 12.5 | 15.7 | 9.3 | 12.3 | 14.3 | 15.6 | 12.9 | 15.2 | 15.1 |
| 65 and over | 35.5 | 21.2 | 28.8 | 29.5 | 24.3 | 10.8 | 20.6 | 22.6 | 29.7 | 17.6 | 25.0 | 26.2 |
| Total | 100.0 | 100.0 | 100.0 | 100.0 | 100.0 | 100.0 | 100.0 | 100.0 | 100.0 | 100.0 | 100.0 | 100.0 |
| **Highest Education Level** | | | | | | | | | | | | |
| 8th Grade or Less | 0.6% | 0.1% | 0.5% | 0.5% | 0.4% | 0.0% | 0.3% | 0.4% | 0.3% | 0.2% | 0.2% | 0.3% |
| Some High School | 1.6 | 0.5 | 1.2 | 1.2 | 2.8 | 0.4 | 1.1 | 2.1 | 1.1 | 0.4 | 0.7 | 0.8 |
| High School Graduate | 20.5 | 5.3 | 12.9 | 13.9 | 22.1 | 3.8 | 11.5 | 17.7 | 17.5 | 4.3 | 11.0 | 12.9 |
| Technical/Trade School | 9.5 | 3.5 | 6.5 | 6.9 | 12.9 | 2.4 | 8.1 | 10.8 | 9.1 | 2.9 | 6.8 | 7.3 |
| Some College | 26.3 | 16.2 | 23.9 | 23.3 | 24.5 | 14.2 | 21.5 | 23.1 | 25.0 | 14.8 | 21.5 | 22.2 |
| College Graduate | 19.3 | 29.0 | 25.8 | 24.4 | 19.7 | 36.8 | 28.6 | 23.5 | 24.4 | 31.4 | 26.6 | 26.2 |
| Post Graduate | 5.4 | 8.2 | 6.6 | 6.5 | 4.7 | 5.4 | 6.0 | 5.2 | 5.1 | 7.4 | 7.0 | 6.3 |
| Advanced Degree | 16.8 | 37.2 | 22.6 | 23.3 | 12.9 | 37.0 | 22.9 | 17.2 | 17.5 | 38.6 | 26.2 | 24.0 |
| Total | 100.0 | 100.0 | 100.0 | 100.0 | 100.0 | 100.0 | 100.0 | 100.0 | 100.0 | 100.0 | 100.0 | 100.0 |
| **Census Region** | | | | | | | | | | | | |
| Northeast | 20.0% | 23.6% | 21.4% | 21.3% | 19.2% | 23.3% | 21.2% | 20.0% | 19.2% | 28.9% | 27.9% | 24.7% |
| Midwest | 38.2 | 13.0 | 17.3 | 22.8 | 32.5 | 10.3 | 16.9 | 26.1 | 38.5 | 14.9 | 21.0 | 27.1 |
| South | 28.8 | 32.5 | 39.6 | 35.2 | 34.1 | 37.7 | 40.8 | 36.7 | 31.3 | 30.8 | 31.9 | 31.6 |
| West | 13.0 | 30.9 | 21.7 | 20.7 | 14.2 | 28.7 | 21.1 | 17.2 | 11.0 | 25.4 | 19.2 | 16.6 |
| Total | 100.0 | 100.0 | 100.0 | 100.0 | 100.0 | 100.0 | 100.0 | 100.0 | 100.0 | 100.0 | 100.0 | 100.0 |
| **Median Household Income** | $72,749 | $142,548 | $78,738 | $83,612 | $94,507 | $342,772 | $104,247 | $99,402 | $90,237 | $174,423 | $93,341 | $95,678 |
| **Initial Quality (Problems per 100 Passenger Cars)** | | | | | | | | | | | | |
| Study Results | 109 | 110 | 95 | 102 | 105 | 115 | 110 | 107 | 124 | 119 | 103 | 112 |

NOTE: Study conducted among personal use buyers of '11 model year vehicles.
(1) Domestic figures include captive import buyers.
(2) Import figures include buyers of North American assembled vehicles.
SOURCE: J.D. Power and Associates, 2011 Initial Quality Study.

# Car Operating Costs

## CAR OPERATING COSTS

| Model Year | Variable Cost in Cents Per Mile | | | | Cost Per 10,000 Miles | | | |
| | Gas & Oil | Maintenance | Tires | Total | Variable Cost | Fixed Cost | Total Cost | Total Cost Per Mile |
|---|---|---|---|---|---|---|---|---|
| 2011 | 12.34 | 4.44 | 0.96 | 17.74 | $1,774 | $5,857 | $7,631 | 76.31¢ |
| 2010 | 11.36 | 4.54 | 0.83 | 16.73 | 1,673 | 5,719 | 7,392 | 73.92 |
| 2009 | 10.09 | 4.56 | 0.77 | 15.42 | 1,542 | 5,526 | 7,068 | 70.68 |
| 2008 | 11.67 | 4.57 | 0.72 | 16.96 | 1,696 | 5,399 | 7,095 | 70.95 |
| 2007 | 8.90 | 4.90 | 0.70 | 14.50 | 1,450 | 4,765 | 6,215 | 62.15 |
| 2006 | 9.50 | 4.90 | 0.70 | 15.10 | 1,510 | 4,686 | 6,196 | 61.96 |
| 2005 | 8.20 | 5.30 | 0.60 | 14.10 | 1,410 | 5,412 | 6,822 | 68.22 |
| 2004 | 6.50 | 5.40 | 0.70 | 12.60 | 1,260 | 5,633 | 6,893 | 68.93 |
| 2003 | 7.20 | 4.10 | 1.80 | 13.10 | 1,310 | 4,884 | 6,194 | 61.94 |
| 2002 | 5.90 | 4.10 | 1.80 | 11.80 | 1,180 | 4,874 | 6,054 | 60.54 |
| 2001 | 7.90 | 3.90 | 1.80 | 13.60 | 1,360 | 4,621 | 5,981 | 59.81 |
| 2000 | 6.90 | 3.60 | 1.70 | 12.20 | 1,220 | 4,724 | 5,944 | 59.44 |
| 1999 | 5.60 | 3.30 | 1.70 | 10.60 | 1,060 | 4,660 | 5,720 | 57.20 |
| 1998 | 6.20 | 3.10 | 1.40 | 10.70 | 1,070 | 4,528 | 5,598 | 55.98 |
| 1997 | 6.60 | 2.80 | 1.40 | 10.80 | 1,080 | 4,348 | 5,428 | 54.28 |
| 1996 | 5.60 | 2.80 | 1.20 | 9.60 | 960 | 4,193 | 5,153 | 51.53 |
| 1995 | 5.80 | 2.60 | 1.20 | 9.60 | 960 | 4,005 | 4,965 | 49.65 |
| 1994 | 5.60 | 2.50 | 1.00 | 9.10 | 910 | 3,836 | 4,746 | 47.46 |
| 1993 | 5.90 | 2.40 | 0.90 | 9.20 | 920 | 3,722 | 4,642 | 46.42 |
| 1992 | 5.90 | 2.20 | 0.90 | 9.00 | 900 | 3,784 | 4,684 | 46.84 |
| 1991 | 6.60 | 2.20 | 0.90 | 9.70 | 970 | 3,566 | 4,536 | 45.36 |
| 1990 | 5.40 | 2.10 | 0.90 | 8.40 | 840 | 3,256 | 4,096 | 40.96 |
| 1989 | 5.30 | 1.90 | 0.80 | 8.00 | 800 | 2,920 | 3,720 | 37.20 |
| 1987 | 4.40 | 1.50 | 0.80 | 6.70 | 670 | 2,328 | 2,998 | 29.98 |
| 1985 | 5.57 | 1.20 | 0.65 | 7.42 | 742 | 2,061 | 2,803 | 28.03 |

## ANNUAL FIXED COST OF OPERATING A CAR

| Model Year | Insurance | | | License, Registration & Taxes | Depreciation | Finance Charge | Total | Average Fixed Cost Per Day |
| | Fire & Theft[2] | Collision[3] | Property Damage & Liability[4] | | | | | |
|---|---|---|---|---|---|---|---|---|
| 2011[1] | NA | $968 | NA | $595 | $3,728 | $823 | $6,114 | $16.75 |
| 2010[1] | NA | 1,031 | NA | 585 | 3,554 | 806 | 5,976 | 16.37 |
| 2009[1] | NA | 976 | NA | 567 | 3,461 | 779 | 5,783 | 15.84 |
| 2008[1] | NA | 943 | NA | 554 | 3,321 | 758 | 5,576 | 15.28 |
| 2007[1] | NA | 985 | NA | 538 | 3,392 | 733 | 5,648 | 15.47 |
| 2006[1] | NA | 926 | NA | 535 | 3,392 | 716 | 5,569 | 15.26 |
| 2005[1] | NA | 1,288 | NA | 389 | 3,879 | 739 | 6,295 | 17.25 |
| 2004[1] | NA | 1,603 | NA | 415 | 3,782 | 741 | 6,541 | 17.92 |
| 2003 | 203 | 401 | 498 | 205 | 3,738 | 744 | 5,789 | 15.86 |
| 2002 | 173 | 357 | 484 | 201 | 3,721 | 828 | 5,764 | 15.79 |
| 2001 | 167 | 345 | 479 | 208 | 3,548 | 866 | 5,613 | 15.38 |
| 2000 | 163 | 326 | 481 | 223 | 3,492 | 849 | 5,534 | 15.16 |
| 1999 | 162 | 324 | 484 | 226 | 3,436 | 828 | 5,460 | 14.96 |
| 1998 | 134 | 287 | 479 | 226 | 3,364 | 813 | 5,303 | 14.53 |
| 1997 | 120 | 326 | 401 | 216 | 3,272 | 768 | 5,103 | 13.98 |
| 1996 | 144 | 275 | 426 | 215 | 3,170 | 718 | 4,948 | 13.56 |
| 1995 | 121 | 252 | 410 | 203 | 3,073 | 686 | 4,745 | 13.00 |
| 1994 | 123 | 246 | 400 | 194 | 2,940 | 648 | 4,551 | 12.47 |
| 1993 | 116 | 243 | 385 | 178 | 2,830 | 670 | 4,422 | 12.12 |
| 1992 | 128 | 286 | 373 | 174 | 2,717 | 796 | 4,474 | 12.26 |
| 1991 | 108 | 247 | 353 | 168 | 2,504 | 266 | 3,646 | 9.99 |
| 1990 | 110 | 245 | 318 | 165 | 2,357 | 680 | 3,875 | 10.62 |
| 1989 | 102 | 234 | 309 | 144 | 2,018 | 588 | 3,395 | 9.30 |
| 1987 | 87 | 196 | 252 | 128 | 1,494 | 526 | 2,683 | 7.35 |
| 1985 | 75 | 177 | 213 | 110 | 1,262 | 534 | 2,371 | 6.50 |

NOTE: Methodology changed beginning in 2004; data is not comparable to prior years. Beginning in 1985 ownership costs are based on a six year/60,000 mile retention cycle rather than four year/60,000 miles.
NA - Not available.
(1) Individual component costs of insurance are no longer available, therefore insurance costs for 2004 forward reflect the total amount of a full coverage policy.
(2) $100 deductible 1981-1992; $250 deductible 1993-2003, $100 deductible 2004-2011.
(3) $250 deductible 1981-1992; $500 deductible 1993-2011.
(4) Coverage: 1967 to 2011-$100,000/$300,000
SOURCE: American Automobile Association.

# Light Truck Operating Costs

## LIGHT TRUCK OPERATING COSTS

| Model Year | Variable Cost in Cents Per Mile | | | | Cost Per 10,000 Miles | | | |
| | Gas & Oil | Maintenance | Tires | Total | Variable Cost | Fixed Cost | Total Cost | Total Cost Per Mile |
| --- | --- | --- | --- | --- | --- | --- | --- | --- |
| 2011 | 17.04 | 4.80 | 1.14 | 22.98 | $2,298 | $7,517 | $9,815 | 98.15 |
| 2010 | 16.38 | 4.95 | 0.98 | 22.31 | 2,231 | 7,463 | 9,694 | 96.94 |
| 2009 | 14.39 | 4.94 | 0.95 | 20.28 | 2,028 | 6,942 | 8,970 | 89.70 |
| 2008 | 17.05 | 5.47 | 0.93 | 23.45 | 2,345 | 6,750 | 9,095 | 90.95 |
| 2007 | 12.60 | 5.50 | 0.90 | 19.00 | 1,900 | 6,247 | 8,147 | 81.47 |
| 2006 | 13.70 | 5.60 | 0.80 | 20.10 | 2,010 | 5,890 | 7,900 | 79.00 |
| 2005 | 10.80 | 5.30 | 0.90 | 17.00 | 1,700 | 6,074 | 7,774 | 77.74 |
| 2004 | 8.40 | 4.30 | 1.00 | 13.70 | 1,370 | 5,903 | 7,273 | 72.73 |
| 2003 | 7.90 | 4.10 | 1.50 | 13.50 | 1,350 | 5,527 | 6,877 | 68.77 |
| 2002 | 5.80 | 4.10 | 1.70 | 11.60 | 1,160 | 4,332 | 5,492 | 54.92 |
| 2001 | 8.05 | 4.00 | 1.60 | 13.65 | 1,365 | 5,197 | 6,562 | 65.62 |

## ANNUAL FIXED COST OF OPERATING A LIGHT TRUCK

| Model Year | Insurance | | | License, Registration & Taxes | Depreciation | Finance Charge | Total | Average Fixed Cost Per Day |
| | Fire & Theft[2] | Collision[3] | Property Damage & Liability[4] | | | | | |
| --- | --- | --- | --- | --- | --- | --- | --- | --- |
| 2011[1] | NA | $912 | NA | $757 | $5,052 | $1,071 | $7,792 | $21.35 |
| 2010[1] | NA | 964 | NA | 735 | 5,003 | 1,036 | 7,738 | 21.20 |
| 2009[1] | NA | 948 | NA | 727 | 4,519 | 1,023 | 7,217 | 19.77 |
| 2008[1] | NA | 888 | NA | 715 | 4,327 | 1,000 | 6,930 | 18.99 |
| 2007[1] | NA | 950 | NA | 695 | 4,531 | 971 | 7,147 | 19.58 |
| 2006[1] | NA | 918 | NA | 683 | 4,254 | 935 | 6,790 | 18.60 |
| 2005[1] | NA | 1,398 | NA | 435 | 4,300 | 891 | 7,024 | 19.24 |
| 2004[1] | NA | 1,491 | NA | 454 | 4,043 | 865 | 6,853 | 18.78 |
| 2003 | 159 | 402 | 389 | 289 | 4,286 | 867 | 6,392 | 17.51 |
| 2002 | 204 | 451 | 389 | 261 | 3,220 | 662 | 5,187 | 14.21 |
| 2001 | 182 | 423 | 389 | 285 | 3,720 | 980 | 5,979 | 16.38 |

NOTE: Methodology changed beginning in 2004; data is not comparable to prior years.
NA - Not available
(1) Individual component costs of insurance are no longer available, therefore insurance costs for 2004 forward reflect the total amount of a full coverage policy.
(2) $250 deductible 2001-2003, $100 deductible 2004-2011.
(3) $$500 deductible 2001-2011.
(4) Coverage: 2001 to 2011-$100,000/$300,000
SOURCE: American Automobile Association.

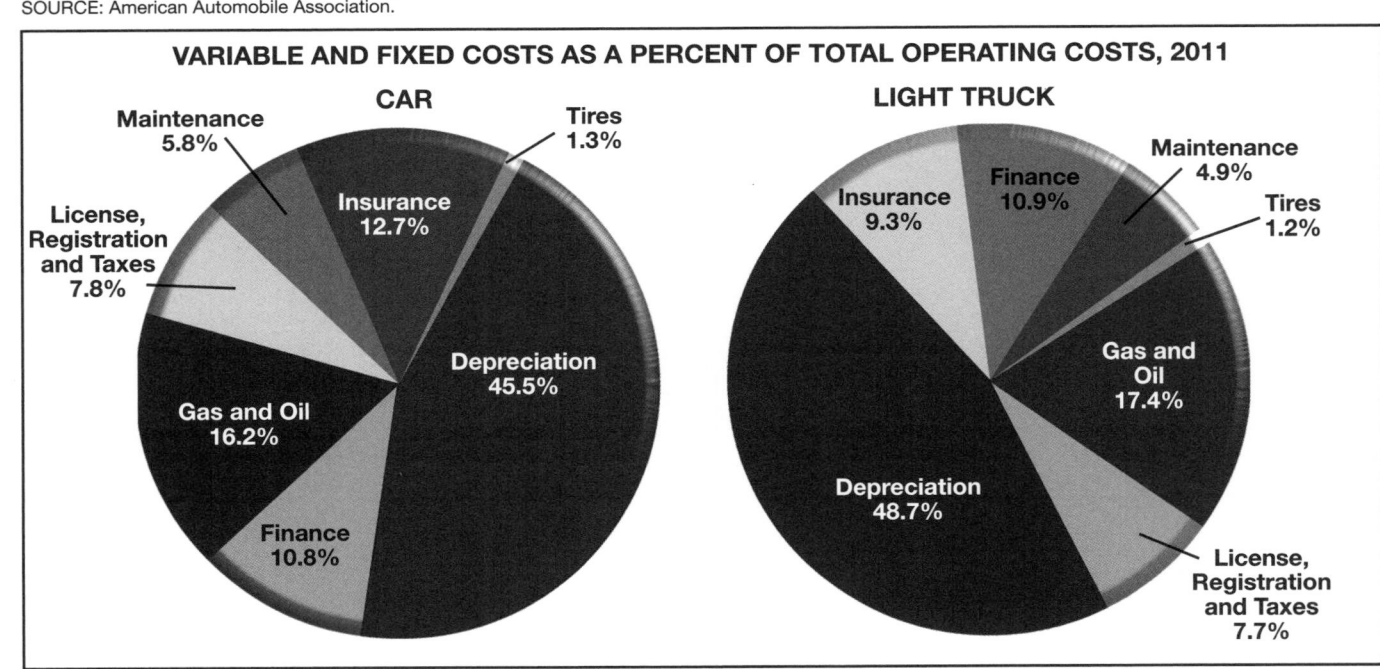

**VARIABLE AND FIXED COSTS AS A PERCENT OF TOTAL OPERATING COSTS, 2011**

CAR
- Maintenance 5.8%
- Tires 1.3%
- Insurance 12.7%
- Depreciation 45.5%
- Gas and Oil 16.2%
- Finance 10.8%
- License, Registration and Taxes 7.8%

LIGHT TRUCK
- Finance 10.9%
- Maintenance 4.9%
- Tires 1.2%
- Insurance 9.3%
- Gas and Oil 17.4%
- Depreciation 48.7%
- License, Registration and Taxes 7.7%

# Automobile Financing

## NEW AND USED CAR FINANCING WITH FINANCE COMPANIES

| Year | % Average Interest Rate | Average Maturity (Months) | Average Amount Financed | Average Monthly Payment | Year | % Average Interest Rate | Average Maturity (Months) | Average Amount Financed | Average Monthly Payment |
|---|---|---|---|---|---|---|---|---|---|
| **NEW CARS** | | | | | **USED CARS** | | | | |
| 2010 | 4.3 | 63.0 | $27,959 | $496.56 | 2010 | 8.2 | 62.6 | $18,124 | $356.82 |
| 2009 | 3.8 | 62.0 | 28,272 | 502.95 | 2009 | 9.4 | 59.2 | 16,225 | 343.57 |
| 2008 | 5.5 | 63.4 | 26,178 | 476.73 | 2008 | 8.7 | 59.8 | 16,664 | 344.41 |
| 2007 | 4.9 | 62.0 | 28,287 | 517.35 | 2007 | 9.2 | 60.7 | 17,095 | 353.29 |
| 2006 | 5.0 | 63.0 | 26,620 | 481.30 | 2006 | 9.6 | 59.4 | 16,671 | 353.70 |
| 2005 | 6.0 | 60.0 | 24,133 | 466.56 | 2005 | 8.8 | 58.6 | 16,228 | 341.68 |
| 2004 | 4.9 | 60.7 | 24,888 | 463.76 | 2004 | 8.8 | 57.9 | 15,136 | 321.77 |
| 2003 | 3.4 | 61.4 | 26,295 | 467.19 | 2003 | 9.7 | 57.7 | 14,613 | 317.90 |
| 2002 | 4.3 | 56.8 | 24,747 | 482.31 | 2002 | 10.7 | 57.6 | 14,532 | 323.70 |
| 2001 | 5.7 | 55.1 | 22,822 | 471.73 | 2001 | 12.2 | 57.5 | 14,416 | 332.33 |
| 2000 | 6.6 | 54.9 | 20,923 | 442.58 | 2000 | 13.6 | 57.0 | 14,058 | 336.16 |
| 1999 | 6.7 | 52.7 | 19,880 | 436.49 | 1999 | 12.6 | 55.9 | 13,642 | 324.15 |
| 1998 | 6.3 | 52.1 | 19,083 | 419.60 | 1998 | 12.6 | 53.5 | 12,691 | 311.51 |
| 1997 | 7.1 | 54.1 | 18,077 | 391.45 | 1997 | 13.3 | 51.0 | 12,281 | 316.54 |
| 1996 | 9.8 | 51.6 | 16,987 | 404.75 | 1996 | 13.5 | 51.4 | 12,182 | 313.39 |
| 1995 | 11.2 | 54.1 | 16,210 | 382.98 | 1995 | 14.5 | 52.2 | 11,590 | 300.66 |
| 1994 | 9.8 | 54.0 | 15,375 | 353.25 | 1994 | 13.5 | 50.2 | 10,709 | 280.37 |
| 1993 | 9.5 | 54.5 | 14,332 | 324.79 | 1993 | 12.8 | 48.8 | 9,875 | 260.63 |
| 1992 | 9.8 | 54.0 | 13,607 | 313.01 | 1992 | 13.7 | 47.9 | 9,211 | 250.70 |
| 1991 | 12.4 | 55.1 | 12,494 | 298.14 | 1991 | 15.6 | 47.2 | 8,884 | 253.11 |
| 1990 | 12.5 | 54.6 | 12,071 | 291.31 | 1990 | 16.0 | 46.1 | 8,289 | 249.35 |
| 1989 | 12.6 | 54.2 | 12,001 | 291.50 | 1989 | 16.2 | 46.6 | 7,954 | 231.08 |
| 1988 | 12.6 | 56.2 | 11,663 | 275.95 | 1988 | 15.1 | 46.7 | 7,824 | 222.68 |
| 1987 | 10.7 | 53.5 | 11,203 | 264.22 | 1987 | 14.6 | 45.2 | 7,420 | 214.39 |
| 1986 | 9.4 | 50.0 | 10,665 | 258.74 | 1986 | 16.0 | 42.6 | 6,555 | 202.52 |
| 1985 | 12.0 | 51.1 | 9,883 | 248.44 | 1985 | 17.6 | 41.2 | 6,091 | 198.03 |
| 1984 | 14.6 | 48.3 | 9,337 | 256.90 | 1984 | 17.9 | 39.7 | 5,691 | 190.92 |
| 1983 | 12.7 | 45.9 | 8,787 | 242.24 | 1983 | 18.8 | 38.0 | 5,033 | 176.77 |
| 1982 | 15.9 | 46.0 | 8,178 | 238.16 | 1982 | 20.8 | 37.0 | 4,746 | 174.84 |
| 1981 | 16.0 | 45.3 | 7,339 | 216.41 | 1981 | 20.0 | 35.8 | 4,339 | 162.02 |
| 1980 | 14.8 | 45.0 | 6,322 | 183.91 | 1980 | 19.1 | 34.8 | 3,810 | 143.44 |

SOURCE: Board of Governors of The Federal Reserve.

# Expenditures for Transportation

## AVERAGE EXPENDITURE PER NEW CAR

| Year | Average Expenditure Per New Car[1] | | | Estimated Average New Car Price for a 1967 "Comparable Car" | | Annual Median Family Earnings[4] | Weeks of Median Family Earnings to Equal Cost of "Comparable Car" | | |
|------|----------|--------|---------|-----------|-----------|----------|---------|-----------|-----------|
| | Domestic* | Import | Average | With Added Safety & Emissions Equipment[2] | Without Added Safety & Emissions Equipment[3] | | Average New Car Expenditure[5] | With Added Safety & Emissions Equipment[6] | Without Added Safety & Emissions Equipment[7] |
| 2010 | $23,095 | $26,808 | $24,296 | $13,722 | $8,807 | $79,541 | 15.9 | 9.0 | 5.8 |
| 2009 | 22,148 | 25,499 | 23,276 | 13,539 | 8,815 | 77,149 | 15.7 | 9.1 | 5.9 |
| 2008 | 22,204 | 25,903 | 23,441 | 13,378 | 8,793 | 78,483 | 15.5 | 8.9 | 5.8 |
| 2007 | 22,284 | 27,465 | 23,892 | 13,364 | 8,797 | 75,610 | 16.4 | 9.2 | 6.1 |
| 2006 | 22,166 | 27,062 | 23,634 | 13,389 | 8,800 | 71,196 | 17.3 | 9.8 | 6.4 |
| 2005 | 21,593 | 26,621 | 23,017 | 13,094 | 8,799 | 66,977 | 17.9 | 10.2 | 6.8 |
| 2003 | 19,971 | 26,081 | 21,646 | 12,923 | 8,838 | 60,135 | 18.7 | 11.2 | 7.6 |
| 2001 | 20,042 | 25,787 | 21,474 | 13,160 | 9,116 | 56,628 | 19.2 | 12.3 | 8.4 |
| 2000 | 19,586 | 25,965 | 21,041 | 13,187 | 9,157 | 53,983 | 19.8 | 12.8 | 8.8 |
| 1999 | 19,032 | 27,542 | 20,710 | 13,164 | 9,157 | 50,784 | 20.9 | 13.6 | 9.4 |
| 1997 | 17,600 | 27,509 | 19,236 | 13,240 | 9,297 | 45,326 | 22.4 | 15.2 | 10.7 |
| 1995 | 16,864 | 23,202 | 17,959 | 12,989 | 9,115 | 40,572 | 23.0 | 16.5 | 11.7 |
| 1993 | 15,976 | 20,261 | 16,871 | 12,153 | 8,631 | 36,764 | 23.9 | 16.7 | 12.2 |
| 1991 | 15,192 | 16,327 | 15,475 | 11,321 | 8,224 | 34,775 | 23.1 | 16.7 | 12.3 |
| 1989 | 13,936 | 15,510 | 14,371 | 10,282 | 7,825 | 32,448 | 23.0 | 16.5 | 12.5 |
| 1987 | 12,922 | 14,470 | 13,386 | 9,775 | 7,518 | 29,744 | 23.4 | 17.1 | 13.1 |
| 1985 | 11,589 | 12,853 | 11,838 | 9,014 | 6,958 | 27,144 | 22.7 | 17.3 | 13.3 |
| 1983 | 10,516 | 10,868 | 10,606 | 8,415 | 6,544 | 24,580 | 22.4 | 17.8 | 13.8 |
| 1981 | 8,912 | 8,896 | 8,910 | 7,726 | 6,115 | 22,388 | 20.7 | 17.9 | 14.2 |
| 1979 | 6,889 | 6,704 | 6,847 | 6,198 | 5,337 | 19,661 | 18.1 | 16.4 | 14.1 |
| 1977 | 5,985 | 5,072 | 5,814 | 5,292 | 4,593 | 16,009 | 18.9 | 17.2 | 14.9 |
| 1967 | 3,313 | 2,276 | 3,216 | 3,196 | 3,185 | 7,933 | 21.1 | 20.9 | 20.9 |

NOTE: *Includes transplants.
(1) U.S. Departments of Commerce, Bureau of Economic Analysis (BEA) , "Average Transaction Price Per New Car." Includes purchases by business, government, and consumers.
(2) 1967 "Average Transaction Price" plus the value of added safety and emissions equipment as determined by the U.S. Bureau of Labor Statistics (BLS), all inflated to current dollars using the BLS, "New Car Consumer Price Index-All Urban Consumers." For example, 1969 is equal to the 1968 value plus the BLS stated value of added safety and emissions equipment for the 1969 model year multiplied by 1968-1969 monthly changes in the New Car Consumer Price Index. The cost to improve fuel economy, which prior to 1980 was included with "Other Quality Adjustments", has since been included by the BLS with the cost of emissions improvements.
(3) 1967 "Average Transaction Price" inflated to current dollars.
(4) BLS, "Median Family Earnings."
(5) "Average Expenditure," as reported by the BEA, divided by "Annual Median Family Earnings", multiplied by 52 weeks. This index is not a good reflection of car prices because it includes upgrading-the purchase of more expensive types of vehicles with more options-and downgrading.
(6) "Estimated Average New Car Price of Comparable Cars With New Safety and Emissions Equipment Added", divided by "Annual Median Family Earnings," multiplied by 52 weeks. This index is a good reflection of price as seen by car purchasers who would not otherwise buy safety/emissions equipment.
(7) "Estimated Average New Car Price of Comparable Cars Without New Safety and Emissions Equipment" divided by "Annual Median Family Earnings," multiplied by 52 weeks. This index is a good reflection of price as seen by purchasers who place full value on new safety/emissions equipment.

## INDICES OF CONSUMER COSTS

| | Consumer Price Index - All Urban Consumers (1982-84 = 100) | | | | | | | |
|------|-----------|---------|----------------|-----------------------|----------|-------------|---------------|----------------------|
| Year | All Items | Housing | Medical Care | Public Transportation | Gasoline | New Cars | New Trucks | Used Cars & Trucks |
| 2010 | 218.1 | 216.2 | 388.4 | 236.4 | 238.6 | 138.1 | 138.8 | 143.1 |
| 2009 | 214.5 | 217.1 | 375.6 | 236.3 | 201.5 | 136.7 | 138.8 | 128.0 |
| 2008 | 215.3 | 216.3 | 364.1 | 250.5 | 277.5 | 135.4 | 137.1 | 134.0 |
| 2007 | 207.3 | 209.6 | 351.1 | 230.0 | 237.9 | 135.9 | 140.7 | 135.7 |
| 2006 | 201.6 | 203.2 | 336.2 | 226.6 | 219.9 | 136.4 | 142.9 | 140.0 |
| 2005 | 195.3 | 195.7 | 323.2 | 217.3 | 194.7 | 135.2 | 145.3 | 139.4 |
| 2004 | 188.9 | 189.5 | 310.1 | 209.1 | 159.7 | 133.9 | 145.0 | 133.3 |
| 2003 | 184.0 | 184.8 | 297.1 | 209.3 | 135.1 | 134.7 | 146.1 | 142.9 |
| 2002 | 179.9 | 180.3 | 285.6 | 207.4 | 116.0 | 137.3 | 147.8 | 152.0 |
| 2001 | 177.1 | 176.4 | 272.8 | 210.6 | 124.0 | 138.9 | 150.7 | 158.7 |
| 2000 | 172.2 | 169.6 | 260.8 | 209.6 | 128.6 | 139.6 | 151.7 | 155.8 |
| 1999 | 166.6 | 163.9 | 250.6 | 197.7 | 100.1 | 139.6 | 153.1 | 152.0 |
| 1998 | 163.0 | 160.4 | 242.1 | 190.3 | 91.6 | 140.7 | 152.1 | 150.6 |
| 1997 | 160.5 | 156.8 | 234.6 | 186.7 | 105.8 | 141.7 | 151.4 | 151.1 |
| 1996 | 156.9 | 152.8 | 228.2 | 181.9 | 105.9 | 141.5 | 149.5 | 157.1 |

NA: Not Available
SOURCE: U.S. Department of Labor, Bureau of Labor Statistics.

# Personal Consumption Expenditures for Transportation

## PERSONAL CONSUMPTION EXPENDITURES FOR TRANSPORTATION

| | 2010 | 2009 | 2008 | 2007 | 2006 | 2005 | 2004 | 2003 |
|---|---|---|---|---|---|---|---|---|
| **User-Operated Transportation** | | | | | | | | |
| New Autos | 69,601 | 72,122 | 85,672 | 95,922 | 99,982 | 97,448 | 91,909 | 91,302 |
| New Light Trucks | 108,207 | 93,197 | 99,193 | 137,230 | 133,065 | 151,447 | 160,522 | 160,305 |
| Net Purchases of Used Motor Vehicles | 114,764 | 104,063 | 106,137 | 116,713 | 113,524 | 112,707 | 107,115 | 106,633 |
| Tires, Tubes, Accessories and Parts | 53,332 | 50,330 | 52,237 | 52,644 | 50,561 | 48,046 | 45,188 | 43,288 |
| Motor Vehicle Maintenance and Repair, Storage, Rental and Leasing | 160,130 | 154,371 | 159,701 | 162,392 | 156,894 | 154,903 | 148,336 | 143,403 |
| Gasoline and Oil | 332,216 | 280,837 | 383,298 | 342,973 | 314,665 | 283,798 | 321,555 | 192,793 |
| Parking Fees and Tolls | 15,233 | 15,588 | 15,585 | 14,702 | 14,778 | 14,771 | 13,722 | 13,152 |
| Insurance Premiums, Less Claims Paid | 61,690 | 60,422 | 61,801 | 61,767 | 56,974 | 57,614 | 53,515 | 49,071 |
| **Total User-Operated Transportation** | **915,173** | **830,930** | **963,624** | **984,343** | **940,443** | **920,734** | **941,862** | **799,947** |
| **Purchased Public Transportation** | | | | | | | | |
| Transit Systems | 15,819 | 15,218 | 15,493 | 14,558 | 14,624 | 13,415 | 12,769 | 11,952 |
| Taxicabs | 4,661 | 4,469 | 4,341 | 4,383 | 4,448 | 4,086 | 3,776 | 3,209 |
| Railway Excluding Commutation | 1,028 | 919 | 996 | 906 | 810 | 733 | 719 | 713 |
| Bus | 1,161 | 1,091 | 1,302 | 1,206 | 1,303 | 1,306 | 1,353 | 1,394 |
| Airline | 50,466 | 45,057 | 51,603 | 51,596 | 49,368 | 47,654 | 46,163 | 43,348 |
| Other | 10,574 | 10,279 | 10,760 | 10,511 | 10,036 | 9,589 | 9,151 | 8,463 |
| **Total Purchased Public Transportation** | **83,709** | **77,033** | **84,495** | **83,160** | **80,589** | **76,783** | **73,931** | **69,079** |
| **Total Transportation Expenditures** | **998,882** | **907,963** | **1,048,119** | **1,067,503** | **1,021,032** | **997,517** | **1,015,793** | **869,026** |
| **Total Personal Consumption Expenditures** | **10,350,589** | **10,001,328** | **10,104,487** | **9,806,312** | **9,322,662** | **8,819,002** | **8,285,080** | **7,804,013** |
| **Transportation spending share of Total PCE** | **9.7%** | **9.1%** | **10.4%** | **10.9%** | **11.0%** | **11.3%** | **12.3%** | **11.1%** |

NOTE: Data in millions of dollars.
SOURCE: U.S. Department of Commerce, Bureau of Economic Analysis.

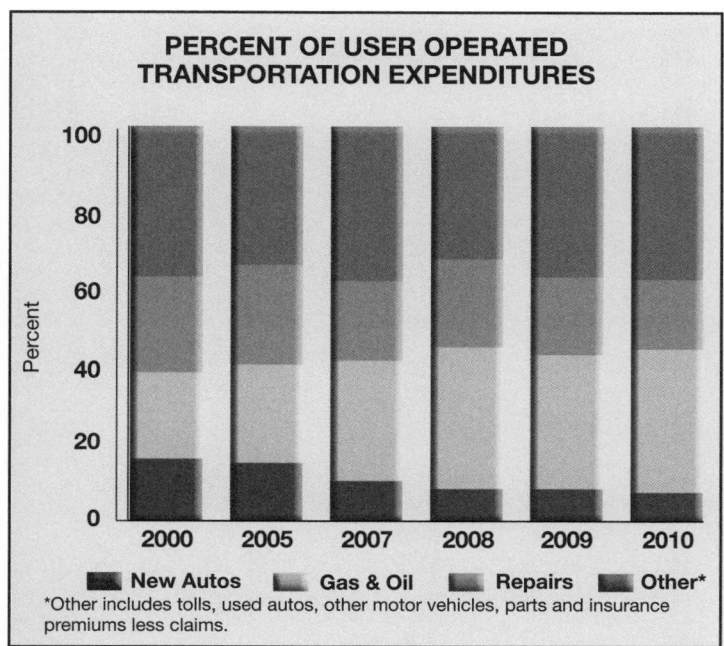

**PERCENT OF USER OPERATED TRANSPORTATION EXPENDITURES**

Legend: New Autos | Gas & Oil | Repairs | Other*

*Other includes tolls, used autos, other motor vehicles, parts and insurance premiums less claims.

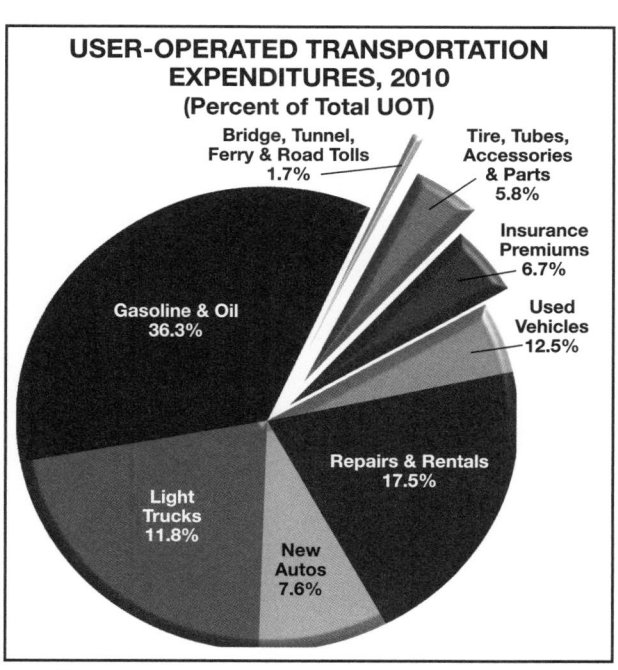

**USER-OPERATED TRANSPORTATION EXPENDITURES, 2010 (Percent of Total UOT)**

- Bridge, Tunnel, Ferry & Road Tolls 1.7%
- Tire, Tubes, Accessories & Parts 5.8%
- Insurance Premiums 6.7%
- Used Vehicles 12.5%
- Gasoline & Oil 36.3%
- Repairs & Rentals 17.5%
- Light Trucks 11.8%
- New Autos 7.6%

# Vehicle Miles of Travel and Fuel Consumption

## VEHICLE MILES OF TRAVEL AND FUEL CONSUMPTION

| | Cars | Light Trucks | Light Vehicle Total | Medium Duty Trucks | Heavy Duty Trucks | Buses | Motorcycles | Total Vehicles |
|---|---|---|---|---|---|---|---|---|
| **Vehicle Miles of Travel (in Millions)** | | | | | | | | |
| 2009 | — | — | 2,630,338 | 120,163 | 167,842 | 14,358 | 20,800 | 2,953,501 |
| 2008 | 1,615,850 | 1,108,603 | 2,724,453 | 83,951 | 143,507 | 7,114 | 14,484 | 2,973,509 |
| 2007 | 1,670,994 | 1,111,277 | 2,782,271 | 81,954 | 145,008 | 6,976 | 13,612 | 3,029,821 |
| 2006 | 1,682,671 | 1,089,013 | 2,771,684 | 80,331 | 142,706 | 6,994 | 12,401 | 3,014,116 |
| 2005 | 1,708,421 | 1,041,051 | 2,749,472 | 79,174 | 144,028 | 6,980 | 10,454 | 2,990,108 |
| 2004 | 1,699,890 | 1,027,164 | 2,727,054 | 78,441 | 142,370 | 6,801 | 10,122 | 2,964,788 |
| 2003 | 1,672,079 | 984,094 | 2,656,173 | 77,757 | 140,160 | 6,783 | 9,577 | 2,890,450 |
| 2002 | 1,658,474 | 966,034 | 2,624,508 | 75,866 | 138,737 | 6,845 | 9,552 | 2,855,508 |
| 2001 | 1,628,332 | 943,207 | 2,571,539 | 72,448 | 136,584 | 7,077 | 9,639 | 2,797,287 |
| 2000 | 1,600,287 | 923,059 | 2,523,346 | 70,500 | 135,020 | 7,590 | 10,469 | 2,746,925 |
| 1990 | 1,417,823 | 574,571 | 1,992,394 | 51,901 | 94,341 | 5,726 | (1) | 2,144,362 |
| 1980 | 1,121,810 | 290,935 | 1,412,745 | 39,813 | 68,678 | 6,059 | (1) | 1,527,295 |
| 1970 | 919,679 | 123,286 | 1,042,965 | 27,081 | 35,134 | 4,544 | (1) | 1,109,724 |
| **Average Annual Miles Traveled Per Vehicle** | | | | | | | | |
| 2009 | — | — | 11,218 | 14,380 | 64,132 | 17,052 | 2,623 | 11,618 |
| 2008 | 11,788 | 10,951 | 11,432 | 12,362 | 64,764 | 8,436 | 1,868 | 11,619 |
| 2007 | 12,293 | 10,952 | 11,720 | 12,040 | 65,290 | 8,360 | 1,907 | 11,910 |
| 2006 | 12,427 | 11,857 | 12,197 | 13,038 | 70,986 | 8,509 | 1,855 | 12,408 |
| 2005 | 12,510 | 10,920 | 11,856 | 12,274 | 69,020 | 8,649 | 1,679 | 12,082 |
| 2004 | 12,460 | 11,184 | 11,946 | 12,732 | 70,819 | 8,552 | 1,755 | 12,200 |
| 2003 | 12,325 | 11,287 | 11,919 | 13,295 | 73,445 | 8,734 | 1,783 | 12,208 |
| 2002 | 12,202 | 11,364 | 11,879 | 13,426 | 60,939 | 8,998 | 1,909 | 12,171 |
| 2001 | 11,831 | 11,204 | 11,593 | 12,702 | 63,404 | 9,442 | 1,966 | 11,887 |
| 2000 | 11,976 | 11,672 | 11,863 | 11,897 | 64,399 | 10,173 | 2,409 | 12,164 |
| 1990 | 10,277 | 11,902 | 10,693 | 11,567 | 55,206 | 9,133 | (1) | 11,107 |
| 1980 | 8,813 | 10,437 | 9,112 | 9,103 | 48,472 | 11,458 | (1) | 9,458 |
| 1970 | 9,989 | 8,676 | 9,821 | 7,356 | 38,819 | 12,035 | (1) | 9,976 |
| **Fuel Consumed (Millions of Gallons)** | | | | | | | | |
| 2009 | — | — | 121,324 | 16,342 | 28,130 | 1,869 | 475 | 168,140 |
| 2008 | 71,947 | 61,199 | 133,146 | 9,889 | 26,814 | 1,110 | 256 | 171,215 |
| 2007 | 74,355 | 61,816 | 136,171 | 10,036 | 28,515 | 1,144 | 242 | 176,108 |
| 2006 | 74,983 | 60,662 | 135,645 | 9,843 | 28,075 | 1,147 | 221 | 174,931 |
| 2005 | 77,418 | 58,869 | 136,287 | 9,501 | 27,689 | 1,120 | 189 | 174,786 |
| 2004 | 75,402 | 63,417 | 138,819 | 8,959 | 24,191 | 1,360 | 202 | 173,531 |
| 2003 | 75,455 | 60,758 | 136,213 | 8,880 | 23,815 | 969 | 192 | 170,069 |
| 2002 | 75,471 | 55,220 | 130,691 | 10,321 | 26,480 | 1,000 | 191 | 168,683 |
| 2001 | 73,559 | 53,522 | 127,081 | 9,667 | 25,512 | 1,026 | 193 | 163,479 |
| 2000 | 73,065 | 52,939 | 126,004 | 9,563 | 25,666 | 1,112 | 209 | 162,554 |
| 1990 | 69,759 | 35,611 | 105,370 | 8,357 | 16,133 | 895 | (1) | 130,755 |
| 1980 | 70,186 | 23,796 | 93,982 | 6,923 | 13,037 | 1,018 | (1) | 114,960 |
| 1970 | 67,879 | 12,313 | 80,192 | 3,968 | 7,348 | 820 | (1) | 92,329 |
| **Average Annual Fuel Consumption Per Vehicle (Gallons)** | | | | | | | | |
| 2009 | — | — | 517 | 1,956 | 10,748 | 2,219 | 60 | 661 |
| 2008 | 522 | 605 | 557 | 1,456 | 12,101 | 1,316 | 33 | 667 |
| 2007 | 547 | 609 | 574 | 1,474 | 12,839 | 1,371 | 34 | 692 |
| 2006 | 554 | 660 | 597 | 1,598 | 13,965 | 1,396 | 33 | 720 |
| 2005 | 567 | 617 | 588 | 1,486 | 13,269 | 1,388 | 30 | 706 |
| 2004 | 553 | 690 | 608 | 1,454 | 12,033 | 1,710 | 35 | 714 |
| 2003 | 556 | 697 | 611 | 1,518 | 12,479 | 1,248 | 36 | 718 |
| 2002 | 555 | 650 | 592 | 1,826 | 11,631 | 1,314 | 38 | 719 |
| 2001 | 534 | 636 | 573 | 1,695 | 11,843 | 1,369 | 39 | 695 |
| 2000 | 547 | 669 | 592 | 1,614 | 12,241 | 1,490 | 48 | 720 |
| 1990 | 506 | 738 | 569 | 1,862 | 9,441 | 1,428 | (1) | 677 |
| 1980 | 551 | 854 | 610 | 1,583 | 9,201 | 1,926 | (1) | 712 |
| 1970 | 737 | 866 | 760 | 1,078 | 8,119 | 2,172 | (1) | 830 |

NOTE: Car and light truck combined into light vehicle beginning in 2009.
NA - Not available. (1) Cars include motorcycles through 1994.
SOURCE: U.S. Department of Transportation, Federal Highway Administration.

# Annual Vehicle Miles of Travel

## VEHICLE MILES OF TRAVEL, 2009

| | Rural Interstate | Total Rural | Urban Interstate | Total Urban | Total |
|---|---|---|---|---|---|
| Alabama | 5,382 | 28,567 | 7,199 | 27,494 | 56,061 |
| Alaska | 860 | 2,316 | 663 | 2,617 | 4,933 |
| Arizona | 6,966 | 18,241 | 5,920 | 43,387 | 61,628 |
| Arkansas | 4,204 | 18,679 | 3,985 | 14,540 | 33,219 |
| California | 17,541 | 58,203 | 68,191 | 266,283 | 324,486 |
| Colorado | 4,287 | 14,565 | 7,260 | 31,711 | 46,276 |
| Connecticut | 718 | 3,971 | 9,562 | 27,449 | 31,420 |
| Delaware | — | 2,742 | 1,230 | 6,338 | 9,080 |
| Dist. of Columbia | — | — | 431 | 3,608 | 3,608 |
| Florida | 9,505 | 35,612 | 24,269 | 159,048 | 194,659 |
| Georgia | 9,671 | 38,681 | 19,203 | 70,577 | 109,258 |
| Hawaii | 113 | 2,423 | 1,786 | 7,550 | 9,973 |
| Idaho | 2,193 | 9,463 | 1,291 | 6,068 | 15,531 |
| Illinois | 8,844 | 27,081 | 22,670 | 78,765 | 105,846 |
| Indiana | 7,014 | 28,574 | 9,712 | 48,054 | 76,628 |
| Iowa | 4,679 | 18,754 | 2,529 | 12,311 | 31,065 |
| Kansas | 3,167 | 14,454 | 3,613 | 15,045 | 29,499 |
| Kentucky | 6,592 | 27,307 | 5,951 | 20,048 | 47,355 |
| Louisiana | 5,416 | 19,359 | 7,187 | 25,504 | 44,863 |
| Maine | 2,171 | 10,442 | 805 | 4,049 | 14,491 |
| Maryland | 3,539 | 14,091 | 13,426 | 41,202 | 55,293 |
| Massachusetts | 1,373 | 4,284 | 15,098 | 50,528 | 54,812 |
| Michigan | 5,276 | 31,444 | 15,389 | 65,325 | 96,769 |
| Minnesota | 4,165 | 24,578 | 8,411 | 32,294 | 56,872 |
| Mississippi | 3,838 | 24,169 | 3,386 | 16,258 | 40,427 |
| Missouri | 5,951 | 29,014 | 12,126 | 39,989 | 69,003 |
| Montana | 2,427 | 8,334 | 360 | 2,677 | 11,011 |
| Nebraska | 2,575 | 10,998 | 1,364 | 8,361 | 19,359 |
| Nevada | 1,959 | 5,092 | 3,407 | 15,362 | 20,454 |
| New Hampshire | 1,261 | 5,701 | 1,569 | 7,274 | 12,975 |
| New Jersey | 1,589 | 6,238 | 13,506 | 66,791 | 73,029 |
| New Mexico | 4,383 | 14,763 | 2,682 | 11,250 | 26,013 |
| New York | 6,088 | 32,963 | 20,440 | 100,528 | 133,491 |
| North Carolina | 6,133 | 39,193 | 14,579 | 89,157 | 128,350 |
| North Dakota | 1,465 | 5,907 | 395 | 2,247 | 8,154 |
| Ohio | 8,991 | 36,367 | 22,170 | 74,275 | 110,642 |
| Oklahoma | 5,088 | 21,444 | 4,761 | 25,553 | 46,997 |
| Oregon | 4,239 | 15,103 | 4,447 | 18,869 | 33,972 |
| Pennsylvania | 10,373 | 37,759 | 14,004 | 66,121 | 103,880 |
| Rhode Island | 404 | 873 | 1,742 | 7,377 | 8,250 |
| South Carolina | 7,411 | 24,252 | 5,989 | 24,878 | 49,130 |
| South Dakota | 1,999 | 6,352 | 616 | 3,254 | 9,607 |
| Tennessee | 8,733 | 28,115 | 11,729 | 42,111 | 70,226 |
| Texas | 14,869 | 67,604 | 39,269 | 162,807 | 230,411 |
| Utah | 3,167 | 7,945 | 5,993 | 18,319 | 26,264 |
| Vermont | 1,202 | 5,779 | 365 | 1,867 | 7,646 |
| Virginia | 9,029 | 29,931 | 14,962 | 50,996 | 80,927 |
| Washington | 4,514 | 16,687 | 10,793 | 39,730 | 56,417 |
| West Virginia | 2,867 | 11,302 | 2,789 | 8,304 | 19,606 |
| Wisconsin | 5,173 | 27,611 | 5,267 | 30,546 | 58,157 |
| Wyoming | 2,470 | 6,899 | 472 | 2,669 | 9,568 |
| **U.S. Total** | **241,873** | **980,227** | **474,963** | **1,997,364** | **2,977,591** |

NOTE: Data in millions. Includes travel by motorcycle.
SOURCE: U.S. Department of Transportation, Federal Highway Administration.

## TOTAL VEHICLE MILES TRAVELED

| Year | Rural | Urban | Total | % Change |
|---|---|---|---|---|
| 2009 | 980 | 1,997 | 2,977 | 0.1 |
| 2008 | 990 | 1,983 | 2,973 | -1.9 |
| 2007 | 1,035 | 1,995 | 3,030 | 0.5 |
| 2006 | 1,037 | 1,977 | 3,014 | 0.8 |
| 2005 | 1,038 | 1,952 | 2,990 | 0.9 |
| 2004 | 1,070 | 1,892 | 2,962 | 2.5 |
| 2003 | 1,085 | 1,806 | 2,891 | 1.2 |
| 2002 | 1,128 | 1,728 | 2,856 | 2.7 |
| 2001 | 1,105 | 1,676 | 2,781 | 1.1 |
| 2000 | 1,085 | 1,665 | 2,750 | 2.2 |
| 1999 | 1,063 | 1,628 | 2,691 | 2.5 |
| 1998 | 1,033 | 1,592 | 2,625 | 3.7 |
| 1997 | 985 | 1,547 | 2,532 | 2.0 |
| 1996 | 960 | 1,522 | 2,482 | 2.5 |
| 1995 | 933 | 1,489 | 2,422 | 2.7 |
| 1994 | 909 | 1,449 | 2,358 | 2.7 |
| 1993 | 887 | 1,410 | 2,297 | 2.2 |
| 1992 | 884 | 1,363 | 2,247 | 3.4 |
| 1991 | 884 | 1,289 | 2,173 | 1.2 |
| 1990 | 870 | 1,277 | 2,147 | 1.9 |
| 1989 | 849 | 1,258 | 2,107 | 4.0 |
| 1988 | 818 | 1,208 | 2,026 | 5.5 |
| 1987 | 780 | 1,141 | 1,921 | 4.7 |
| 1986 | 748 | 1,087 | 1,835 | 3.4 |
| 1985 | 730 | 1,044 | 1,774 | 3.1 |
| 1984 | 718 | 1,002 | 1,720 | 4.1 |
| 1983 | 701 | 952 | 1,653 | 3.6 |
| 1982 | 689 | 906 | 1,595 | 2.7 |
| 1981 | 686 | 867 | 1,553 | 1.7 |
| 1980 | 672 | 855 | 1,527 | -0.2 |
| 1979 | 676 | 854 | 1,530 | -0.9 |
| 1978 | 682 | 862 | 1,544 | 5.2 |
| 1977 | 651 | 816 | 1,467 | 4.6 |
| 1976 | 625 | 777 | 1,402 | 5.6 |
| 1975 | 602 | 726 | 1,328 | 3.8 |
| 1974 | 585 | 695 | 1,280 | -2.5 |
| 1973 | 606 | 707 | 1,313 | 4.2 |
| 1972 | 590 | 670 | 1,260 | 6.9 |
| 1971 | 573 | 606 | 1,179 | 6.3 |
| 1970 | 539 | 570 | 1,109 | 4.5 |
| 1969 | 524 | 537 | 1,061 | 4.4 |
| 1968 | 506 | 510 | 1,016 | 5.4 |
| 1967 | 481 | 483 | 964 | 4.1 |
| 1966 | 476 | 450 | 926 | 4.3 |
| 1965 | 464 | 424 | 888 | 5.0 |
| 1964 | 441 | 405 | 846 | 5.1 |
| 1963 | 420 | 385 | 805 | 5.0 |
| 1962 | 399 | 368 | 767 | 3.9 |
| 1961 | 398 | 340 | 738 | 2.6 |
| 1960 | 387 | 332 | 719 | 2.6 |
| 1959 | 377 | 324 | 701 | 5.4 |
| 1958 | 358 | 307 | 665 | 2.8 |
| 1957 | 350 | 297 | 647 | 2.5 |
| 1956 | 344 | 287 | 631 | 4.1 |
| 1955 | 331 | 275 | 606 | 7.8 |
| 1954 | 314 | 248 | 562 | 3.3 |
| 1953 | 308 | 236 | 544 | 6.0 |
| 1952 | 289 | 224 | 513 | 4.5 |
| 1951 | 268 | 223 | 491 | 7.2 |
| 1950 | 240 | 218 | 458 | 8.0 |

NOTE: Data in billions.
SOURCE: U.S. Department of Transportation, Federal Highway Administration.

# Selected Travel Data by State

## TRAVEL DATA BY STATE, 2009

| State | Resident Population in Thousands | Population Per Vehicle | Annual Miles Traveled | | Public Road and Street Mileage | | | State Gasoline Tax Rate |
| --- | --- | --- | --- | --- | --- | --- | --- | --- |
| | | | Per Vehicle | Per Licensed Driver | Rural | Urban | Total | |
| Alabama | 4,709 | 1.02 | 12,158 | 14,822 | 73,283 | 20,536 | 93,820 | 18.0 |
| Alaska | 698 | 1.00 | 7,095 | 9,715 | 13,300 | 2,419 | 15,719 | 8.0 |
| Arizona | 6,596 | 1.51 | 14,143 | 13,996 | 37,523 | 22,917 | 60,440 | 18.0 |
| Arkansas | 2,889 | 1.42 | 16,305 | 16,086 | 87,255 | 12,845 | 100,100 | 21.5 |
| California | 36,962 | 1.07 | 9,424 | 13,703 | 81,831 | 90,043 | 171,874 | 18.0 |
| Colorado | 5,025 | 0.95 | 8,775 | 12,492 | 68,903 | 19,375 | 88,278 | 22.0 |
| Connecticut | 3,518 | 1.15 | 10,229 | 10,775 | 6,245 | 15,162 | 21,407 | 25.0 |
| Delaware | 885 | 1.05 | 10,766 | 12,976 | 3,309 | 2,993 | 6,302 | 23.0 |
| District of Columbia | 600 | 2.76 | 16,577 | 9,594 | — | 1,505 | 1,505 | 20.0 |
| Florida | 18,538 | 1.21 | 12,711 | 13,899 | 40,407 | 81,040 | 121,447 | 15.6 |
| Georgia | 9,829 | 1.16 | 12,843 | 17,301 | 83,023 | 38,608 | 121,631 | 7.5 |
| Hawaii | 1,295 | 1.45 | 11,139 | 11,207 | 2,052 | 2,319 | 4,371 | 17.0 |
| Idaho | 1,546 | 1.12 | 11,296 | 14,718 | 42,437 | 5,743 | 48,180 | 25.0 |
| Illinois | 12,910 | 1.31 | 10,701 | 12,751 | 98,144 | 41,433 | 139,577 | 19.0 |
| Indiana | 6,423 | 1.11 | 13,200 | 13,806 | 68,901 | 26,778 | 95,679 | 18.0 |
| Iowa | 3,008 | 0.89 | 9,237 | 14,480 | 102,992 | 11,355 | 114,347 | 21.0 |
| Kansas | 2,819 | 1.16 | 12,163 | 14,422 | 127,821 | 12,932 | 140,753 | 24.0 |
| Kentucky | 4,314 | 1.20 | 13,211 | 16,110 | 66,380 | 12,583 | 78,963 | 22.5 |
| Louisiana | 4,492 | 1.11 | 11,123 | 14,538 | 44,996 | 16,339 | 61,335 | 20.0 |
| Maine | 1,318 | 1.25 | 13,724 | 14,298 | 19,843 | 2,996 | 22,839 | 28.4 |
| Maryland | 5,699 | 1.27 | 12,332 | 14,161 | 14,072 | 17,389 | 31,461 | 23.5 |
| Massachusetts | 6,594 | 1.25 | 10,417 | 11,839 | 7,980 | 28,197 | 36,177 | 21.0 |
| Michigan | 9,970 | 1.26 | 12,229 | 13,662 | 85,791 | 35,860 | 121,651 | 19.0 |
| Minnesota | 5,266 | 1.10 | 11,858 | 17,524 | 117,130 | 20,802 | 137,932 | 22.5 |
| Mississippi | 2,952 | 1.46 | 19,957 | 20,940 | 63,960 | 11,025 | 74,985 | 18.4 |
| Missouri | 5,988 | 1.22 | 14,070 | 16,360 | 106,767 | 23,592 | 130,359 | 17.0 |
| Montana | 975 | 1.05 | 11,904 | 14,921 | 70,552 | 3,075 | 73,627 | 27.8 |
| Nebraska | 1,797 | 1.00 | 10,797 | 14,347 | 87,217 | 6,414 | 93,631 | 26.0 |
| Nevada | 2,643 | 1.89 | 14,638 | 12,100 | 27,561 | 7,283 | 34,844 | 24.0 |
| New Hampshire | 1,325 | 1.09 | 10,701 | 12,545 | 11,113 | 4,928 | 16,041 | 19.6 |
| New Jersey | 8,708 | 1.42 | 11,945 | 12,329 | 7,278 | 31,557 | 38,835 | 10.5 |
| New Mexico | 2,010 | 1.24 | 16,050 | 18,878 | 60,391 | 7,993 | 68,384 | 18.9 |
| New York | 19,541 | 1.74 | 11,871 | 11,783 | 66,115 | 48,431 | 114,546 | 24.5 |
| North Carolina | 9,381 | 1.55 | 21,224 | 19,733 | 69,450 | 35,867 | 105,317 | 30.2 |
| North Dakota | 647 | 0.90 | 11,293 | 17,110 | 84,945 | 1,898 | 86,843 | 23.0 |
| Ohio | 11,543 | 1.05 | 10,038 | 13,939 | 78,242 | 44,783 | 123,024 | 28.0 |
| Oklahoma | 3,687 | 1.09 | 13,837 | 20,249 | 97,077 | 18,774 | 115,851 | 17.0 |
| Oregon | 3,826 | 1.26 | 11,152 | 11,954 | 46,234 | 12,894 | 59,128 | 24.0 |
| Pennsylvania | 12,605 | 1.28 | 10,538 | 11,958 | 76,478 | 45,302 | 121,780 | 30.0 |
| Rhode Island | 1,053 | 1.34 | 10,461 | 11,059 | 1,212 | 5,188 | 6,400 | 30.0 |
| South Carolina | 4,561 | 1.26 | 13,593 | 15,031 | 49,841 | 16,422 | 66,263 | 16.0 |
| South Dakota | 812 | 0.88 | 10,372 | 15,954 | 79,368 | 2,986 | 82,354 | 22.0 |
| Tennessee | 6,296 | 1.22 | 13,664 | 15,688 | 69,594 | 23,658 | 93,252 | 20.0 |
| Texas | 24,782 | 1.37 | 12,733 | 14,987 | 213,733 | 97,117 | 310,850 | 20.0 |
| Utah | 2,785 | 1.13 | 10,703 | 15,270 | 33,731 | 11,146 | 44,877 | 24.5 |
| Vermont | 622 | 1.12 | 13,718 | 15,082 | 13,012 | 1,424 | 14,436 | 21.0 |
| Virginia | 7,883 | 1.25 | 12,842 | 15,133 | 50,387 | 23,795 | 74,182 | 17.5 |
| Washington | 6,664 | 1.19 | 10,109 | 11,224 | 60,316 | 23,191 | 83,507 | 37.5 |
| West Virginia | 1,820 | 1.29 | 13,881 | 14,753 | 33,232 | 5,366 | 38,598 | 32.2 |
| Wisconsin | 5,655 | 1.16 | 11,931 | 14,167 | 92,530 | 22,380 | 114,910 | 30.9 |
| Wyoming | 544 | 0.83 | 14,668 | 23,290 | 25,392 | 2,713 | 28,105 | 14.0 |
| **Total** | **307,007** | **1.23** | **11,912** | **14,205** | **2,969,346** | **1,081,371** | **4,050,717** | **21.7** |

SOURCE: U.S. Department of Commerce, Bureau of the Census, and U.S. Department of Transportation.

# State Highway Agency Capital Outlay and Maintenance

## STATE HIGHWAY AGENCY CAPITAL OUTLAY AND MAINTENANCE

| | Capital Outlay | | Maintenance | | Total | | '09 vs. '08 Percent Change |
|---|---|---|---|---|---|---|---|
| | 2009 | 2008 | 2009 | 2008 | 2009 | 2008 | |
| Alabama | 1,182,119 | 1,170,599 | 158,245 | 182,085 | 1,340,364 | 1,352,684 | -0.9 |
| Alaska | 578,918 | 379,094 | 72,610 | 71,876 | 651,528 | 450,970 | 44.5 |
| Arizona | 1,273,127 | 1,133,353 | 117,821 | 112,901 | 1,390,948 | 1,246,254 | 11.6 |
| Arkansas | 561,904 | 630,837 | 240,028 | 231,195 | 801,932 | 862,032 | -7.0 |
| California | 6,198,986 | 5,144,804 | 963,106 | 500,728 | 7,162,092 | 5,645,532 | 26.9 |
| Colorado | 925,307 | 741,595 | 101,393 | 114,242 | 1,026,700 | 855,837 | 20.0 |
| Connecticut | 659,277 | 553,557 | 71,838 | 84,469 | 731,115 | 638,026 | 14.6 |
| Delaware | 334,746 | 247,399 | 54,261 | 55,917 | 389,007 | 303,316 | 28.3 |
| District of Columbia | 285,947 | 247,863 | 55,108 | 62,883 | 341,055 | 310,746 | 9.8 |
| Florida | 4,589,386 | 5,381,502 | 685,611 | 854,822 | 5,274,997 | 6,236,324 | -15.4 |
| Georgia | 2,198,897 | 2,674,700 | 156,094 | 164,897 | 2,354,991 | 2,839,597 | -17.1 |
| Hawaii | 276,618 | 260,763 | 36,969 | 30,739 | 313,587 | 291,502 | 7.6 |
| Idaho | 537,617 | 453,111 | 82,842 | 87,068 | 620,459 | 540,179 | 14.9 |
| Illinois | 3,000,966 | 3,112,997 | 429,340 | 383,896 | 3,430,306 | 3,496,893 | -1.9 |
| Indiana | 1,823,311 | 1,823,311 | 65,495 | 65,495 | 1,888,806 | 1,888,806 | — |
| Iowa | 680,583 | 526,150 | 87,774 | 93,353 | 768,357 | 619,503 | 24.0 |
| Kansas | 904,092 | 844,916 | 133,294 | 137,594 | 1,037,386 | 982,510 | 5.6 |
| Kentucky | 1,735,079 | 1,745,629 | 354,691 | 332,732 | 2,089,770 | 2,078,361 | 0.5 |
| Louisiana | 2,973,935 | 1,867,305 | 226,341 | 197,794 | 3,200,276 | 2,065,099 | 55.0 |
| Maine | 299,913 | 283,437 | 121,667 | 158,397 | 421,580 | 441,834 | -4.6 |
| Maryland | 1,474,659 | 1,474,464 | 116,675 | 130,779 | 1,591,334 | 1,605,243 | -0.9 |
| Massachusetts | 1,046,031 | 912,288 | 114,500 | 62,450 | 1,160,531 | 974,738 | 19.1 |
| Michigan | 2,260,625 | 2,321,864 | 192,948 | 199,365 | 2,453,573 | 2,521,229 | -2.7 |
| Minnesota | 848,952 | 945,278 | 344,285 | 291,805 | 1,193,237 | 1,237,083 | -3.5 |
| Mississippi | 867,005 | 964,864 | 101,583 | 88,990 | 968,588 | 1,053,854 | -8.1 |
| Missouri | 1,595,920 | 1,337,453 | 390,532 | 352,261 | 1,986,452 | 1,689,714 | 17.6 |
| Montana | 435,888 | 401,116 | 64,764 | 63,688 | 500,652 | 464,804 | 7.7 |
| Nebraska | 606,510 | 567,602 | 273,790 | 248,957 | 880,300 | 816,559 | 7.8 |
| Nevada | 738,746 | 465,116 | 89,267 | 84,899 | 828,013 | 550,015 | 50.5 |
| New Hampshire | 230,115 | 259,987 | 120,100 | 150,519 | 350,215 | 410,506 | -14.7 |
| New Jersey | 1,594,245 | 1,790,173 | 185,605 | 96,908 | 1,779,850 | 1,887,081 | -5.7 |
| New Mexico | 528,548 | 253,991 | 147,028 | 120,178 | 675,576 | 374,169 | 80.6 |
| New York | 3,229,953 | 3,060,882 | 698,057 | 762,793 | 3,928,010 | 3,823,675 | 2.7 |
| North Carolina | 1,989,813 | 2,083,426 | 609,270 | 623,815 | 2,599,083 | 2,707,241 | -4.0 |
| North Dakota | 314,349 | 320,586 | 17,355 | 18,201 | 331,704 | 338,787 | -2.1 |
| Ohio | 2,068,001 | 2,091,603 | 341,647 | 163,051 | 2,409,648 | 2,254,654 | 6.9 |
| Oklahoma | 1,040,529 | 919,510 | 129,856 | 152,110 | 1,170,385 | 1,071,620 | 9.2 |
| Oregon | 820,255 | 839,822 | 161,803 | 189,553 | 982,058 | 1,029,375 | -4.6 |
| Pennsylvania | 3,638,187 | 2,714,483 | 1,026,411 | 1,055,208 | 4,664,598 | 3,769,691 | 23.7 |
| Rhode Island | 153,323 | 189,344 | 80,049 | 70,432 | 233,372 | 259,776 | -10.2 |
| South Carolina | 645,602 | 549,986 | 387,342 | 365,653 | 1,032,944 | 915,639 | 12.8 |
| South Dakota | 349,865 | 290,825 | 49,593 | 51,090 | 399,458 | 341,915 | 16.8 |
| Tennessee | 1,035,883 | 898,313 | 305,894 | 251,537 | 1,341,777 | 1,149,850 | 16.7 |
| Texas | 5,364,789 | 7,101,872 | 1,133,383 | 1,300,886 | 6,498,172 | 8,402,758 | -22.7 |
| Utah | 911,965 | 524,841 | 202,917 | 97,937 | 1,114,882 | 622,778 | 79.0 |
| Vermont | 191,853 | 172,848 | 71,851 | 66,057 | 263,704 | 238,905 | 10.4 |
| Virginia | 1,091,029 | 1,355,251 | 1,052,926 | 1,038,727 | 2,143,955 | 2,393,978 | -10.4 |
| Washington | 1,981,924 | 1,728,938 | 509,519 | 564,000 | 2,491,443 | 2,292,938 | 8.7 |
| West Virginia | 841,764 | 734,389 | 216,260 | 196,360 | 1,058,024 | 930,749 | 13.7 |
| Wisconsin | 1,369,599 | 1,285,906 | 64,735 | 66,713 | 1,434,334 | 1,352,619 | 6.0 |
| Wyoming | 429,025 | 361,366 | 39,446 | 81,824 | 468,471 | 443,190 | 5.7 |
| **Total** | **70,715,680** | **68,141,309** | **13,453,919** | **12,929,829** | **84,169,599** | **81,071,138** | **3.8** |

NOTE: Data in thousands of dollars.
SOURCE: U.S. Department of Transportation, Federal Highway Administration.

# Vehicle and Equipment Manufacturing Employment by State

## VEHICLE AND EQUIPMENT MANUFACTURING EMPLOYMENT BY STATE, 2008

| State | Vehicle Manufacturing | Vehicle Body & Trailer | Engine & Engine Parts | Electrical Components | Transmission, Brake & Suspension Parts | Other Vehicle Parts Manufacturing |
|---|---|---|---|---|---|---|
| Alabama | 11,434 | 4,553 | 1,300 | 2,750 | 2,884 | 8,284 |
| Alaska | — | 25 | — | — | — | — |
| Arizona | 39 | 1,014 | 140 | 56 | 246 | 2,151 |
| Arkansas | 510 | 1,696 | 1,232 | 150 | 2,120 | 2,717 |
| California | 11,000 | 9,219 | 2,194 | 2,412 | 2,616 | 12,315 |
| Colorado | 5 | 568 | 84 | 16 | 42 | 865 |
| Connecticut | — | 52 | 110 | 881 | 595 | 1,430 |
| Delaware | 1,200 | 8 | 7 | 5 | — | 169 |
| District of Columbia | — | — | — | — | — | — |
| Florida | 260 | 3,595 | 517 | 607 | 478 | 1,996 |
| Georgia | 1,300 | 3,217 | 501 | 1,165 | 2,513 | 3,713 |
| Hawaii | — | 10 | 9 | 5 | 8 | 5 |
| Idaho | — | 1,354 | 5 | 8 | 10 | 56 |
| Illinois | 6,432 | 2,933 | 2,153 | 6,584 | 3,705 | 8,075 |
| Indiana | 14,061 | 34,366 | 6,287 | 8,768 | 22,689 | 15,489 |
| Iowa | 33 | 7,440 | 650 | 1,054 | 730 | 2,731 |
| Kansas | 1,050 | 2,348 | 66 | 1,394 | 46 | 1,203 |
| Kentucky | 15,195 | 1,468 | 1,862 | 3,259 | 10,015 | 12,950 |
| Louisiana | 1,200 | 600 | 140 | 24 | 55 | 385 |
| Maine | — | 203 | 11 | 25 | 270 | 30 |
| Maryland | 30 | 109 | 40 | 300 | 337 | 567 |
| Massachusetts | 25 | 456 | 242 | 1,650 | 41 | 187 |
| Michigan | 33,737 | 2,631 | 12,694 | 3,614 | 24,001 | 34,161 |
| Minnesota | 1,060 | 2,550 | 620 | 356 | 793 | 968 |
| Mississippi | 2,600 | 612 | 159 | 1,170 | 885 | 1,530 |
| Missouri | 9,053 | 2,198 | 1,300 | 982 | 3,456 | 4,811 |
| Montana | 140 | 221 | 30 | 5 | 4 | 44 |
| Nebraska | 40 | 1,807 | 650 | 260 | 765 | 1,750 |
| Nevada | 111 | 52 | 168 | 170 | 11 | 155 |
| New Hampshire | 10 | 159 | 5 | 744 | 200 | 610 |
| New Jersey | 152 | 433 | 217 | 103 | 168 | 283 |
| New Mexico | 30 | 88 | 19 | 20 | 5 | 35 |
| New York | 550 | 1,398 | 3,522 | 3,143 | 5,448 | 3,621 |
| North Carolina | 6,000 | 2,670 | 1,787 | 1,400 | 6,681 | 8,100 |
| North Dakota | 270 | 524 | 8 | 600 | 4 | 204 |
| Ohio | 22,382 | 5,752 | 6,020 | 8,210 | 20,135 | 19,931 |
| Oklahoma | 1,060 | 3,486 | 294 | 600 | 855 | 506 |
| Oregon | 2,650 | 5,264 | 131 | 578 | 77 | 894 |
| Pennsylvania | 922 | 7,614 | 382 | 3,570 | 3,397 | 2,106 |
| Rhode Island | — | 86 | 5 | 200 | — | 145 |
| South Carolina | 6,000 | 750 | 2,750 | 1,054 | 3,001 | 5,980 |
| South Dakota | 140 | 989 | 140 | 40 | 50 | 954 |
| Tennessee | 5,050 | 2,344 | 2,016 | 2,670 | 10,285 | 15,861 |
| Texas | 9,488 | 6,367 | 935 | 2,017 | 982 | 8,113 |
| Utah | 8 | 1,361 | 26 | 5 | 247 | 3,504 |
| Vermont | — | 45 | 5 | — | — | — |
| Virginia | 2,570 | 1,942 | 1,450 | 1,125 | 2,905 | 1,301 |
| Washington | 644 | 1,025 | 295 | 279 | 62 | 1,341 |
| West Virginia | 30 | 175 | 1,300 | 145 | 60 | 300 |
| Wisconsin | 5,070 | 4,862 | 5,050 | 1,500 | 1,031 | 5,782 |
| Wyoming | — | 270 | 30 | 5 | 5 | 40 |
| **Total** | **182,072** | **136,404** | **60,550** | **66,128** | **140,068** | **199,913** |

NOTE: In some cases, an average was taken based on the Bureau of the Census employment range.
Omission of data for individual states is due to either the absences of such business from the state or the necessity of withholding the data to avoid disclosure of individual firms data.
SOURCE: U.S. Department of Commerce, Bureau of the Census.

# Vehicle and Equipment Manufacturing Employment by State

**VEHICLE AND EQUIPMENT MANUFACTURING EMPLOYMENT BY STATE, 2008 — continued**

| State | Vehicle Metal Stamping | Tire Manufacturing | Storage Batteries | Total Vehicle & Equipment Manufacturing | Total State Manufacturing Employment | Vehicle and Equipment % of Total State Manufacturing Employment |
|---|---|---|---|---|---|---|
| Alabama | 2,977 | 5,442 | — | 39,624 | 278,608 | 14.2 |
| Alaska | — | 5 | — | 30 | 12,028 | 0.2 |
| Arizona | 30 | 96 | 5 | 3,777 | 165,910 | 2.3 |
| Arkansas | 5 | 1,111 | 200 | 9,741 | 183,494 | 5.3 |
| California | 1,403 | 789 | 1,047 | 42,995 | 1,383,918 | 3.1 |
| Colorado | 45 | 113 | 290 | 2,028 | 139,427 | 1.5 |
| Connecticut | 743 | 78 | 125 | 4,014 | 178,239 | 2.3 |
| Delaware | — | 5 | 150 | 1,544 | 32,956 | 4.7 |
| District of Columbia | — | — | — | — | 2,011 | — |
| Florida | 546 | 481 | 341 | 8,821 | 341,607 | 2.6 |
| Georgia | 981 | 3,246 | 600 | 17,236 | 397,930 | 4.3 |
| Hawaii | — | 5 | — | 42 | 14,190 | 0.3 |
| Idaho | 5 | 6 | — | 1,444 | 63,460 | 2.3 |
| Illinois | 4,835 | 4,136 | 265 | 39,118 | 644,978 | 6.1 |
| Indiana | 9,648 | 2,130 | 624 | 114,062 | 523,683 | 21.8 |
| Iowa | 1,200 | 1,300 | 564 | 15,702 | 228,190 | 6.9 |
| Kansas | 25 | 1,060 | 1,111 | 8,303 | 183,411 | 4.5 |
| Kentucky | 4,796 | 181 | 270 | 49,996 | 247,611 | 20.2 |
| Louisiana | — | 142 | — | 2,546 | 143,245 | 1.8 |
| Maine | — | 33 | — | 572 | 58,774 | 1.0 |
| Maryland | 265 | 30 | 140 | 1,818 | 122,213 | 1.5 |
| Massachusetts | 300 | 61 | 108 | 3,070 | 263,538 | 1.2 |
| Michigan | 33,259 | 278 | 165 | 144,540 | 560,342 | 25.8 |
| Minnesota | 287 | 147 | — | 6,781 | 333,501 | 2.0 |
| Mississippi | 275 | 1,500 | 30 | 8,761 | 162,615 | 5.4 |
| Missouri | 1,174 | 526 | 2,078 | 25,578 | 291,156 | 8.8 |
| Montana | 5 | 30 | — | 479 | 20,156 | 2.4 |
| Nebraska | 160 | 106 | — | 5,538 | 104,997 | 5.3 |
| Nevada | — | 25 | 5 | 697 | 49,972 | 1.4 |
| New Hampshire | 33 | 25 | — | 1,786 | 83,459 | 2.1 |
| New Jersey | 72 | 300 | 20 | 1,748 | 284,494 | 0.6 |
| New Mexico | 6 | 5 | — | 208 | 34,925 | 0.6 |
| New York | 1,450 | 1,860 | 125 | 21,117 | 511,209 | 4.1 |
| North Carolina | 333 | 6,203 | 561 | 33,735 | 502,878 | 6.7 |
| North Dakota | — | 25 | — | 1,635 | 27,755 | 5.9 |
| Ohio | 20,324 | 3,452 | 1,200 | 107,406 | 742,787 | 14.5 |
| Oklahoma | 37 | 2,650 | 35 | 9,523 | 148,669 | 6.4 |
| Oregon | 50 | 273 | 295 | 10,212 | 182,031 | 5.6 |
| Pennsylvania | 688 | 1,553 | 6,000 | 26,232 | 638,681 | 4.1 |
| Rhode Island | 5 | — | 5 | 446 | 49,585 | 0.9 |
| South Carolina | 1,551 | 4,703 | — | 25,789 | 256,729 | 10.0 |
| South Dakota | 3 | 2 | 5 | 2,323 | 43,276 | 5.4 |
| Tennessee | 3,507 | 5,150 | 1,016 | 47,899 | 363,793 | 13.2 |
| Texas | 1,524 | 964 | 165 | 30,555 | 849,300 | 3.6 |
| Utah | 35 | 30 | — | 5,216 | 123,684 | 4.2 |
| Vermont | 125 | 5 | 300 | 480 | 36,500 | 1.3 |
| Virginia | 5 | 2,850 | 5 | 14,153 | 277,232 | 5.1 |
| Washington | 50 | 70 | 50 | 3,816 | 253,102 | 1.5 |
| West Virginia | 128 | 50 | — | 2,188 | 59,700 | 3.7 |
| Wisconsin | 1,229 | 35 | 842 | 25,401 | 482,775 | 5.3 |
| Wyoming | — | 5 | — | 355 | 11,435 | 3.1 |
| **Total** | **94,263** | **58,207** | **19,848** | **957,453** | **13,096,159** | **7.3** |

NOTE: In some cases, an average was taken based on the Bureau of the Census employment range.
Omission of data for individual states is due to either the absences of such business from the state or the necessity of withholding the data to avoid disclosure of individual firms data.
SOURCE: U.S. Department of Commerce, Bureau of the Census.

# U.S. Vehicle and Related Industries Employment

## U.S. EMPLOYMENT IN VEHICLE AND RELATED INDUSTRIES, 2008

| Industry | Companies | Employees | Payrolls $ (000) |
|---|---|---|---|
| **Motor Vehicle and Equipment Manufacturing** | | | |
| Light vehicle manufacturing | 277 | 153,426 | 10,549,876 |
| Heavy truck manufacturing | 100 | 28,646 | 1,320,594 |
| Motor vehicle body & trailers | 2,156 | 136,404 | 4,780,522 |
| Motor vehicle engine and engine parts | 949 | 60,550 | 3,174,570 |
| Motor vehicle electrical & electrical equipment | 792 | 66,128 | 3,050,159 |
| Motor vehicle suspension, brake and powertrains | 1,018 | 140,068 | 7,094,452 |
| Motor vehicle seating and Interior trim | 409 | 49,958 | 1,993,185 |
| Other motor vehicle parts manufacturing | 1,748 | 149,955 | 5,957,204 |
| Motor vehicle metal stamping | 788 | 94,263 | 4,444,796 |
| Tires and Inner Tubes | 643 | 58,207 | 2,969,322 |
| Storage Batteries | 116 | 19,848 | 933,070 |
| **Subtotal** | **8,996** | **957,453** | **46,267,750** |
| **Motor Freight Transportation and Related Services** | | | |
| Trucking and courier services[1] | 129,720 | 2,023,135 | 78,271,551 |
| Road transportation support activities | 10,112 | 78,043 | 2,311,097 |
| Arrangement of transportation of freight & cargo | 21,418 | 264,104 | 11,970,392 |
| Misc. services incidental to transportation | 1,496 | 27,637 | 1,218,918 |
| **Subtotal** | **162,746** | **2,392,919** | **93,771,958** |
| **Petroleum Refining and Wholesale Distribution** | | | |
| Petroleum Refining | 311 | 65,303 | 6,156,588 |
| Asphalt paving mixtures and blocks | 1,380 | 14,441 | 792,195 |
| Lubricating oils and greases | 347 | 10,250 | 613,353 |
| Petroleum bulk stations and terminals | 4,546 | 73,119 | 4,068,965 |
| Petroleum and petroleum products wholesalers, except bulk stations and terminals | 2,793 | 31,851 | 2,233,119 |
| **Subtotal** | **9,377** | **194,964** | **13,864,220** |
| **Passenger Transportation** | | | |
| Local and suburban transportation | 2,583 | 70,571 | 2,474,307 |
| Taxi & Limousine service | 7,413 | 71,025 | 1,626,641 |
| Intercity and rural bus transportation | 487 | 15,016 | 421,877 |
| Bus charter service | 1,335 | 30,693 | 757,043 |
| School and Employee bus transportation | 4,501 | 219,610 | 3,886,849 |
| Arrangement of passenger transportation | 22,497 | 259,310 | 12,666,039 |
| Passenger car rental | 6,991 | NA | NA |
| Passenger car leasing | 557 | 7,208 | 405,367 |
| Truck, utility trailer and RV rental | 6,305 | 54,837 | 2,214,909 |
| Automobile parking | 13,181 | 133,202 | 2,220,797 |
| Recreational vehicle parks and campsites | 7,270 | 39,550 | 1,121,259 |
| **Subtotal** | **73,120** | **901,022** | **27,795,088** |
| **Automotive Sales and Servicing** | | | |
| Retail automotive dealers-New | 24,200 | 1,125,163 | 47,150,010 |
| Retail automotive dealers-Used | 25,324 | 128,553 | 3,969,182 |
| Auto parts, accessories and tire stores | 56,115 | 465,879 | 12,347,080 |
| Gasoline service stations[2] | 114,144 | 896,590 | 15,313,367 |
| Recreational vehicle dealers | 2,966 | 40,453 | 1,406,215 |
| Wholesale trade in motor vehicles | 25,963 | 394,728 | 17,932,473 |
| Automotive repair and maintenance | 160,915 | 866,431 | 25,063,805 |
| Motor Vehicle Towing | 8,400 | 55,257 | 1,629,500 |
| **Subtotal** | **418,027** | **3,973,054** | **124,811,632** |
| **Total of Motor Vehicle and Related Industries** | **672,266** | **8,419,412** | **306,510,648** |
| **U.S. Total** | **7,601,169** | **120,903,551** | **5,130,509,178** |
| **Motor Vehicle Percent of U.S. Total** | **8.8%** | **7.0%** | **6.0%** |

NA is not available.
(1) Except by air or by the U.S. Postal Service. (2) Includes truck stops and stations with and without convenience stores.
SOURCE: U.S. Department of Commerce, Bureau of the Census.

# New Car Dealerships

## FRANCHISED NEW CAR DEALERSHIPS BY STATE, 2010

| State | Dealer-ships[1] | Sales (Millions $) | Paid Employees | Payrolls (Millions $) | State | Dealer-ships[1] | Sales (Millions $) | Paid Employees | Payrolls (Millions $) |
|---|---|---|---|---|---|---|---|---|---|
| Alabama | 304 | 7,678 | 12,925 | 562 | Nebraska | 186 | 4,130 | 6,557 | 279 |
| Alaska | 32 | 1,245 | 2,245 | 108 | Nevada | 97 | 3,622 | 6,236 | 331 |
| Arizona | 233 | 10,965 | 18,641 | 896 | New Hampshire | 143 | 3,908 | 6,089 | 311 |
| Arkansas | 227 | 4,781 | 7,166 | 307 | New Jersey | 474 | 21,006 | 26,815 | 1,565 |
| California | 1,303 | 57,659 | 90,616 | 4,675 | New Mexico | 115 | 2,826 | 5,218 | 223 |
| Colorado | 253 | 9,961 | 14,553 | 729 | New York | 918 | 34,813 | 44,246 | 2,360 |
| Connecticut | 264 | 7,875 | 12,093 | 660 | North Carolina | 586 | 16,576 | 28,082 | 1,230 |
| Delaware | 55 | 1,957 | 3,948 | 189 | North Dakota | 89 | 2,090 | 3,502 | 147 |
| Florida | 842 | 38,928 | 61,116 | 2,924 | Ohio | 763 | 21,019 | 36,522 | 1,524 |
| Georgia | 511 | 17,101 | 28,601 | 1,351 | Oklahoma | 280 | 17,746 | 15,967 | 709 |
| Hawaii | 63 | 1,682 | 3,094 | 162 | Oregon | 240 | 5,390 | 10,377 | 457 |
| Idaho | 108 | 2,174 | 4,065 | 173 | Pennsylvania | 956 | 23,638 | 41,476 | 1,827 |
| Illinois | 774 | 23,385 | 38,366 | 1,825 | Rhode Island | 51 | 1,719 | 2,736 | 132 |
| Indiana | 438 | 10,372 | 17,649 | 725 | South Carolina | 266 | 6,551 | 12,176 | 524 |
| Iowa | 325 | 6,294 | 11,073 | 463 | South Dakota | 100 | 1,988 | 3,311 | 141 |
| Kansas | 236 | 4,967 | 8,580 | 373 | Tennessee | 348 | 10,231 | 18,759 | 855 |
| Kentucky | 259 | 6,022 | 10,749 | 455 | Texas | 1,197 | 46,677 | 70,419 | 3,564 |
| Louisiana | 296 | 7,680 | 12,714 | 575 | Utah | 141 | 4,462 | 7,121 | 317 |
| Maine | 131 | 2,772 | 4,765 | 206 | Vermont | 85 | 1,438 | 2,531 | 111 |
| Maryland | 302 | 11,705 | 20,262 | 999 | Virginia | 493 | 14,925 | 26,570 | 1,265 |
| Massachusetts | 404 | 13,862 | 19,892 | 1,101 | Washington | 335 | 9,421 | 17,180 | 826 |
| Michigan | 656 | 12,314 | 28,095 | 1,346 | West Virginia | 141 | 3,128 | 5,673 | 211 |
| Minnesota | 371 | 6,839 | 14,460 | 626 | Wisconsin | 508 | 9,749 | 19,259 | 731 |
| Mississippi | 200 | 3,667 | 6,252 | 256 | Wyoming | 65 | 1,060 | 1,912 | 82 |
| Missouri | 417 | 10,823 | 17,955 | 812 | **Total** | **17,699** | **552,888** | **892,300** | **42,364** |
| Montana | 118 | 2,064 | 3,691 | 145 | | | | | |

(1) The number of establishments are NADA estimates as of Jan. 1, 2011.
SOURCE: National Automobile Dealers Assn.

## DEALER SERVICE AND PARTS SALES

| Year | $ Billions | % Change |
|---|---|---|
| 2010 | 77.63 | 1.8 |
| 2009 | 76.21 | -7.4 |
| 2008 | 81.84 | -1.8 |
| 2007 | 83.35 | 3.5 |
| 2006 | 80.45 | -5.5 |
| 2005 | 85.16 | -0.4 |
| 2004 | 85.48 | 0.2 |
| 2003 | 85.35 | 2.7 |
| 2002 | 83.11 | 3.8 |
| 2001 | 80.10 | 8.5 |
| 2000 | 73.83 | 9.1 |

SOURCE: National Automobile Dealers Assn.

## DEALER SERVICE AND PARTS SALES BY TYPE
(Billions of Dollars)

| Service Labor Sales | 2010 | % Chg. '10 vs. '09 | 2009 |
|---|---|---|---|
| Customer Mechanical | $15.59 | -4.8 | $16.38 |
| Customer Body | 3.85 | 2.7 | 3.75 |
| Warranty | 6.29 | 15.6 | 5.44 |
| Sublet | 2.34 | 18.2 | 1.98 |
| Internal | 5.10 | 11.4 | 4.58 |
| Other | 1.37 | -6.2 | 1.46 |
| **Total Service Labor** | **34.55** | **2.9** | **33.59** |

| Parts Sales | 2010 | % Chg. '10 vs. '09 | 2009 |
|---|---|---|---|
| Customer Mechanical | $12.87 | — | $12.87 |
| Customer Body | 3.00 | 1.7 | 2.95 |
| Wholesale | 11.51 | 1.1 | 11.39 |
| Counter | 2.49 | 6.4 | 2.34 |
| Warranty | 7.45 | -0.5 | 7.49 |
| Internal | 3.60 | 14.3 | 3.15 |
| Other | 2.16 | -11.5 | 2.44 |
| **Total Parts** | **43.08** | **1.1** | **42.63** |

SOURCE: National Automobile Dealers Association.

## SHARE OF TOTAL DEALERSHIP SALES DOLLARS BY DEPARTMENT, 2010

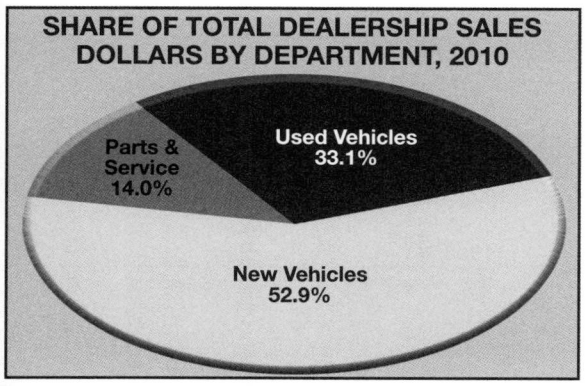

Used Vehicles 33.1%
Parts & Service 14.0%
New Vehicles 52.9%

## PROFILE OF FRANCHISED DEALER SERVICE AND PARTS OPERATIONS, 2010

| | Average Dealership | All Dealers |
|---|---|---|
| Total service and parts sales | $4,386,547 | $77.63 Billion |
| Total gross profit as percent of service and parts sales | 46.5% | — |
| Total net profit as percent of service and parts sales | 7.9% | — |
| Total number of repair orders written | 13,818 | 245 Million |
| Total service and parts sales per customer repair order | $228 | — |
| Total service and parts sales per warranty repair order | $258 | — |
| Number of technicians | 14 | 248,100 |
| Number of service bays (excluding body) | 18 | 309,750 |
| Total parts inventory | $275,370 | $4.87 |
| Average customer mechanical labor rate | $93 | — |

SOURCE: National Automobile Dealers Assn.

# Personal Income of Vehicle and Equipment Manufacturing Employees by State

## PERSONAL INCOME OF VEHICLE AND EQUIPMENT MANUFACTURING EMPLOYEES

| | Personal Income (in Millions of Dollars) | | | | 2009 Vehicle & Equipment Percent of Total Manufacturing | 2008 Vehicle & Equipment Percent of Total Manufacturing |
|---|---|---|---|---|---|---|
| | Vehicle and Equipment Manufacturing Employees | | All Manufacturing Employees | | | |
| State | 2009 | 2008 | 2009 | 2008 | | |
| Alabama | 1,942 | 2,318 | 15,357 | 17,051 | 12.6% | 13.6% |
| Alaska | — | — | 695 | 733 | — | — |
| Arizona | — | — | 12,714 | 13,908 | — | — |
| Arkansas | — | — | 8,316 | 9,182 | — | — |
| California | 2,258 | 2,598 | 119,103 | 125,793 | 1.9% | 2.1% |
| Colorado | 114 | 119 | 10,282 | 11,313 | 1.1% | 1.1% |
| Connecticut | — | — | 16,334 | 17,716 | — | — |
| Delaware | — | — | 2,325 | 2,546 | — | — |
| District of Columbia | — | — | 155 | 165 | — | — |
| Florida | 640 | 598 | 22,934 | 24,916 | 2.8% | 2.4% |
| Georgia | 778 | 982 | 23,517 | 25,965 | 3.3% | 3.8% |
| Hawaii | — | — | 789 | 874 | — | — |
| Idaho | — | — | 3,525 | 4,049 | — | — |
| Illinois | 2,014 | 2,469 | 44,909 | 50,231 | 4.5% | 4.9% |
| Indiana | 6,334 | 7,536 | 32,569 | 37,074 | 19.4% | 20.3% |
| Iowa | — | — | 1,275 | 13,990 | — | — |
| Kansas | 519 | — | 11,746 | 12,737 | — | — |
| Kentucky | 2,737 | 3,147 | 13,830 | 15,321 | 19.8% | 20.5% |
| Louisiana | — | — | 11,495 | 11,955 | — | — |
| Maine | 21 | 26 | 3,415 | 3,798 | 0.6% | 0.7% |
| Maryland | — | — | 10,135 | 10,644 | — | — |
| Massachusetts | — | — | 23,313 | 25,266 | — | — |
| Michigan | 12,571 | 16,619 | 37,701 | 46,205 | 33.3% | 36.0% |
| Minnesota | 305 | 356 | 21,398 | 23,411 | 1.4% | 1.5% |
| Mississippi | — | — | 7,757 | 8,362 | — | — |
| Missouri | 1,576 | 1,956 | 17,344 | 19,796 | 9.1% | 9.9% |
| Montana | — | — | 1,060 | 1,165 | — | — |
| Nebraska | — | — | 5,274 | 56,568 | — | — |
| Nevada | — | — | 2,781 | 3,233 | — | — |
| New Hampshire | 27 | 21 | 5,212 | 5,789 | 0.5% | 0.4% |
| New Jersey | 161 | 195 | 26,416 | 29,122 | 0.6% | 0.7% |
| New Mexico | — | — | 2,096 | 2,341 | — | — |
| New York | 1,182 | 1,577 | 37,825 | 41,875 | 3.1% | 3.8% |
| North Carolina | 1,453 | 1,671 | 30,075 | 33,199 | 4.8% | 5.0% |
| North Dakota | — | — | 1,355 | 1,495 | — | — |
| Ohio | 6,179 | 8,031 | 44,935 | 51,613 | 13.8% | 15.6% |
| Oklahoma | 367 | 486 | 10,884 | 12,000 | 3.4% | 4.1% |
| Oregon | 285 | 456 | 12,152 | 13,840 | 2.3% | 3.3% |
| Pennsylvania | — | 1,077 | 40,833 | 45,105 | 0.0% | 2.4% |
| Rhode Island | 9 | 9 | 2,792 | 3,095 | 0.3% | 0.3% |
| South Carolina | — | — | 14,117 | 15,303 | — | — |
| South Dakota | — | — | 1,970 | 2,175 | — | — |
| Tennessee | 2,842 | — | 20,793 | 23,312 | — | — |
| Texas | 2,233 | 2,251 | 74,433 | 81,200 | 3.0% | 2.8% |
| Utah | — | — | 7,531 | 8,043 | — | — |
| Vermont | — | 51 | 2,143 | 2,319 | 0.0% | 2.2% |
| Virginia | — | — | 16,026 | 17,362 | — | — |
| Washington | — | — | 22,463 | 23,702 | — | — |
| West Virginia | — | — | 3,355 | 3,639 | — | — |
| Wisconsin | — | — | 28,703 | 31,835 | — | — |
| Wyoming | — | 22 | 693 | 727 | 0.0% | 3.0% |
| **Total** | **54,877** | **67,216** | **900,278** | **992,143** | **6.1%** | **6.8%** |

NOTE: Personal Income is measured as the sum of wage and salary disbursements, other labor income, proprietors' income, rental income, personal dividend income and personal interest income.
Omission of data for individual state is due to either the absences of such business from the state or the necessity of withholding the data to avoid disclosure of individual firm's data. Total includes states not listed individually.
SOURCE: U.S. Department of Commerce, Bureau of Economic Analysis.

# Automotive Employment and Compensation

## HOURLY COMPENSATION OF AUTOMOTIVE PRODUCTION EMPLOYMENT IN SELECTED COUNTRIES

| Country | National Currency | 2009 Exchange Rate Per U.S. Dollar | Hourly Compensation | | | | | | 2009 Percent of U.S. Earnings |
|---|---|---|---|---|---|---|---|---|---|
| | | | National Currency | | | U.S. Currency | | | |
| | | | 2009 | 2008 | 2007 | 2009 | 2008 | 2007 | |
| France | Euro | 0.718 | 24.73 | 24.66 | 23.99 | 34.47 | 40.96 | 32.89 | 97.0 |
| Germany | Euro | 0.718 | 38.72 | 39.00 | NA | 53.96 | 55.94 | NA | 151.8 |
| Ireland | Euro | 0.718 | 20.44 | 19.52 | NA | 28.48 | 29.18 | NA | 80.1 |
| Italy | Euro | 0.718 | 22.83 | 22.10 | NA | 31.82 | 32.55 | NA | 89.5 |
| Japan | Yen | 93.680 | 2,901.40 | 3,046.36 | NA | 32.18 | 31.14 | NA | 90.5 |
| Korea | Won | 1,274.630 | 19,730.55 | 20,909.07 | 19,597.00 | 15.48 | 17.73 | 21.10 | 43.6 |
| Mexico | Peso | 13.489 | 48.69 | 45.66 | 43.17 | 3.60 | 4.10 | 3.95 | 10.1 |
| Spain | Euro | 0.718 | 22.90 | 21.57 | 20.77 | 31.90 | 31.77 | 28.48 | 89.8 |
| Taiwan | Dollar | 33.020 | 275.40 | 287.39 | NA | 8.15 | 9.11 | NA | 22.9 |
| United Kingdom | Pound | 0.639 | 18.27 | 18.51 | NA | 29.55 | 34.32 | NA | 83.1 |
| United States | Dollar | 1.000 | 35.54 | 34.16 | 33.33 | 35.54 | 34.16 | 33.33 | 100.0 |

NA: Not available.
NOTE: Compensation data estimated for 2008 and 2009.
SOURCE: U.S. Department of Labor, Bureau of Labor Statistics.

## U.S. VEHICLE AND EQUIPMENT MANUFACTURING EMPLOYMENT

| Year | All Employees (000) | Production Workers | | |
|---|---|---|---|---|
| | | Number (000) | Percent of Total Employees | Average Hourly Earnings |
| 2010 | 674.0 | 521.6 | 77.4% | $22.00 |
| 2009 | 664.1 | 510.0 | 76.8% | 21.86 |
| 2008 | 875.5 | 695.5 | 79.4% | 22.21 |
| 2007 | 994.2 | 804.2 | 80.9% | 22.00 |
| 2006 | 1,070.0 | 872.7 | 81.6% | 22.14 |
| 2005 | 1,096.7 | 892.3 | 81.4% | 22.26 |
| 2004 | 1,112.8 | 902.9 | 81.1% | 21.71 |
| 2003 | 1,125.3 | 906.3 | 80.5% | 21.68 |
| 2002 | 1,151.2 | 931.0 | 80.9% | 21.09 |
| 2001 | 1,212.8 | 986.7 | 81.4% | 19.62 |
| 2000 | 1,313.6 | 1,073.0 | 81.7% | 19.07 |
| 1999 | 1,312.6 | 1,075.7 | 82.0% | 18.45 |
| 1998 | 1,271.5 | 1,050.3 | 82.6% | 18.19 |
| 1997 | 1,253.9 | 1,062.5 | 84.7% | 18.35 |
| 1996 | 1,240.3 | 1,052.3 | 84.8% | 18.07 |
| 1995 | 1,241.5 | 1,048.9 | 84.5% | 17.63 |
| 1994 | 1,168.5 | 978.4 | 83.7% | 17.28 |

NOTE: The basis for industry classification has changed from the Standard Industrial Classification System (SIC) to the North American Industry Classification System (NAICS).
SOURCE: U.S. Department of Labor, Bureau of Labor Statistics.

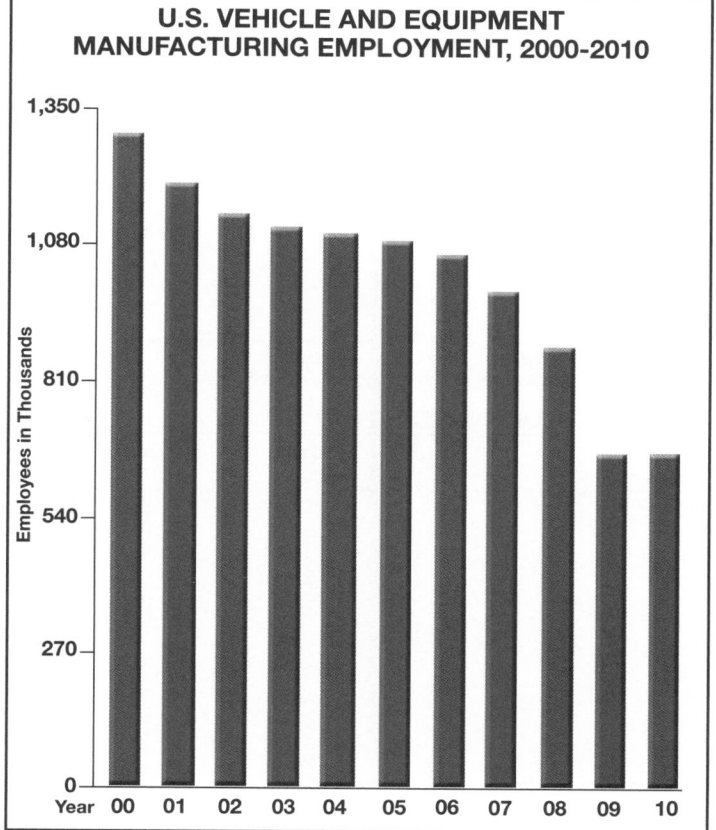

**U.S. VEHICLE AND EQUIPMENT MANUFACTURING EMPLOYMENT, 2000-2010**

# Industrial Production and Capacity Utilization

## INDUSTRIAL PRODUCTION INDEX FOR VEHICLE AND PARTS MANUFACTURERS

| | Industrial Production Index | | | |
|---|---|---|---|---|
| | Total | | Vehicle and Parts | |
| Year | Index | Percent Change | Index | Percent Change |
| 2010 | 87.3 | -8.4 | 76.1 | -4.9 |
| 2009 | 95.3 | -12.7 | 80.0 | -4.0 |
| 2008 | 109.2 | 9.2 | 83.3 | -16.7 |
| 2007 | 100.0 | -0.8 | 100.0 | 3.6 |
| 2006 | 100.8 | -1.5 | 96.5 | 2.2 |
| 2005 | 102.3 | 0.7 | 94.4 | 4.2 |
| 2004 | 101.6 | 0.5 | 90.6 | 3.0 |
| 2003 | 101.1 | 3.6 | 88.0 | 1.5 |
| 2002 | 97.6 | 9.9 | 86.7 | 0.6 |
| 2001 | 88.8 | -8.8 | 86.2 | -4.0 |
| 2000 | 97.4 | 13.4 | 89.8 | -8.5 |
| 1999 | 85.9 | -2.2 | 98.1 | 11.0 |

NOTE: "Industrial Production" is an index benchmarked to 2007=100.
SOURCE: Board of Governors of the Federal Reserve System.

## CAPACITY UTILIZATION FOR VEHICLE AND PARTS MANUFACTURING

| Year | All Manufac- turing | Percent Change | Vehicle & Parts Mfg. | Percent Change |
|---|---|---|---|---|
| 2010 | 71.7 | 8.3 | 60.2 | 35.3 |
| 2009 | 66.2 | -11.6 | 44.5 | -22.1 |
| 2008 | 74.9 | -5.4 | 57.1 | -28.6 |
| 2007 | 79.2 | 0.8 | 80.0 | 11.7 |
| 2006 | 78.6 | 0.5 | 71.6 | -6.9 |
| 2005 | 78.2 | 2.8 | 76.9 | -0.1 |
| 2004 | 76.1 | 3.0 | 77.0 | -1.8 |
| 2003 | 73.9 | 1.4 | 78.4 | -0.4 |
| 2002 | 72.9 | -1.1 | 78.7 | 8.1 |
| 2001 | 73.7 | -7.9 | 72.8 | -10.6 |
| 2000 | 80.0 | -0.9 | 81.4 | -3.3 |
| 1999 | 80.7 | -1.3 | 84.2 | 4.7 |

NOTE: "Capacity Utilization" is a percent of capacity.
SOURCE: Board of Governors of the Federal Reserve System.

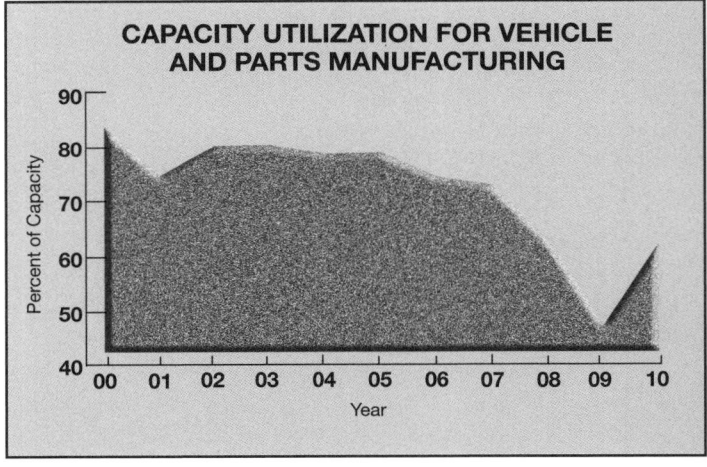

## CAR AND TRUCK OUTPUT

| Year | Car Output | Car Percent of GDP | Truck Output | Truck Percent of GDP | Total Vehicle Output | Percent of GDP | Gross Domestic Product (GDP) |
|---|---|---|---|---|---|---|---|
| 2010 | 111.9 | 0.8 | 208.7 | 1.4 | 320.6 | 2.2 | 14,660.4 |
| 2009 | 94.7 | 0.7 | 154.3 | 1.1 | 249.0 | 1.8 | 14,119.0 |
| 2008 | 138.7 | 1.0 | 186.3 | 1.3 | 325.0 | 2.3 | 14,369.1 |
| 2007 | 152.4 | 1.1 | 257.5 | 1.8 | 409.9 | 2.9 | 14,061.8 |
| 2006 | 155.4 | 1.2 | 257.2 | 1.9 | 412.7 | 3.1 | 13,398.9 |
| 2005 | 150.3 | 1.2 | 268.7 | 2.1 | 418.9 | 3.3 | 12,638.4 |
| 2004 | 129.8 | 1.1 | 264.4 | 2.3 | 394.2 | 3.4 | 11,685.9 |
| 2003 | 130.1 | 1.2 | 248.5 | 2.3 | 378.6 | 3.5 | 10,971.2 |
| 2002 | 148.0 | 1.4 | 233.7 | 2.2 | 381.7 | 3.6 | 10,469.6 |
| 2001 | 141.4 | 1.4 | 203.1 | 2.0 | 344.5 | 3.4 | 10,128.0 |
| 2000 | 151.1 | 1.2 | 213.9 | 2.4 | 365.0 | 3.6 | 9,817.0 |
| 1999 | 150.4 | 1.4 | 221.5 | 2.4 | 371.9 | 3.7 | 9,268.4 |

NOTE: Data in billions of dollars.
SOURCE: U.S. Department of Commerce, Bureau of Economic Analysis.

# Corporate Profits

## SELECTED AUTOMAKERS' REVENUES/NET INCOME

| Year | Chrysler[1] Revenues | Net Income | Ford Revenues | Net Income | General Motors[2] Revenues | Net Income | Honda Revenues | Net Income |
|------|------|------|------|------|------|------|------|------|
| 2010 | 41,946 | -652 | 128,954 | 7,149 | 135,592 | 4,668 | 92,210 | 2,885 |
| 2009 | NA | NA | 118,308 | 2,717 | 47,115 | 109,118 | 101,916 | 1,395 |
| 2008 | NA | NA | 146,277 | -14,672 | 148,979 | -30,860 | 119,801 | 5,989 |
| 2007 | NA | NA | 172,455 | -2,723 | 178,199 | -38,732 | 93,919 | 5,018 |
| 2006 | 200,138 | 4,261 | 160,065 | -12,613 | 171,179 | -1,978 | 84,345 | 5,082 |
| 2005 | 177,402 | 3,371 | 176,835 | 1,440 | 158,623 | -10,417 | 80,429 | 4,521 |
| 2004 | 192,319 | 3,338 | 172,255 | 3,487 | 195,351 | 2,701 | 77,268 | 4,395 |
| 2003 | 171,870 | 564 | 166,040 | 495 | 185,837 | 2,899 | — | — |
| 2002 | 156,838 | 4,947 | 162,256 | -9,800 | 186,763 | 1,736 | — | — |
| 2001 | 136,072 | -589 | 162,412 | -5,453 | 177,260 | 601 | — | — |
| 2000 | 152,446 | 7,411 | 170,064 | 3,467 | 184,632 | 4,452 | — | — |
| 1999 | 151,035 | 5,785 | 160,658 | 7,237 | 176,558 | 6,002 | — | — |
| 1998 | 154,615 | 5,656 | 143,350 | 22,071 | 155,445 | 2,956 | — | — |
| 1997 | 61,147 | 2,805 | 153,627 | 6,920 | 178,174 | 6,698 | — | — |
| 1996 | 61,397 | 3,529 | 146,991 | 4,446 | 164,013 | 4,963 | — | — |
| 1995 | 53,195 | 2,025 | 137,137 | 4,139 | 160,254 | 6,881 | — | — |
| 1994 | 52,235 | 3,713 | 128,439 | 5,308 | 154,951 | 4,901 | — | — |
| 1993 | 43,596 | -2,551 | 108,521 | 2,529 | 138,676 | 2,466 | — | — |
| 1992 | 36,897 | 723 | 100,132 | -7,385 | 132,429 | -23,498 | — | — |
| 1991 | 29,370 | -795 | 88,286 | -2,258 | 123,056 | -4,453 | — | — |
| 1990 | 30,620 | 68 | 97,650 | 860 | 124,705 | -1,986 | — | — |
| 1989 | 35,186 | 359 | 96,146 | 3,835 | 126,932 | 4,224 | — | — |
| 1988 | 34,421 | 1,050 | 92,446 | 5,300 | 123,642 | 4,856 | — | — |
| 1987 | 28,353 | 1,290 | 79,893 | 4,625 | 114,870 | 3,551 | — | — |
| 1986 | 24,569 | 1,389 | 69,695 | 3,285 | 115,610 | 2,945 | — | — |
| 1984 | 19,717 | 2,373 | 56,323 | 2,907 | 93,145 | 4,517 | — | — |
| 1983 | 13,240 | 701 | 44,500 | 1,867 | 74,582 | 3,730 | — | — |

| Year | Hyundai Revenues | Net Income | Nissan Revenues | Net Income | Toyota Revenues | Net Income | Volkswagen Revenues | Net Income |
|------|------|------|------|------|------|------|------|------|
| 2010 | 32,431 | 4,610 | 18,897 | 3,362 | 232,375 | 1,808 | 168,128 | 9,057 |
| 2009 | 27,329 | 2,540 | 86,720 | 2,402 | 222,566 | -4,448 | 150,756 | 2,659 |
| 2008 | 25,430 | 1,144 | 108,242 | 4,823 | 262,394 | 17,146 | 160,440 | 6,609 |
| 2007 | 32,695 | 1,796 | 88,717 | 3,905 | 202,864 | 13,927 | 160,389 | 6,071 |
| 2006 | 29,096 | 1,624 | 80,584 | 4,428 | 179,083 | 11,681 | 138,463 | 3,631 |
| 2005 | 57,636 | 2,277 | 80,152 | 4,788 | 172,749 | 10,907 | 111,344 | 1,327 |
| 2004 | 50,693 | 1,567 | 70,087 | 4,752 | 163,637 | 10,995 | 120,405 | 969 |
| 2003 | NA | NA | 56,905 | 4,126 | 128,965 | 6,247 | 109,786 | 1,408 |
| 2002 | NA | NA | 46,588 | 2,799 | 107,443 | 4,177 | 82,958 | 2,478 |
| 2001 | 17,003 | 880 | 48,204 | 2,462 | 106,030 | 5,447 | 78,446 | 4,806 |
| 2000 | 14,389 | 527 | 56,649 | 6,486 | 119,656 | 4,540 | 78,314 | 3,791 |
| 1999 | 12,468 | 769 | 57,471 | 233 | 100,990 | 3,747 | 75,525 | 2,534 |
| 1998 | 11,921 | -28 | 49,361 | 105 | 88,473 | 3,442 | 80,395 | 1,343 |
| 1997 | — | — | — | — | 99,730 | 3,143 | 63,664 | 765 |
| 1996 | — | — | — | — | 101,177 | 2,426 | 64,491 | 437 |
| 1995 | — | — | — | — | 89,715 | 1,458 | 61,168 | 233 |
| 1994 | — | — | — | — | 91,317 | 1,227 | 50,930 | 95 |
| 1993 | — | — | — | — | 95,063 | 1,643 | 44,774 | -1,134 |
| 1992 | — | — | — | — | 80,128 | 1,875 | 53,977 | 93 |
| 1991 | — | — | — | — | 71,731 | 3,140 | 48,826 | 713 |
| 1990 | — | — | — | — | 59,962 | 2,878 | 45,429 | 725 |
| 1989 | — | — | — | — | 61,440 | 2,652 | 37,606 | 597 |
| 1988 | — | — | — | — | — | — | — | — |
| 1987 | — | — | — | — | — | — | — | — |
| 1986 | — | — | — | — | — | — | — | — |
| 1984 | — | — | — | — | — | — | — | — |
| 1983 | — | — | — | — | — | — | — | — |

NA - Not available.
NOTE: Data in millions of U.S. dollars.
(1) Data for DaimlerChrysler for 1998-2006. (2) Data for General Motors Corp. from Jan 1 through July 9, 2009, and General Motors Co. in 2010.
SOURCE: Compiled by *Ward's* Automotive Group from company annual reports.

# Use Tax Revenues by State

## STATE USE TAX REVENUES, 2010

| State | Total State Tax Revenue | State Tax on Vehicle Fuel | State License Tax on Vehicles | State License Tax on Vehicle Operators | Total Vehicle Fuel and License Taxes | Percent Vehicle of Total Taxes |
|---|---|---|---|---|---|---|
| Alabama | 8,181,918 | 558,476 | 200,285 | 19,148 | 777,909 | 9.5 |
| Alaska | 4,518,023 | 23,834 | 63,692 | -- | 87,526 | 1.9 |
| Arizona | 10,199,338 | 796,560 | 176,095 | 23,701 | 996,356 | 9.8 |
| Arkansas | 7,279,215 | 466,482 | 139,582 | 16,871 | 622,935 | 8.6 |
| California | 104,840,520 | 3,163,694 | 3,108,956 | 270,344 | 6,542,994 | 6.2 |
| Colorado | 8,586,401 | 602,347 | 379,611 | 20,937 | 1,002,895 | 11.7 |
| Connecticut | 12,285,994 | 498,177 | 196,778 | 37,251 | 732,206 | 6.0 |
| Delaware | 2,769,731 | 112,889 | 47,375 | 4,356 | 164,620 | 5.9 |
| Florida | 31,498,998 | 2,266,814 | 1,282,832 | 310,101 | 3,859,747 | 12.3 |
| Georgia | 14,782,779 | 854,360 | 282,516 | 42,648 | 1,179,524 | 8.0 |
| Hawaii | 4,837,862 | 86,370 | 100,575 | 241 | 187,186 | 3.9 |
| Idaho | 2,951,703 | 230,377 | 120,275 | 7,676 | 358,328 | 12.1 |
| Illinois | 29,761,862 | 1,339,228 | 1,446,595 | 92,484 | 2,878,307 | 9.7 |
| Indiana | 13,796,427 | 759,959 | 393,350 | 214,505 | 1,367,814 | 9.9 |
| Iowa | 6,809,344 | 437,763 | 466,982 | 14,428 | 919,173 | 13.5 |
| Kansas | 6,492,996 | 424,703 | 174,932 | 18,222 | 617,857 | 9.5 |
| Kentucky | 9,531,507 | 655,245 | 194,027 | 16,537 | 865,809 | 9.1 |
| Louisiana | 8,757,557 | 587,995 | 109,388 | 12,758 | 710,141 | 8.1 |
| Maine | 3,489,953 | 241,687 | 94,633 | 8,400 | 344,720 | 9.9 |
| Maryland | 15,223,923 | 722,597 | 433,777 | 28,554 | 1,184,928 | 7.8 |
| Massachusetts | 20,050,292 | 654,649 | 362,053 | 104,298 | 1,121,000 | 5.6 |
| Michigan | 22,626,247 | 988,069 | 868,467 | 56,212 | 1,912,748 | 8.5 |
| Minnesota | 17,208,877 | 832,291 | 557,733 | 46,189 | 1,436,213 | 8.3 |
| Mississippi | 6,268,804 | 393,363 | 124,437 | 33,255 | 551,055 | 8.8 |
| Missouri | 9,703,459 | 721,917 | 265,623 | 17,215 | 1,004,755 | 10.4 |
| Montana | 2,142,809 | 204,390 | 142,189 | 8,500 | 355,079 | 16.6 |
| Nebraska | 3,809,266 | 298,805 | 79,479 | 10,858 | 389,142 | 10.2 |
| Nevada | 5,835,963 | 292,804 | 158,987 | 20,136 | 471,927 | 8.1 |
| New Hampshire | 2,124,984 | 147,805 | 131,100 | 12,122 | 291,027 | 13.7 |
| New Jersey | 25,927,891 | 535,281 | 578,968 | 50,345 | 1,164,594 | 4.5 |
| New Mexico | 4,413,988 | 227,633 | 121,770 | 3,705 | 353,108 | 8.0 |
| New York | 63,529,354 | 509,687 | 965,000 | 136,785 | 1,611,472 | 2.5 |
| North Carolina | 21,511,278 | 1,551,660 | 548,379 | 127,096 | 2,227,135 | 10.4 |
| North Dakota | 2,645,695 | 151,050 | 87,145 | 4,040 | 242,235 | 9.2 |
| Ohio | 23,583,596 | 1,727,242 | 832,589 | 89,456 | 2,649,287 | 11.2 |
| Oklahoma | 7,079,985 | 431,151 | 579,380 | 15,916 | 1,026,447 | 14.5 |
| Oregon | 7,475,135 | 403,284 | 496,097 | 28,501 | 927,882 | 12.4 |
| Pennsylvania | 30,169,122 | 2,020,099 | 800,432 | 60,995 | 2,881,526 | 9.6 |
| Rhode Island | 2,568,851 | 123,805 | 53,385 | 626 | 177,816 | 6.9 |
| South Carolina | 6,803,724 | 521,215 | 147,405 | 51,121 | 719,741 | 10.6 |
| South Dakota | 1,304,487 | 125,223 | 52,822 | 3,611 | 181,656 | 13.9 |
| Tennessee | 10,513,788 | 824,795 | 249,577 | 45,118 | 1,119,490 | 10.6 |
| Texas | 39,399,251 | 3,043,495 | 1,542,188 | 101,229 | 4,686,912 | 11.9 |
| Utah | 5,092,415 | 351,449 | 292,359 | 13,806 | 657,614 | 12.9 |
| Vermont | 2,511,387 | 99,278 | 72,214 | 7,241 | 178,733 | 7.1 |
| Virginia | 16,411,055 | 882,919 | 339,581 | 58,743 | 1,281,243 | 7.8 |
| Washington | 16,106,154 | 1,196,688 | 463,075 | 66,666 | 1,726,429 | 10.7 |
| West Virginia | 4,655,034 | 391,995 | 86,691 | 3,900 | 482,586 | 10.4 |
| Wisconsin | 14,368,569 | 972,979 | 471,556 | 42,309 | 1,486,844 | 10.3 |
| Wyoming | 2,117,100 | 25,617 | 65,895 | 2,188 | 93,700 | 4.4 |
| **Total** | **704,554,611** | **35,480,195** | **20,948,832** | **2,381,344** | **58,810,371** | **8.3** |

NOTE: Data in thousands of dollars.
SOURCE: U.S. Department of Commerce, Bureau of the Census.

# New Car Corporate Average Fuel Economy

## NEW CAR U.S. CORPORATE AVERAGE FUEL ECONOMY PERFORMANCE BY MANUFACTURER (Miles Per Gallon)

| Manufacturer | Preliminary '10 mpg | '09 mpg | '08 mpg | Final Sales Basis '07 mpg | '05 mpg | '03 mpg | '01 mpg | '99 mpg | '97 mpg | '95 mpg | '93 mpg |
|---|---|---|---|---|---|---|---|---|---|---|---|
| **Domestic Fleet** | | | | | | | | | | | |
| Chrysler | 28.0 | 28.1 | 29.3 | — | — | — | — | — | 27.6 | 28.4 | 27.8 |
| DaimlerChrysler[1][2] | — | — | — | 28.5 | 28.8 | 29.7 | 27.9 | 27.2 | — | — | — |
| Ford[1] | 32.3 | 31.5 | 30.1 | 29.0 | 28.6 | 27.9 | 27.7 | 27.6 | 27.2 | 27.7 | 28.8 |
| General Motors[1] | 30.6 | 31.3 | 29.6 | 30.0 | 29.2 | 28.9 | 28.3 | 27.7 | 28.2 | 27.4 | 27.4 |
| Honda | 34.7 | 34.3 | 36.0 | 33.5 | 33.2 | 34.4 | 32.7 | 33.5 | 28.5 | — | — |
| Mazda | 31.4 | 30.9 | — | — | — | — | — | — | — | — | — |
| Mitsubishi | — | — | — | — | 27.6 | — | — | — | — | — | — |
| Nissan | 34.8 | 33.9 | 33.9 | 33.4 | 30.4 | 28.9 | 27.9 | 29.9 | — | — | — |
| Subaru | — | 29.0 | 29.0 | 29.5 | — | — | — | — | — | — | — |
| Toyota | 36.4 | 32.5 | 34.0 | 31.3 | 34.4 | 28.1 | 34.2 | 28.3 | 28.8 | 28.5 | — |
| **Import Fleet** | | | | | | | | | | | |
| Alfa Romeo | — | — | — | — | — | — | — | — | — | — | — |
| AMC-Renault | — | — | — | — | — | — | — | — | — | — | — |
| BMW | 28.7 | 29.0 | 27.4 | 27.7 | 27.2 | 26.8 | 25.0 | 25.4 | 25.7 | 25.3 | 25.2 |
| Chrysler | — | — | 26.5 | — | — | — | — | — | — | — | — |
| Daimler | 26.9 | 27.1 | 26.9 | — | — | — | — | — | — | — | — |
| DaimlerChrysler[2] | — | — | — | 24.7 | 25.9 | 26.3 | 26.5 | 26.5 | 25.7 | 28.6 | 31.0 |
| Ford | 27.6 | 27.6 | 31.1 | 30.0 | 28.4 | 28.2 | 27.9 | 30.1 | 31.3 | 34.0 | 26.7 |
| General Motors | 34.0 | 30.3 | 31.5 | 32.3 | 30.5 | 28.3 | 26.5 | 25.5 | 32.1 | 36.7 | 30.5 |
| Honda | 40.9 | 39.0 | 33.5 | 39.3 | 33.1 | 31.9 | 29.3 | 29.4 | 32.4 | 32.7 | 32.5 |
| Hyundai | 36.0 | 34.1 | 34.2 | 32.4 | 30.3 | 30.4 | 31.3 | 30.8 | 31.4 | 31.2 | 31.3 |
| Isuzu | — | — | — | — | — | — | — | — | — | — | 34.8 |
| Kia | 36.6 | 35.2 | 33.6 | 33.4 | 29.5 | 30.4 | 30.5 | 30.9 | 31.0 | — | — |
| Mercedes-Benz | — | — | — | — | — | — | — | — | 25.2 | 24.7 | 22.9 |
| Mitsubishi | 31.7 | 30.4 | 30.0 | 28.7 | 30.2 | — | 29.4 | 30.0 | 30.0 | 29.9 | 29.4 |
| Nissan | 32.5 | 33.3 | 29.2 | 29.6 | 24.8 | 27.4 | 28.7 | 29.9 | 29.9 | 29.5 | 29.4 |
| Peugeot | — | — | — | — | — | — | — | — | — | — | 26.2 |
| Subaru | 29.7 | 29.2 | 28.9 | 28.5 | 27.9 | 27.6 | 27.8 | 27.7 | 28.3 | 28.9 | 29.6 |
| Suzuki | 34.5 | 32.7 | 31.6 | 30.3 | 29.6 | 33.0 | 35.1 | 35.5 | 35.2 | 40.8 | 45.6 |
| Toyota | 44.4 | 39.4 | 38.3 | 38.3 | 36.6 | 32.4 | 30.6 | 29.9 | 30.1 | 30.4 | 29.1 |
| Volvo | — | — | — | — | — | — | — | 26.2 | 25.8 | 26.0 | 25.9 |
| Volkswagen | 32.9 | 31.2 | 29.1 | 28.8 | 29.1 | 29.8 | 28.5 | 28.2 | 29.0 | 29.0 | 27.2 |
| Yugo | — | — | — | — | — | — | — | — | — | — | — |

NOTE: Data are for model years.
(1) Domestic fleet excludes captive imports after '79.
(2) DaimlerChrysler includes Mercedes-Benz and the Chrysler Group from '99-'07.
SOURCE: U.S. Department of Transportation.

## NEW CAR U.S. CORPORATE AVERAGE FUEL ECONOMY (Sales Weighted Combined City/Highway Miles Per Gallon)

| Model Year | Federal Standard | Domestic Fleet | Import Fleet | Total Fleet |
|---|---|---|---|---|
| 2010 (prelim.) | 27.5 | 32.9 | 35.1 | 33.7 |
| 2009 | 27.5 | 32.1 | 33.8 | 32.9 |
| 2008 | 27.5 | 31.2 | 31.8 | 31.5 |
| 2007 | 27.5 | 30.6 | 32.2 | 31.2 |
| 2006 | 27.5 | 30.3 | 29.7 | 30.1 |
| 2005 | 27.5 | 30.5 | 29.9 | 30.3 |
| 2004 | 27.5 | 29.9 | 28.7 | 29.5 |
| 2003 | 27.5 | 29.1 | 29.9 | 29.5 |
| 2002 | 27.5 | 29.1 | 28.8 | 29.0 |
| 2000 | 27.5 | 28.7 | 28.3 | 28.5 |
| 1998 | 27.5 | 28.6 | 29.2 | 28.8 |
| 1996 | 27.5 | 28.1 | 29.6 | 28.5 |
| 1995 | 27.5 | 27.7 | 30.3 | 28.6 |
| 1994 | 27.5 | 27.5 | 29.7 | 28.3 |
| 1992 | 27.5 | 27.0 | 29.2 | 27.9 |
| 1990 | 27.5 | 26.9 | 29.9 | 28.0 |
| 1988 | 26.0 | 27.4 | 31.5 | 28.8 |
| 1986 | 26.0 | 26.6 | 31.6 | 28.2 |
| 1984 | 27.0 | 25.6 | 32.0 | 26.9 |
| 1982 | 24.0 | 25.0 | 31.1 | 26.6 |
| 1980 | 20.0 | 22.6 | 29.6 | 24.3 |
| 1978 | 18.0 | 18.7 | 27.3 | 19.9 |
| 1976 | | 16.6 | 25.4 | 17.5 |

NOTE: After 1979, domestic fleet excludes captive imports.
SOURCE: U.S. Department of Transportation.

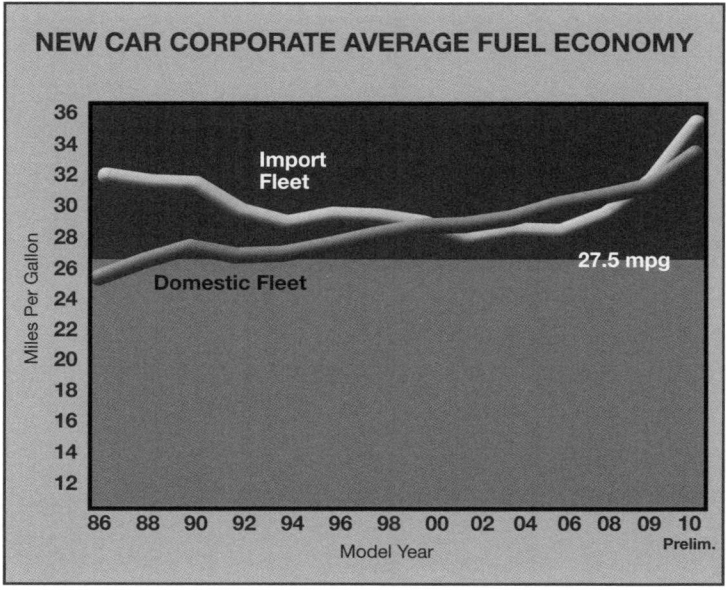

NEW CAR CORPORATE AVERAGE FUEL ECONOMY

# New Light Truck Corporate Average Fuel Economy

## NEW LIGHT TRUCK[1] U.S. CORPORATE AVERAGE FUEL ECONOMY
### (Sales Weighted Combined City/Highway Miles Per Gallon)

| Model Year | Federal Standard | Other[3] | Captive Import[4] | Total Fleet |
|---|---|---|---|---|
| 2010 (prelim.) | 23.5 | — | — | 25.1 |
| 2009 | 23.1 | — | — | 24.8 |
| 2008 | 22.5 | — | — | 23.6 |
| 2007 | 22.2 | — | — | 23.1 |
| 2006 | 21.6 | — | — | 22.5 |
| 2005 | 21.0 | — | — | 22.1 |
| 2004 | 20.7 | — | — | 21.5 |
| 2003 | 20.7 | — | — | 21.8 |
| 2001 | 20.7 | — | — | 20.9 |
| 1999 | 20.7 | — | — | 20.9 |
| 1997 | 20.7 | 20.4 | — | 20.6 |
| 1995 | 20.6 | 20.5 | — | 20.5 |

| | 2-Wheel Drive | | | 4-Wheel Drive | | |
|---|---|---|---|---|---|---|
| | Federal | Sales Weighted Average | | Federal | Sales Weighted Average | |
| | Standard | Domestic[1] | Import | Standard | Domestic* | Import |
| 1991* | 20.7 | 20.9[2] | 23.0[2] | 19.1 | 20.9[2] | 23.0[2] |
| 1990* | 20.5 | 20.3[2] | 23.0[2] | 19.0 | 20.3[2] | 23.0[2] |
| 1989* | 21.5 | 20.4[2] | 23.5[2] | 19.0 | 20.4[2] | 23.5[2] |
| 1987* | 21.0 | 20.4 | 27.5 | 19.5 | 19.4 | 25.3 |
| 1985* | 19.7 | 19.9 | 27.4 | 18.9 | 19.6 | 24.7[2] |
| 1983* | 19.5 | 19.6[2] | 27.1[2] | 17.5 | 19.6[2] | 27.1 |

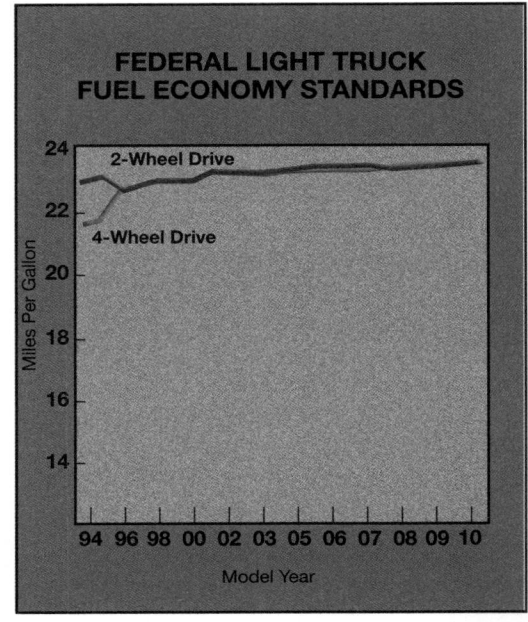

**FEDERAL LIGHT TRUCK FUEL ECONOMY STANDARDS**

Light truck defined as 0-8,500 lbs.
* Manufacturers may elect to meet a single combined corporate fleet average of 19 mpg in 1983, 19.5 mpg. in 1985, 20.5 mpg in 1987-89, 20 in 1990, and 20.2 in 1991.
(1) Captive imports are excluded.
(2) Combined 2-wheel and 4-wheel drive fleet average.
(3) Not a captive import light truck; 2 and 4 wheel drive combined.
(4) A light truck which is not domestically manufactured but imported by a manufacturer whose principal place of business is the United States; 2 and 4 wheel drive combined.
SOURCE: U.S. Department of Transportation.

## NEW LIGHT TRUCK U.S. CORPORATE AVERAGE FUEL ECONOMY
### PERFORMANCE BY MANUFACTURER (Miles Per Gallon)

| Manufacturer | Preliminary '10 mpg | Final Sales Basis '09 mpg | '08 mpg | '07 mpg | '06 mpg | '05 mpg | '04 mpg | '03 mpg |
|---|---|---|---|---|---|---|---|---|
| BMW | 23.6 | 22.7 | 22.9 | 23.4 | 21.2 | 21.3 | 21.5 | 20.0 |
| Chrysler | 24.1 | 23.9 | 23.6 | — | — | — | — | — |
| Daimler | 21.5 | 20.8 | 20.8 | — | — | — | — | — |
| DaimlerChrysler[1][2] | — | — | — | 22.9 | 21.7 | 21.4 | 20.5 | 22.2 |
| Ford[1] | 24.0 | 24.6 | 23.6 | 22.3 | 21.1 | 21.6 | 21.1 | 21.3 |
| General Motors[1] | 25.4 | 23.6 | 22.8 | 22.4 | 22.8 | 21.8 | 21.4 | 21.3 |
| Honda | 26.9 | 26.1 | 25.5 | 25.1 | 24.7 | 24.9 | 24.6 | 24.7 |
| Hyundai | 30.0 | 25.9 | 25.6 | 25.5 | 25.2 | 24.7 | 24.2 | 24.4 |
| Isuzu | — | — | — | — | — | — | 23.1 | 22.3 |
| Kia | 25.7 | 25.0 | 24.2 | 24.2 | 22.8 | 21.4 | 20.5 | 19.7 |
| Land Rover | 18.7 | 19.1 | 19.3 | — | — | — | — | — |
| Mazda | 26.6 | 26.6 | — | — | — | — | — | — |
| Mitsubishi | 28.3 | 27.4 | 24.7 | 24.7 | 23.9 | 23.6 | — | — |
| Nissan | 24.9 | 25.7 | 23.1 | 22.9 | 21.9 | 21.6 | 21.2 | 21.9 |
| Porsche | 20.5 | 20.1 | 20.0 | — | 18.5 | 18.5 | 18.3 | — |
| Subaru | 29.9 | 28.5 | 27.3 | 27.1 | — | — | — | — |
| Suzuki | 26.3 | 25.6 | 23.7 | 23.8 | 24.0 | 22.8 | 22.8 | 21.9 |
| Toyota | 26.0 | 26.2 | 23.9 | 23.7 | 23.7 | 23.1 | 22.7 | 21.9 |
| Volkswagen | 25.2 | 24.5 | 20.2 | 19.5 | 20.1 | 20.1 | 19.2 | 21.3 |

NOTE: Data are for vehicles with gross vehicle weight of 8,500 lbs. or less by model years.
(1) Captive imports are excluded.
(2) DaimlerChrysler includes Mercedes-Benz and the Chrysler Group from '99-'07.
SOURCE: U.S. Department of Transportation.

# Gas Guzzler Tax Receipts, Automotive Fuel Prices and New Car Quality Improvements

## NEW CAR GAS GUZZLER TAX

| Miles Per Gallon* | 1991-11 | 1986-90 | 1985 | 1984 | 1983 | 1982 | 1981 | 1980 |
|---|---|---|---|---|---|---|---|---|
| Under 12.5 | $7,700 | $3,850 | $2,650 | $2,150 | $1,550 | $1,200 | $650 | $550 |
| 12.5-13.0 | 6,400 | 3,200 | 2,650 | 1,750 | 1,550 | 950 | 650 | 550 |
| 13.0-13.5 | 6,400 | 3,200 | 2,200 | 1,750 | 1,250 | 950 | 550 | 300 |
| 13.5-14.0 | 5,400 | 2,700 | 2,200 | 1,450 | 1,250 | 750 | 550 | 300 |
| 14.0-14.5 | 5,400 | 2,700 | 1,800 | 1,450 | 1,000 | 750 | 450 | 200 |
| 14.5-15.0 | 4,500 | 2,250 | 1,800 | 1,150 | 1,000 | 600 | 450 | 200 |
| 15.0-15.5 | 4,500 | 2,250 | 1,500 | 1,150 | 800 | 600 | 350 | 0 |
| 15.5-16.0 | 3,700 | 1,850 | 1,500 | 950 | 800 | 450 | 350 | 0 |
| 16.0-16.5 | 3,700 | 1,850 | 1,200 | 950 | 650 | 450 | 200 | 0 |
| 16.5-17.0 | 3,000 | 1,500 | 1,200 | 750 | 650 | 350 | 200 | 0 |
| 17.0-17.5 | 3,000 | 1,500 | 1,000 | 750 | 500 | 350 | 0 | 0 |
| 17.5-18.0 | 2,600 | 1,300 | 1,000 | 600 | 500 | 200 | 0 | 0 |
| 18.0-18.5 | 2,600 | 1,300 | 800 | 600 | 350 | 0 | 0 | 0 |
| 18.5-19.0 | 2,100 | 1,050 | 800 | 450 | 350 | 0 | 0 | 0 |
| 19.0-19.5 | 2,100 | 1,050 | 600 | 450 | 0 | 0 | 0 | 0 |
| 19.5-20.0 | 1,700 | 850 | 600 | 0 | 0 | 0 | 0 | 0 |
| 20.0-20.5 | 1,700 | 850 | 500 | 0 | 0 | 0 | 0 | 0 |
| 20.5-21.0 | 1,300 | 650 | 500 | 0 | 0 | 0 | 0 | 0 |
| 21.0-21.5 | 1,300 | 650 | 0 | 0 | 0 | 0 | 0 | 0 |
| 21.5-22.0 | 1,000 | 500 | 0 | 0 | 0 | 0 | 0 | 0 |
| 22.0-22.5 | 1,000 | 500 | 0 | 0 | 0 | 0 | 0 | 0 |
| 22.5 & Over | 0 | 0 | 0 | 0 | 0 | 0 | 0 | 0 |

NOTE: New car purchaser pays tax if car's combined city/highway fuel economy rating is lower than standard. * Combined city/highway rating.
SOURCE: Internal Revenue Service.

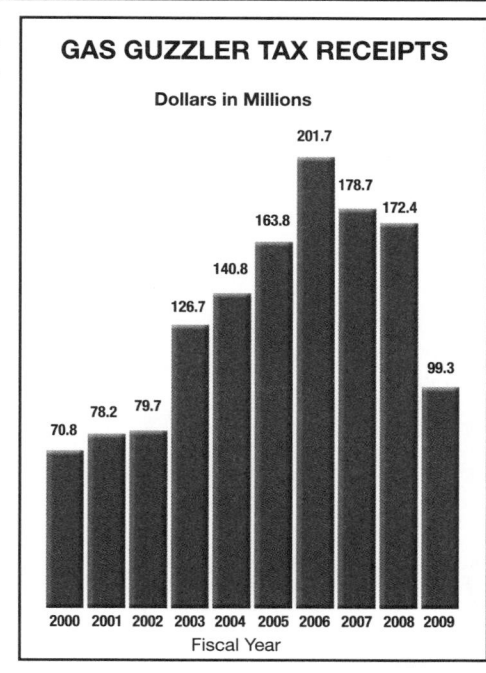

### GAS GUZZLER TAX RECEIPTS

Dollars in Millions

| Fiscal Year | |
|---|---|
| 2000 | 70.8 |
| 2001 | 78.2 |
| 2002 | 79.7 |
| 2003 | 126.7 |
| 2004 | 140.8 |
| 2005 | 163.8 |
| 2006 | 201.7 |
| 2007 | 178.7 |
| 2008 | 172.4 |
| 2009 | 99.3 |

## U.S. CITY AVERAGE RETAIL PRICES FOR AUTOMOTIVE FUEL

| Year | Unleaded Regular | Unleaded Premium | All Types[1] | Diesel |
|---|---|---|---|---|
| 2010 | 278.8 | 304.7 | 283.6 | 301.7 |
| 2009 | 235.0 | 260.7 | 240.1 | 252.7 |
| 2008 | 326.6 | 351.9 | 331.7 | 391.5 |
| 2007 | 280.1 | 303.3 | 284.9 | 296.4 |
| 2006 | 258.9 | 280.5 | 263.5 | 281.4 |
| 2005 | 229.5 | 249.1 | 233.8 | 252.0 |
| 2004 | 188.0 | 206.8 | 192.3 | 192.1 |
| 2003 | 159.1 | 177.7 | 163.8 | 164.5 |
| 2002 | 135.8 | 155.6 | 144.1 | 142.6 |
| 2001 | 146.1 | 165.7 | 153.1 | 153.4 |
| 2000 | 138.2 | 169.3 | 156.3 | 151.1 |
| 1999 | 116.5 | 135.7 | 122.1 | 112.0 |
| 1998 | 105.9 | 125.0 | 111.5 | 104.5 |
| 1997 | 120.0 | 138.1 | 124.5 | 120.0 |
| 1996 | 123.1 | 141.3 | 128.8 | 123.6 |
| 1995 | 114.7 | 133.6 | 120.5 | 110.9 |
| 1994 | 111.2 | 130.5 | 117.4 | 112.0 |
| 1993 | 110.8 | 130.2 | 117.3 | 114.8 |
| 1992 | 112.7 | 131.6 | 119.0 | 114.5 |
| 1991[2] | 114.0 | 132.1 | 119.6 | 124.3 |
| 1990 | 116.4 | 134.9 | 121.7 | 134.3 |
| 1985 | 120.2 | 134.0 | 119.6 | 129.5 |

NOTE: Prices are based on city averages, cents per gallon including taxes.
NA - Not available. (1) Includes types of motor gasoline not shown separately.
(2) Price calculations changed from "Full Service" to "Self Service." SOURCE: U.S. Department of Transportation.

## AVERAGE RETAIL PRICE INCREASES FOR NEW CAR QUALITY IMPROVEMENTS

| | Adjusted to 2010 Dollars | | | |
|---|---|---|---|---|
| Model Year | Safety | Emissions[1] | Other[2] | Total |
| 2011 | 4.83 | — | 105.96 | 110.79 |
| 2010 | — | — | 249.69 | 249.69 |
| 2009 | — | — | 187.08 | 187.08 |
| 2008 | 84.03 | — | 89.53 | 173.56 |
| 2007 | 57.49 | — | 95.87 | 153.36 |
| 2006 | — | 27.12 | 2.48 | 29.60 |
| 2005 | 197.25 | 119.91 | — | 317.16 |
| 2004 | 38.33 | 22.48 | 24.75 | 85.56 |
| 2003 | — | — | 25.67 | 25.67 |
| 2002 | — | — | 68.70 | 68.70 |
| 2001 | 25.02 | 67.26 | 119.17 | 211.45 |
| 2000 | 15.10 | — | — | 15.10 |
| 1999 | — | 75.79 | 403.86 | 479.65 |
| 1998 | — | 51.18 | 175.37 | 226.55 |
| 1997 | 8.88 | 20.23 | 151.71 | 180.82 |
| 1996 | 16.13 | 86.30 | 85.96 | 188.39 |
| 1995 | 119.06 | 53.16 | — | 172.22 |
| 1994 | 186.91 | 40.07 | 142.26 | 369.24 |
| 1993 | — | — | 93.57 | 93.57 |
| 1992 | 37.28 | — | 242.14 | 279.42 |
| 1991 | 237.03 | — | — | 237.03 |
| 1990 | 203.05 | — | 43.93 | 246.98 |
| 1989 | 26.82 | — | 185.07 | 211.89 |
| 1988 | 77.28 | — | 212.81 | 290.09 |
| 1987 | — | — | 56.79 | 56.79 |
| 1986 | 34.24 | — | 198.63 | 232.87 |
| 1985 | — | 26.12 | 171.00 | 197.12 |
| 1984 | -16.24 | 79.11 | 85.01 | 147.88 |
| 1983 | — | 89.37 | 87.63 | 177.00 |
| 1982 | — | 120.06 | 59.04 | 179.10 |

(1) Includes changes to improve fuel economy and emissions control.
(2) Includes improved warranties, corrosion protection and changes in standard equipment.
SOURCE: U.S. Department of Labor, Bureau of Labor Statistics.

# Federal Exhaust Emission Standards for Cars and Light Trucks

## FEDERAL EXHAUST EMISSION STANDARDS FOR CONVENTIONALLY FUELED CARS AND LIGHT TRUCKS (Grams Per Mile)

### EPA Tier 1 Emission Standards for Passenger Cars and Light-Duty Trucks, FTP 75, (grams/mile)

| Category | 50,000 miles/5 years | | | | | | 100,000 miles/10 years[1] | | | | | |
|---|---|---|---|---|---|---|---|---|---|---|---|---|
| | THC | NMHC | CO | NOx diesel | NOx gasoline | PM | THC | NMHC | CO | NOx diesel | NOx gasoline | PM |
| LDV (Passenger cars) | 0.41 | 0.25 | 3.4 | 1 | 0.4 | 0.08 | — | 0.31 | 4.2 | 1.25 | 0.6 | 0.1 |
| LDT1 (LLDT, LVW <3,750 lbs) | — | 0.25 | 3.4 | 1 | 0.4 | 0.08 | 0.8 | 0.31 | 4.2 | 1.25 | 0.6 | 0.1 |
| LDT2 (LLDT, LVW >3,750 lbs) | — | 0.32 | 4.4 | — | 0.7 | 0.08 | 0.8 | 0.4 | 5.5 | 0.97 | 0.97 | 0.1 |
| LDT3 (HLDT, ALVW <5,750 lbs) | — | 0.32 | 4.4 | — | 0.7 | — | 0.8 | 0.46 | 6.4 | 0.98 | 0.98 | 0.1 |
| LDT4 (HLDT, ALVW >5,750 lbs) | — | 0.39 | 5 | — | 1.1 | — | 0.8 | 0.56 | 7.3 | 1.53 | 1.53 | 0.12 |

1 - Useful life 120,000 miles/11 years for all HLDT standards and for THC standards for LDT

**Abbreviations:**
 LVW - loaded vehicle weight (curb weight + 300 lbs)
 ALVW - adjusted LVW (the numerical average of the curb weight and the GVWR)
 LLDT - light light-duty truck (below 6,000 lbs GVWR)
 HLDT - heavy light-duty truck (above 6,000 lbs GVWR)

### EPA Tier 2 Emission Standards, FTP 75, (grams/mile)

| Bin# | 50,000 miles | | | | | 120,000 miles | | | | |
|---|---|---|---|---|---|---|---|---|---|---|
| | NMOG | CO | NOx | PM | HCHO | NMOG | CO | NOx* | PM | HCHO |
| **Temporary Bins** | | | | | | | | | | |
| 11[c,g] | | | | | | 0.28 | 7.3 | 0.9 | 0.12 | 0.032 |
| 10[a,b,d,f] | 0.125 | 3.4 (0.160) | 0.4 (4.4) | — | 0.015 | 0.156 (0.018) | 4.2 (0.230) | 0.6 (6.4) | 0.08 | 0.018 (0.027) |
| 9[a,b,e] | 0.075 (0.140) | 3.4 | 0.2 | — | 0.015 | 0.090 (0.180) | 4.2 | 0.3 | 0.06 | 0.018 |
| **Permanent Bins** | | | | | — | | | | | |
| 8[b] | 0.100 | 3.4 (0.125) | 0.14 | — | 0.015 | 0.125 | 4.2 (0.156) | 0.2 | 0.02 | 0.018 |
| 7 | 0.075 | 3.4 | 0.11 | — | 0.015 | 0.09 | 4.2 | 0.15 | 0.02 | 0.018 |
| 6 | 0.075 | 3.4 | 0.08 | — | 0.015 | 0.09 | 4.2 | 0.1 | 0.01 | 0.018 |
| 5 | 0.075 | 3.4 | 0.05 | — | 0.015 | 0.09 | 4.2 | 0.07 | 0.01 | 0.018 |
| 4 | — | — | — | — | — | 0.07 | 2.1 | 0.04 | 0.01 | 0.011 |
| 3 | — | — | — | — | — | 0.055 | 2.1 | 0.03 | 0.01 | 0.011 |
| 2 | — | — | — | — | — | 0.01 | 2.1 | 0.02 | 0.01 | 0.004 |
| 1 | — | — | — | — | — | — | — | — | — | — |

* - average manufacturer fleet NOx standard is 0.07 g/mi

NOTE: Tier 2 standards were phased in between 2004 and 2009. For new passenger cars and light LDT's, Tier 2 standards phased in beginning in 2004, with the standards fully phased in during 2007. For heavy LDT's and MDPV's, the Tier 2 standards were phased in beginning in 2008, with full compliance in 2009

a - Bin deleted at end of 2006 model year (2008 for HLDTs)
b - The higher temporary NMOG, CO and HCHO values applying to HLDTs expired after 2008
c - An additional temporary bin restricted to MDPVs expired after model year 2008
d - Optional temporary NMOG standard of 0.195 g/mi (50,000) and 0.280 g/mi (120,000) applies for qualifying LDT4s and MDPVs only
e - Optional temporary NMOG standard of 0.100 g/mi (50,000) and 0.130 g/mi (120,000) applies for qualifying LDT2s only
f - 50,000 mile standard optional for diesels certified to bin 10
g - Bins 9-11 expired in 2006 for light-duty vehicles and light-duty trucks and 2008 for heavy-duty light trucks and medium-duty passenger vehicles.

# Traffic Deaths in Selected Countries and Countries with Safety Belt Use Laws

## STATES WITH STANDARD/PRIMARY SEAT BELT ENFORCEMENT LAWS*

| | |
|---|---|
| Alabama | Maine |
| Alaska | Maryland |
| Arkansas | Michigan |
| California | Minnesota |
| Connecticut | Mississippi |
| Delaware | New Jersey |
| District of Columbia | New Mexico |
| Florida | New York |
| Georgia | North Carolina |
| Hawaii | Oklahoma |
| Illinois | Oregon |
| Indiana | South Carolina |
| Iowa | Tennessee |
| Kansas | Texas |
| Kentucky | Washington |
| Louisiana | Wisconsin |

*The safety belt use law may be enforced independent of another violation.
SOURCE: National Highway Traffic Safety Administration.

## VEHICLE DEATHS IN SELECTED COUNTRIES

| | 2009 | 2008 | Traffic Fatalities Per 100,000 Registered Vehicles 2009 | 2008 |
|---|---|---|---|---|
| Australia | 1,492 | 1,466 | 9.9 | 10.0 |
| Austria | 633 | 679 | 13.3 | 14.6 |
| Belgium | 955 | 922 | 16.0 | 15.7 |
| Canada | 2,130 | 2,371 | 10.2 | 11.6 |
| China | 67,759 | 73,484 | 110.8 | 156.3 |
| Denmark | 303 | 406 | 11.5 | 15.4 |
| Finland | 279 | 344 | 8.7 | 10.9 |
| France | 4,273 | 4,274 | 11.4 | 11.5 |
| Germany | 4,152 | 4,477 | 9.3 | 10.1 |
| Hungary | 822 | 996 | 23.8 | 28.5 |
| Italy | 4,237 | 4,731 | 10.3 | 11.6 |
| Japan | 5,772 | 6,023 | 7.8 | 8.1 |
| Netherlands | 644 | 677 | 7.2 | 7.6 |
| Norway | 212 | 255 | 7.6 | 9.3 |
| Poland | 4,572 | 5,437 | 23.6 | 28.8 |
| Portugal | 840 | 885 | 14.5 | 15.4 |
| Spain | 2,714 | 3,100 | 9.8 | 11.2 |
| Sweden | 358 | 397 | 7.4 | 8.3 |
| Switzerland | 349 | 357 | 8.0 | 8.2 |
| Turkey | 4,300 | NA | 40.5 | NA |
| United Kingdom | 2,337 | 2,645 | 6.6 | 7.4 |
| United States | 33,808 | 37,261 | 13.6 | 14.9 |

NA - Not available.
NOTE: Data varies significantly between countries both definitionally and quantitatively
SOURCE: Compiled by *Ward's* from various sources.

## COUNTRIES WITH SAFETY BELT USE LAWS

| Country | Effective Date | Country | Effective Date |
|---|---|---|---|
| Argentina | 7/1/92 | United States & Territories | |
| Australia | 1/72 | Alabama | 7/18/91 |
| Austria | 7/76 | Alaska | 9/12/90 |
| Belgium | 6/75 | Arizona | 1/1/91 |
| Brazil | 6/72 | Arkansas | 7/15/91 |
| Bulgaria | 1976 | California | 1/1/86 |
| Canadian Provinces | | Colorado | 7/1/87 |
| Alberta | 7/87 | Connecticut | 1/1/86 |
| British Columbia | 10/77 | Delaware | 1/1/92 |
| Manitoba | 4/84 | District of Columbia | 12/12/85 |
| Newfoundland | 7/82 | Florida | 7/1/86 |
| New Brunswick | 11/83 | Georgia | 9/1/88 |
| Nova Scotia | 1/85 | Hawaii | 2/16/85 |
| Ontario | 1/76 | Idaho | 7/1/86 |
| Prince Edward Island | 1/88 | Illinois | 7/1/85 |
| Quebec | 7/76 | Indiana | 7/1/87 |
| Saskatchewan | 7/77 | Iowa | 7/1/86 |
| Croatia | — | Kansas | 7/1/86 |
| Cyprus | 1/8/87 | Kentucky | 7/13/94 |
| Czech Republic | 1/69 | Louisiana | 7/1/86 |
| Denmark | 1/76 | Maine | 12/26/95 |
| Finland | 7/75 | Maryland | 7/1/86 |
| France | 10/79 | Massachusetts | 2/1/94 |
| Germany | 1/76 | Michigan | 7/1/85 |
| Greece | 12/79 | Minnesota | 8/1/86 |
| Hong Kong | 10/83 | Mississippi | 3/20/90 |
| Hungary | 7/77 | Missouri | 9/28/85 |
| Iceland | 10/81 | Montana | 10/1/87 |
| India | — | Nebraska | 1/1/93 |
| Ireland | 2/79 | Nevada | 7/1/87 |
| Israel | 7/75 | New Hampshire | — |
| Italy | 7/03 | New Jersey | 3/1/85 |
| Ivory Coast | 1970 | New Mexico | 1/1/86 |
| Japan | 12/71 | New York | 12/1/84 |
| Jordan | 12/83 | North Carolina | 10/1/85 |
| Luxembourg | 6/75 | North Dakota | 7/14/94 |
| Malaysia | 4/79 | Ohio | 5/6/86 |
| Netherlands | 6/75 | Oklahoma | 2/1/87 |
| New Zealand | 6/72 | Oregon | 12/7/90 |
| Norway | 9/75 | Pennsylvania | 11/23/87 |
| Peru | — | Puerto Rico | 1/19/75 |
| Poland | 1/84 | Rhode Island | 6/18/91 |
| Portugal | 1/78 | South Carolina | 7/1/89 |
| Singapore | 7/81 | South Dakota | 1/1/95 |
| Slovenia | — | Tennessee | 4/21/86 |
| South Africa | 12/77 | Texas | 9/1/85 |
| Spain | 10/74 | Utah | 4/28/86 |
| Sweden | 1/75 | Vermont | 1/1/94 |
| Switzerland | 1/76 | Virginia | 1/1/88 |
| Turkey | 10/84 | Washington | 6/11/86 |
| United Kingdom | 1/83 | West Virginia | 9/1/93 |
| USSR | 1/76 | Wisconsin | 12/1/87 |
| Zimbabwe | 7/80 | Wyoming | 6/8/89 |

SOURCE: Compiled by *Ward's* from various sources.

# INDEX

# INDEX

**Our news, data and analysis in one subscription puts you in the driver's seat.**

# WARDSAUTO.COM

**Subscribe today for unrestricted online access to all the auto data, breaking news, analysis and archives from Ward's -- the industry's most trusted source.**

WardsAuto.com is updated throughout the day, provides all of Ward's content in one location, is easy to use, and offers the most powerful automotive-focused search capabilities available anywhere!

- Sales, production, inventory by country
- Production forecasts
- Production & marketing strategies
- Market share analysis
- Automaker earnings
- Key economic data
- Engine/original equipment installations
- Safety and emissions recalls
- New vehicle introductions
- WARD'S vehicle segmentations
- And much, much more!

To learn more visit www.WardsAuto.com or contact Amber McLincha at 248-799-2622 or AMcLincha@wardsauto.com

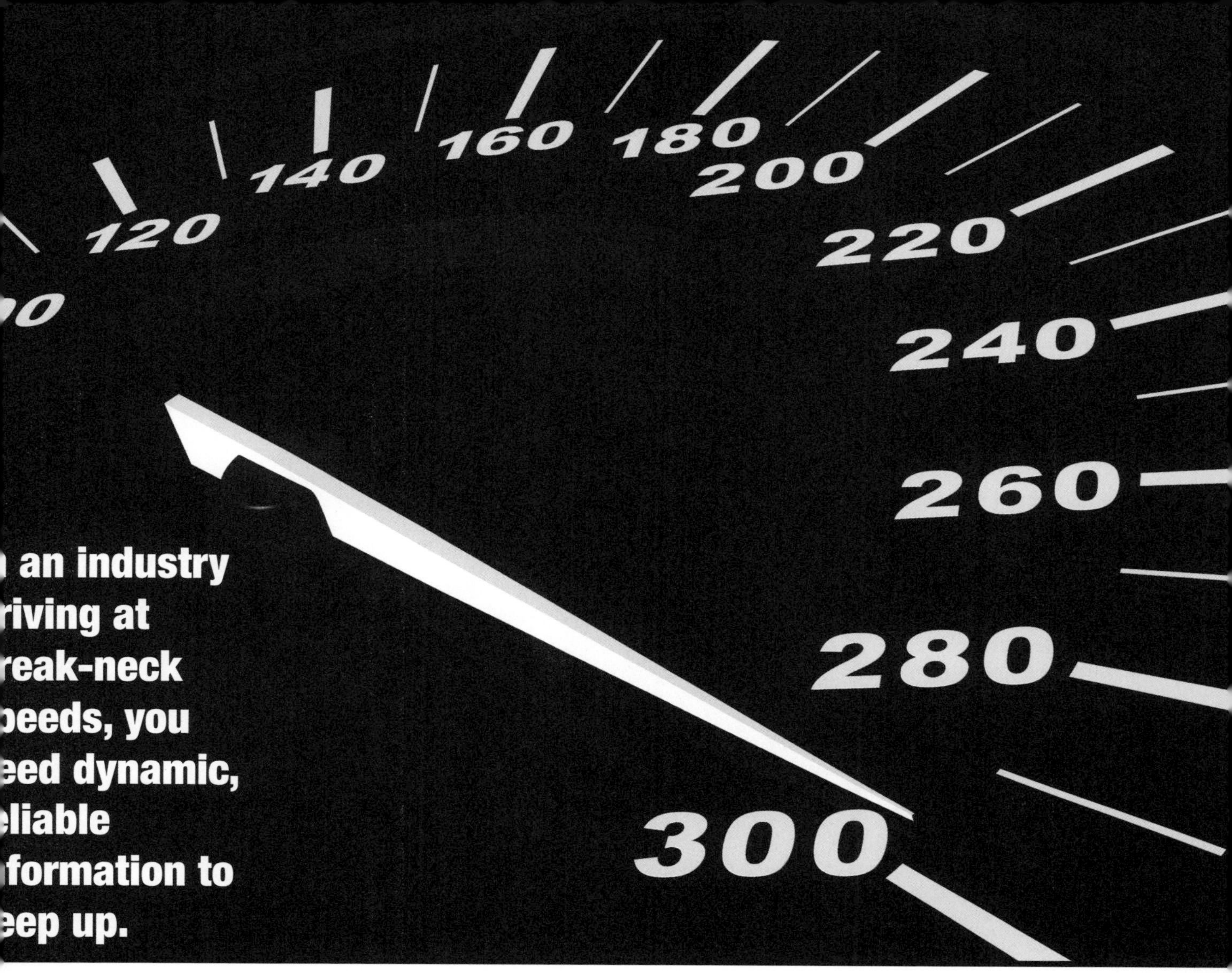

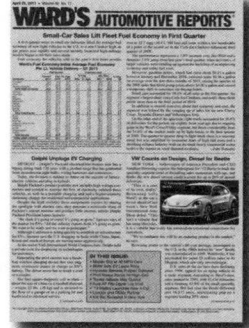

# WARD'S® AUTOMOTIVE GROUP

## THE POWER OF AUTOMOTIVE INFORMATIO

Contact Ward's Information Products for
more details or pricing on the products below:
Amber McLincha • 248.799.2622 • amclincha@wardsauto.com

Contact Customer Service for more
details or pricing on the products below.
Barbara Liske • 248.799-2645 • bliske@wardsauto.com

## Online Subscription Services

Call for pricing
(based on number
of users)

**WardsAuto.com**
All of Ward's in one online subscription --
news, data, analysis and more.

_____

**Ward's AutoInfoBank™ on the web**
Powerful web-based data reporting tool

_____

## Forecast Report Products

Call for pricing
(multiple forecast
products available)

**Ward's AutoForecasts**
Knowledgable forecasts on where the
automotive manufacturing industry is headed

_____

## Ward's Monthly Auto Data Reports

**Call for details and pricing on these reports:**
- Retail sales
- Production/factory sales

## Magazines

**Call 866-505-7173 to order or for more details:**

| | US & Mexico | Canada | Airmail Overseas |
|---|---|---|---|
| **Ward's AutoWorld**®*  1 yr. (12 issues) | $80 | $85 | $104 |
| **Ward's Dealer Business**®*  1 yr. (12 issues) | $52 | $72 | $104 |

## Newsletters

### Ward's Automotive Reports®*
- ❏ One year (52 issues) with Yearbook  $1,540 (airmail overseas, add $
- ❏ 13-week trial .......................................$295 (airmail overseas, add $

### Ward's Engine and Vehicle Technology Update®*
- ❏ One year (24 issues)................................$1,110 (airmail overseas, add $
- ❏ Half-year (12 issues) ..........................$525 (airmail overseas, add $

## Reference Annuals

### Ward's Automotive Yearbook®**
- ❏ 2011 Yearbook ...............................$580 (airmail overseas, add $
- ❏ 2011 Yearbook and CD-ROM set.........$910 (airmail overseas, add $
- ❏ 2010 Yearbook ...............................$570 (airmail overseas, add $
- ❏ 2010 Yearbook and CD-ROM set.........$895 (airmail overseas, add $

### Ward's World Motor Vehicle Data™**
- ❏ 2011 Data Book ..................................$325 (airmail overseas, add
- ❏ 2011 Data Book and CD-ROM set........$395 (airmail overseas, add
  (2011 version available Sept., 2011)
- ❏ 2010 Data Book ..................................$310 (airmail overseas, add
- ❏ 2010 Data Book and CD-ROM set........$395 (airmail overseas, add

ALL ORDERS MUST INCLUDE APPLICABLE TAXES. If tax-exempt and not a govt.
agency, please provide copy of tax exempt certificate.
* Subject to sales tax in AL, CO, FL, GA, IN, KS, KY, MO, SC, TN, WA and Canada.
** Subject to sales tax in AL, AK, CA, CO, CT, FL, GA, IL, IN, KS, KY, MA, MI, MN,
MO, MS, NE, NJ, NY, OH, PA, SC, TN, TX, VA, WA, WI and Canada.

---

Bill to my:     ☐ VISA     ☐ Mastercard     ☐ American Express     ☐ Discover

Amount enclosed $ _____  Signature _____
(Please do not use this form to order Ward's AutoWorld or Ward's Dealer Business.
Please call 866-505-7173 to order either monthly magazine.)

Card number_____  Exp. Date _____

Name/Title (Please print) _____

Company/Division_____

Street Address _____

City_____  State/Province _____

Zip/Postal Code_____  Country_____

Phone _____  Fax _____

E-mail Address _____

Mail Orders to:  Penton Media, Inc. - Ward's Automotive Group • 24653 Network Place • Chicago, IL 60673-1246
Please make checks payable to:  Penton Media, Inc. in U.S. funds, drawn on a U.S. bank.
**Customer Service Inquiries:** Contact Barbara Liske by phone: (248) 799-2645, by fax: (248) 357-9747, or email: bliske@wardsauto.com